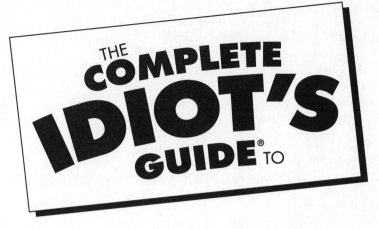

THE

COMPLETE

IDIOT'S

GUIDE® TO

Personal Finance in Your 20s and 30s

Third Edition

by Sarah Young Fisher and Susan Shelly

ALPHA

A member of Penguin Group (USA) Inc.

This book is dedicated to my 20something children: Rob and Catie, the best of the best!

ALPHA BOOKS

Published by the Penguin Group

Penguin Group (USA) Inc., 375 Hudson Street, New York, New York 10014, U.S.A.

Penguin Group (Canada), 10 Alcorn Avenue, Toronto, Ontario, Canada M4V 3B2 (a division of Pearson Penguin Canada Inc.)

Penguin Books Ltd, 80 Strand, London WC2R 0RL, England

Penguin Ireland, 25 St Stephen's Green, Dublin 2, Ireland (a division of Penguin Books Ltd)

Penguin Group (Australia), 250 Camberwell Road, Camberwell, Victoria 3124, Australia (a division of Pearson Australia Group Pty Ltd)

Penguin Books India Pvt Ltd, 11 Community Centre, Panchsheel Park, New Delhi—110 017, India

Penguin Group (NZ), cnr Airborne and Rosedale Roads, Albany, Auckland 1310, New Zealand (a division of Pearson New Zealand Ltd)

Penguin Books (South Africa) (Pty) Ltd, 24 Sturdee Avenue, Rosebank, Johannesburg 2196, South Africa

Penguin Books Ltd, Registered Offices: 80 Strand, London WC2R 0RL, England

Copyright © 2005 by Susan Shelly and Sarah Young Fisher

International Standard Book Number: 978-1-59257-332-5
Library of Congress Catalog Card Number: 2005920504

09 08   8 7

Interpretation of the printing code: The rightmost number of the first series of numbers is the year of the book's printing; the rightmost number of the second series of numbers is the number of the book's printing. For example, a printing code of 05-1 shows that the first printing occurred in 2005.

Printed in the United States of America

Note: This publication contains the opinions and ideas of its authors. It is intended to provide helpful and informative material on the subject matter covered. It is sold with the understanding that the authors and publisher are not engaged in rendering professional services in the book. If the reader requires personal assistance or advice, a competent professional should be consulted.

The authors and publisher specifically disclaim any responsibility for any liability, loss, or risk, personal or otherwise, which is incurred as a consequence, directly or indirectly, of the use and application of any of the contents of this book.

Most Alpha books are available at special quantity discounts for bulk purchases for sales promotions, premiums, fundraising, or educational use. Special books, or book excerpts, can also be created to fit specific needs.

For details, write: Special Markets, Alpha Books, 375 Hudson Street, New York, NY 10014.

Publisher: *Marie Butler-Knight*
Product Manager: *Phil Kitchel*
Senior Managing Editor: *Jennifer Bowles*
Acquisitions Editor: *Paul Dinas*
Development Editor: *Ginny Bess Munroe*
Production Editor: *Megan Douglass*

Copy Editor: *Emily Bell*
Cartoonist: *Shannon Wheeler*
Cover/Book Designer: *Trina Wurst*
Indexer: *Angie Bess*
Layout: *Angela Calvert*
Proofreading: *Donna Martin*

Contents at a Glance

Contents

Foreword

For more than 30 years, I have advised thousands of people who sought help managing their finances. Some were fortunate enough to have accumulated sizeable portfolios that they wanted my firm to manage. Others had less money but an array of concerns from how to save for retirement or a new house to whether they had appropriate insurance coverage. Regardless of their particular financial situation, all these people shared a common need for advice about their money and finances.

That's why Sarah Young Fisher and Susan Shelly's book is so important. All too often, people in their 20s and 30s are so intimidated by the thought of managing their finances that they make no decisions, the wrong choices, or seek advice from parents, spouses, or friends … people who often have only limited knowledge of money matters. Many times, the most basic strategies of personal finance prove elusive, yet taking control of one's money is vital to one's long-term financial health. In user-friendly, nonintimidating language, this book walks readers through the essentials of basic money management, from setting financial goals and creating a budget to opening the right type of bank account. Once these nuts-and-bolts strategies are mastered, readers can learn about investing, insurance, getting a mortgage, paying down debt, and other money issues.

Given the stressful, fast-paced lives that are all too common these days, it's not surprising that so many young people never learn about managing money. Our high schools and colleges teach very little, if anything, about personal finances. Many baby boomer parents still consider the subject of money taboo, so we learn very little from them as well. However, recent college or graduate school graduates must navigate their way through complex decisions for the first time. They may go from living in a dorm or a frat house and eating in a cafeteria to having to find an apartment and put down a deposit while getting a job, buying a car, paying off their own credit cards, and more. That doesn't even include other key money decisions such as selecting the right health and car insurance, or participating in a company savings plan.

The Complete Idiot's Guide to Personal Finance in Your 20s and 30s, Third Edition, is an invaluable book for people who are ready to take charge of their own finances—either because they are truly on their own for the first time, or they no longer want to be dependent on parents or a spouse regarding financial decisions. By walking readers through—slowly—the all-important money decisions, the authors help people learn the basics, which they will be able to use throughout their lives. By mastering the basics—wise budgeting, investing for the future, and getting out of debt—readers will be well on their way to a lifetime of financial security. This book provides the reader with the financial foundation to make smart financial choices and develop a solid financial plan for their future.

Stewart H. Welch III, CFP, AEP, is the founder of The Welch Group, LLC, which specializes in providing fee-only Wealth Management services. Mr. Welch has been recognized by *Money, Worth, Mutual Funds Magazine,* and *Medical Economics* as one of the top financial advisors in the country. He is a financial columnist for the *Birmingham Post Herald* and a member of the Editorial Board for *Physician's Money Digest* and *Dentist's Money Digest.* Visit his website, www.welchgroup.com.

Introduction

If personal finance is so important, how come so many people pay so little attention to it? The biggest reason, we think, is because they're intimidated. Why? Because they're not taking their finances personally enough.

Your personal finances are all about you, not the guy you work with, not your mom and dad, and not that nosy neighbor on the third floor of your apartment building. They're not about the stock market, capital gains, or compounding interest, either. Although those things all factor into your personal finances, they are not the essence.

Personal finance is attitude and mindset. It's being able to look down the road and sacrifice a bit now for big returns later. It's knowing when to go for the new car and when to buy a used one. It's a matter of knowing how to make the right choices and doing just that.

To know how to make those choices you need some financial education, and that's what you'll find in this book. You'll also need to examine your financial attitudes and mindsets and be prepared to make some adjustments to them, when necessary. Your personal finances affect the way you live now, and how you'll live in the future. How much more personal can you get?

What You'll Find in This Book

The Complete Idiot's Guide to Personal Finance in Your 20s and 30s, Third Edition, is written in five sections. Each section covers a different time of your life.

Part 1, "The Real World," deals with personal financial issues that come up when you're just starting out. You've just hung the old college diploma on your wall or finished the technical school program. You're ready to set the world on fire, but there are a few details you need to attend to first.

You need a place to live, a car to drive, the right bank accounts and credit cards—help! Relax. This section gives you all the info you need to make your way through these thorny issues without a scratch. We also take a look at the deplorable lack of financial education in American schools. (That's fancy talk for why the heck you haven't learned this stuff before now!)

Things are a little more laid back in **Part 2, "On Your Own and Loving It."** This part covers some pretty exciting life events. You get your first real job with a salary, benefits, and everything. No more flipping burgers for you!

Now that you're making some money, we want you to think about how you're using it. That's where the "b word" (budget) comes in. We'll help you to examine your attitudes concerning spending, saving, and using credit. We'll explain how credit works, and tell you how many people know all about your spending habits. You'll see that your finances might be personal, but they're not all that private! We'll also give you lots of good tips for saving money on just about everything.

By now, you have a pretty good feel for this financial stuff, and you're ready for **Part 3, "Coasting Along."** Here, we broach some subjects that are important to consider once you're doing okay with the day-to-day expenses and managing to save some money: investments, taxes, and insurance.

There are better places for your money than your piggy bank or a savings account, and we'll tell you what to consider when you start looking at where to put it. We'll also talk about some fun stuff, such as vacations, your own apartment, and that cool new modem you've been looking at.

Things get moving pretty fast in **Part 4, "To Everything There Is a Season."** Don't worry. We're not going to have you doing estate planning—you're way too young for that. We will, however, talk about things such as working from home, buying an engagement ring, paying for a wedding, and pumping up your retirement account. If all that makes you too nervous, try to calm down and persevere. These are important issues to consider during this time of your life. This is also the section in which we'll introduce you to Wall Street and tell you how to find a financial advisor, if you need one.

In **Part 5, "So You're Thinking of Buying a House,"** we talk about the financial, practical, and psychological aspects of buying and owning a home. We'll tell you what to look for when you're choosing a real estate agent, how to come up with more money for a down payment, and how to find that house of your dreams. We also cover mortgage talk, tell you how owning a home affects your taxes, and explain what insurance you'll need to protect your investment.

When you finish the last part, you'll have a basic, sound understanding of how your personal finances work in various stages of your life. You won't be an expert, but you'll have a lot more confidence about handling your money and building a financially secure future.

More Bang for Your Buck

You'll find four types of sidebars in this book. These little snippets of information are geared toward keeping you out of trouble, providing tips, telling you what something means, or just giving you something to talk about with your friends.

Money Pit

Be sure to read these gems of wisdom, because they could keep you from making some common mistakes regarding your personal finances.

Pocket Change

Wow everybody at the next party with these snippets of little-known information. You'll impress your friends and sound oh-so-smart.

Show Me the Money

There's a lot of financial mumbo-jumbo out there, and these sidebars will help you through it. We give you clear definitions for some of the financial jargon you'll encounter.

Dollars and Sense

These tips or bits of upbeat information keep you on top of and up to date with your personal finances.

Acknowledgments

The authors would like to thank the many people who provided time, information, and resources for this book. Especially, we thank our editors at Alpha Books. Thanks also go to our technical reviewer, for his expertise and patience, and to Gene Brissie of James Peter Associates.

A very special thank-you goes to our families and friends, especially to Dallas (Chuck) Fisher, who went above and beyond the call of duty as data processing expert. Thanks also go to Lois Young, who, as always, took precious time to review material and share her knowledge and insights.

And a very, very special thank-you to Michael, Sara, and Ryan McGovern.

Special Thanks to the Technical Reviewer

The Complete Idiot's Guide to Personal Finance in Your 20s and 30s, Third Edition, was reviewed by an expert who double-checked the accuracy of what you'll learn here, to help us ensure that this book gives you everything you need to know about the topics that affect your bank accounts—and your future. Special thanks are extended to Kenneth Kaplan.

Trademarks

All terms mentioned in this book that are known to be or are suspected of being trademarks or service marks have been appropriately capitalized. Alpha Books and Penguin Group (USA) Inc. cannot attest to the accuracy of this information. Use of a term in this book should not be regarded as affecting the validity of any trademark or service mark.

Part 1

The Real World

"Nobody told me it was gonna be like this!" If you've uttered that or a similar phrase recently, take comfort in knowing that you're not the only one. This can be a rough period in your life. You're out of college, and anxious to get started on your own. You just didn't think there would be so much to think about, or so many responsibilities.

You thought all those term papers were bad, but now you've got to think about different kinds of bank accounts, and getting the best deal on (not to mention paying off) your credit cards. And, you need to find a place to live and a car to drive! You can't imagine how you'll pay for everything.

Relax. Chapters 1 through 6 give you all the information you need on these and other mind-boggling financial topics. You'll feel a lot better when you're finished with this section, so settle in and start reading.

Personal Finance: The Stuff They Didn't Teach You in College

In This Chapter

◆ The meaning of personal finance

◆ Finding out how much (or little) you know about personal finance

◆ Money attitudes

◆ Starting to save and plan now

◆ Navigating the misleading: The confusing world of personal finance information

If the phrase *personal finance* makes you think of long and serious (read boring) discussions about stocks, bonds, annuities, and interest rates, well, your impression is partially correct—all those subjects do have their place in the vast world of money and finance. In most ways, however, the emphasis in personal finance is on the first word, *personal*, which means it's all about what *you* do with *your* money. What could be more interesting than that?

Exactly What Is Personal Finance?

Simply put, *personal finance* is every aspect of your life that deals with money—everything from buying a ticket to the movies, to finding an affordable apartment, to leasing that new BMW or Explorer you've had your eye on, to putting money into a retirement plan. Your personal finances affect your relationships, your lifestyle, and very possibly, your self-perception.

Let's face it, money is extremely important in our society. We place great emphasis on owning big homes in the right neighborhoods, high-status cars, labels on our clothing, and vacations to the right places. Even kids as young as six and seven are affected. Look at a group of kids sometime and see how many are wearing hats or shirts bearing trademark logos.

Show Me the Money

Personal finance includes every aspect of your life that deals with money. The emphasis of the phrase is definitely on the word *personal*.

No doubt about it, money is a big motivator in America. People work for money, gamble for money, marry for money, fight for money, and even kill for money. Money commands respect, even when the person who has the money doesn't.

However, it's important to keep money in perspective, and polls show that people in their 20s and 30s are tending to do so more than their baby boomer counterparts have. Studies show that family, spirituality, and personal satisfaction were important to many Generation Xers, even before the events of 9/11. Sociologists explain these priorities as a generation's backlash to the high divorce rate, obvious consumption, and get-ahead mentality of their baby boomer parents. Who knows? But if money is of any importance to you, then personal finance must be important to you, too. You can't separate them.

Show Me the Money

There are mentions throughout this book of *baby boomers* and *Generation Xers*, even though Gen Xers are now sometimes referred to as the New Power Generation, due to their increasingly important roles in business and society. Generation X loosely refers to those 50 million men and women born between 1965 and 1980. Baby boomers are defined as those 78 million Americans who are in the mid 40s to late 50s range.

Personal finance is planning and implementing financial goals. It's putting away some money each week for that Jeep you've been looking at. It's whether you shop at Sam's Club or the gourmet specialty shop, and it's whether your vacation is one week or two. How well you accomplish your personal financial goals determines whether you buy a house or keep renting the condo, and eventually it will influence where your kids will go to school and the quality of your retirement.

Why Don't I Already Know This Stuff?

In many ways, we live in a strange society. At an early age, we learn the capitals of every state and can recite the nightly television schedule without consulting *TV Guide*. We debate the merits of dozens of different cell phone plans and spout Red Sox batting averages from 1996. When it comes to our personal finances, however, many of us are lost. We've never learned the basics of managing our money.

On the surface, personal finance sounds complicated. It sounds scary. It sounds like something we'd rather not have to deal with. So we let our hard-earned money lie in a bank account, making little or no interest, while we go about our day-to-day routines.

It's not that we *can't* learn about personal finance and managing our money. For one reason or another, we just *don't* learn about it. The thing is, your personal finances are extremely important, because your future depends on how you handle them. Left unattended, you might financially survive, but you surely won't prosper. Financial experts agree hands-down that the earlier you get a financial plan in place, the better off you'll be later on.

> **Pocket Change**
>
> More than 1.6 million American households filed for personal bankruptcy protection in 2003, according to the American Bankruptcy Institute. The agency also reports an increasing amount of delinquent credit card and home equity debt among Americans.

Whatever Happened to Personal Finance 101?

You learn all sorts of interesting information in high school and college. But, unless you were the business major type, I bet money, personal finance, and *financial planning* weren't even part of the curriculum.

> **Show Me the Money**
>
> **Financial planning** is the process of evaluating your present financial situation, identifying financial goals, preparing a plan (often written) to achieve those goals, and carrying out the plan.

A recent survey of high school seniors showed that (no surprise here) the majority have many misconceptions about investing and saving money, using credit cards, and preparing for retirement. Many did not know how a checking account works and had little knowledge about interest, bank fees, and other issues.

This lack of knowledge, experts say, should not be a surprise. Kids can't know what they've never been taught. Experts say that kids aren't learning responsible personal finance from their schools or their parents, either. Kids often pick up bad money habits at home and continue those habits when they're on their own.

Those who do realize the importance of financial planning, like you (after all, you bought this book), are to be congratulated. By taking time to learn how to make the most of your money, you're giving yourself a huge advantage over those who aren't paying attention.

But I Don't Think I'll Be Able to Understand It

The subject of personal finance can seem intimidating. It includes topics such as taxes, insurance, investments, and interest. But when you begin learning about each of these topics, you'll find that personal finance is not all that complicated. A lot of personal finance and money management is just good common sense. Sure, mastering all the nuances of Wall Street would be a major challenge, but you don't need to do that to manage your own finances and ensure your future financial health.

As you move through different stages and situations in your life, you'll need to know different things concerning personal finances. Say, for instance, that you're in your early 20s and just out of college. You've just landed your first job, which is a notable accomplishment, but the salary isn't as much as you had hoped. In fact, you're trying to figure out how you'll get enough money together for a security deposit on that apartment you've been looking at.

At this point in your life, you don't need to learn about dividend reinvestment plans or dollar-cost averaging. You do, however, need to worry about budgeting your income to meet all your expenses, finding some transportation to and from work, and paying off college debt.

Money's Not a Dirty Word

Before the 1960s, sex wasn't an acceptable topic of conversation. Young women who "got into trouble" disappeared for six or seven months under the pretense of visiting long-lost relatives in Peoria. Forty years later, sex talk is as commonplace as mosquitoes in a swamp. No longer a taboo topic, sex is everywhere.

Although sex has become an acceptable conversation topic, talk about some aspects of money is still somewhat taboo. Studies have shown that parents are more likely to talk with their kids about sex than about money.

Couples fight more about money than any other issue, mostly because they don't talk about it unless it gets to be a problem in their marriage. Money problems are blamed for much of the marital strife that leads one out of every two married couples in this country down the road to divorce court.

To your credit, Gen Xers tend to be more open about financial matters than previous generations. Perhaps by 2010 or so, money talk will be as common as talk about sex.

Pocket Change

In a survey of married couples, more than half of them said that, sooner or later, money is the most important concern in a marriage. Yet most couples don't talk about it until it becomes an issue.

Dollars and Sense

Alarmingly, participation in 401(k) plans has been dropping off for the past couple of years, according to a survey by the Profit Sharing/401(k) Council of America. The survey, reported in 2004, showed that 76 percent of eligible employees participated in 401(k) plans in 2003, down from 80 percent in 2002.

Personal Finance Is for My Parents

Who needs to think about personal finance? Anyone with any money at all should be concerned about where it's going and whether it's being managed to its best advantage. Sure, that includes your parents, but it also includes you. If your parents are nearing retirement age, or perhaps still have a child in college or approaching college age, they're probably painfully aware of their personal finances. This book, however, is for 20- and 30-somethings who traditionally are notorious for not paying much attention to their personal finances. Polls do show that Generation Xers are saving more money than baby boomers did in their 20s and 30s, but that's not exactly great news. Baby boomers are notorious spenders, and many of them are still not saving any money. Still, there are many Gen Xers who aren't saving anything either. The decision to not save or the lack of a decision to save occurs for various reasons, including the following:

◆ You're too busy having a great time spending the first real money you've ever made to worry about saving any of it.

◆ You figure you'll have plenty of time to worry about saving later (like after you get married).

◆ You've got an apartment, a car, and plenty of spending money; what else could anyone want?

Keep the mistakes of your elders in mind as you cruise on through your 20s, spending just about every dollar you make from that job you landed. In the back of your mind, you probably know you should be saving some money, and many people your age are. But too often, saving just doesn't seem to happen. There's always something else to buy. But you're not too worried about it. You figure you'll probably be married in 5 or 10 years, and then you'll have to get serious about many things, money included.

You're being shortsighted if you don't save something from these years. What happens if you're waiting to start saving money until you're married, but Mr. or Ms. Right doesn't show up for another 8 or 10 years? You will have lost a lot of savings time and interest.

Even if you can't save a lot, you should be saving something in your 20s and 30s. No one is saying you have to save half of each paycheck. Small savings don't add up as quickly as big savings, but they do add up. Remember, saving money is a big aspect (but not the only aspect) of personal finance.

There's no denying that there's a lot to learn about personal finance.

> **Pocket Change**
>
> A poll by marketing consultants Roper ASW showed that in 2003, only 42 percent of Americans were routinely putting aside money for retirement. That's the lowest rate since 1980, according to Roper.

> **Dollars and Sense**
>
> If you start saving $2,000 a year in an IRA when you're 25, and you save that much for 10 consecutive years, earning about 9 percent total return per year, you'll have $440,000 when you turn 65. That should be a pretty good incentive to put some money away!

The Least You Need to Know

- Personal finance is every aspect of your life that deals with money.

- Personal finance is an often overlooked or ignored topic by people of all ages.

- Talking about money is sometimes still considered impolite or even taboo, but it shouldn't be.

- There's a glut of information about personal finance, much of which is confusing and inaccurate.

- The younger you are when you learn about personal finance and managing money, the better off you'll be later in your life.

You're Out Here—Now What Are You Gonna Do?

In This Chapter

- ◆ The financial challenges of living on your own
- ◆ Being on your own versus living with Mom and Dad
- ◆ Striking a balance between lifestyle and finances
- ◆ The low salary and high debt pitfalls
- ◆ Your financial situation will improve, really
- ◆ Testing your financial knowledge

You now have a good understanding of why learning about personal finance is important and how the way you handle your personal finances has a major effect on the way you live. Personal finance will become increasingly important to you as you get established on your own. You'll probably have more money during the next few years than you did in high school or college, and additional responsibilities, such as repayment of college loans, as well. You'll need to know the best way to handle your money and your debts.

Hey! Nobody Told Me It Was Gonna Be Like This!

Remember when you were in school? Sure, there was a lot to do, but looking back, it probably seems that life was a breeze. Sure, you had tests and term papers to do, but chances are that you're facing way more responsibility now than you did then.

> **Dollars and Sense** _____
>
> Finishing school and moving out on your own is a major life transition and, therefore, a time of high stress. If you feel overly anxious or unable to handle the situation, it's important to find some help. Your employer may offer counseling as a benefit, or you can talk to someone at your church or synagogue or confide in a trusted friend.

It's easy to get overwhelmed as your responsibilities mount, but try to relax and enjoy yourself. Getting started career-wise, socially, and financially might be unsettling, but once you've lived on your own for a while you'll become savvy and streetwise—and do just fine.

Mom and Dad, Where Are You?

Finishing college is a milestone, and, for many new graduates, figuring out what to do after college is the biggest initial challenge. Our society has this expectation that when somebody graduates from college, she'll find a job, move out on her own, and begin advancing her career. But it doesn't always work like that.

Studies show that most college graduates do not make a seamless transition from student to employed person living on their own. If their degree is not in a field where employment is readily available, it can take a while to find a job. If there's no job, there's no money. Having no money delays the process of getting out into the world on your own.

> **Pocket Change**
>
> The National Opinion Research Center at the University of Chicago reports that most Americans consider 26 the age at which adulthood begins. But, only 45 percent of women and 31 percent of men had completed the five widely recognized transitions to adulthood by age 30. Those transitions are: finishing school, leaving home, gaining financial independence, getting married, and having a baby.

As a result, more young people are moving home with Mom and Dad after graduating from college or having been away for another reason.

The U.S. Bureau of the Census reported that in 2002, 55 percent of men and 46 percent of women between the ages of 18 and 24 were still living at home. Among 25- to 34-year-olds, 14 percent of men and 8 percent of women still lived at home. Not having to pay rent, or paying just minimal rent to parents, gives recent grads a lot more money to save—or to spend. Many of these stay-at-home grads are the ones with the fancy electronic equipment or sport utility vehicles. Others, though, use the money they save on living expenses to pay back college loans or to put into a fund for a down payment on a house.

If you have a job, but are living rent-free, or nearly rent-free, at your parents' house, realize that you're in a great position to save money.

> **Pocket Change**
>
> An increase in the average age that people are marrying is partially attributed to young people living at home longer than their parents did. In 1970, the median age for first marriages was 20.8 for women and 22.5 for men. In 2002, it was 25.1 for women and 26.8 for men, according to U.S. Census figures.

It's a Big, Cold World Out Here

If you have made it out of your parents' house, you don't expect life on your own to be perfect. Still, you didn't realize it would be so much hassle. If living independently isn't turning out to be what you had expected, try to relax.

No two people want to live exactly the same way. Some prefer living with a group of roommates; others just want to be by themselves. Some follow orderly, strict schedules; others eat and sleep when the mood strikes. There are as many lifestyles as there are people. The trick is to find out how you want to live and how it's most financially feasible for you to live in that way.

If you live by yourself and are lonely or worried about your safety or your financial situation, maybe you should think about getting a roommate. Even if you have to move to a bigger place and don't end up saving much money, you may be more comfortable and happier living with someone.

> **CAUTION** **Money Pit**
>
> If you're considering a lifestyle change, be sure you take time to figure out how it will affect your wallet. If you make a decision based strictly on emotion, you could compound your woes by ending up in financial trouble.

If, on the other hand, you live with someone or with a group and are unhappy because of that, it's time to start looking for your own place. You'll probably have to move to a smaller, less expensive apartment, but you'll probably think it's worthwhile to be able to live by yourself. Only you can know what's best for you both personally and financially. You must reach a balance between the two in order to achieve maximum happiness.

A Look at Where You Are

Starting out on your own in 2004 might be a bit more difficult than it would have been four or five years ago. The 9/11 attacks left an already weakened economy floundering, and many employers responded by laying off workers and downsizing operations.

However, economists now say the economy is in recovery and we can expect to see jobs returning. That's good news for everyone, and perhaps particularly good news to young workers, who can be starting out with very significant debt. More than half of the college grads in this country have borrowed money to pay for their educations, and the amount owed upon graduation can be staggering—especially for students completing graduate work. *U.S. News and World Report*, which does an annual ranking of various aspects of American colleges and universities, reports that students graduating in 2001 with doctoral degrees from national universities carry debt that can top $30,000.

Debt was generally less for undergraduate students, but still very significant, sometimes $20,000 or more. And your college loans might not be the only money you owe. Because credit cards are so accessible to students these days, and because marketers are so good at making us think we have to have so many things, credit card debt among recent college grads is at an all-time high. The situation has gotten so bad that some students are leaving college to get full-time jobs in order to pay off their credit cards.

In addition to worrying about paying off debt, you're looking at a lot of expenses at this point of your life. If you're just renting an apartment, you need a couple of months' rent, plus a security deposit just to move in. A little furniture would be nice, too. We're talking significant money.

Maybe you need to buy a car to get to and from work, or at least round up enough money to pay for the bus every day. Also, you'll probably have to replace some of your jeans and sweaters with career clothes. Speaking of careers, you probably won't be pulling in $60,000 or $70,000 to start. Your salary doesn't seem to stretch very far when you think about all the things it has to pay for.

Pocket Change

Loan provider Nellie Mae reported that by the time a student graduates from college, he has twice as much credit card debt and three times as many credit cards as when he arrived on campus. Thirty-one percent of college seniors have credit card debt of between $3,000 and $7,000, according to Nellie Mae. Kiplinger.com reported the average college student graduates with $3,000 in credit card debt.

Mom and Dad might be pretty interested in your new job and where you're living and with whom, but they probably aren't being much help financially these days. Better face it; your time of being fully financially supported is over.

Lest we paint too glum an economic picture, you should know that many 20-somethings are on their own and doing just fine. Let's take a look at the flip side.

A Look at Where You're Going

If you're a bit financially strapped at the moment, consider it a temporary situation and focus on the future. If you have a job and are making enough money to support yourself, you're off to a great start. Sure, there'll be things you'd like to have that you can't afford—but that's okay. Keep telling yourself that you'll be in better financial shape next year, and enjoy the experience of being out on your own.

To stay on the right financial track, remember these two things:

1. Resist the temptation to use credit cards to buy what you want but can't afford. You'll get yourself in a huge rut if you do this and end up with less in the future. Be patient and know that eventually, you'll have more buying power.

2. Be aware of financial opportunities, and take advantage of them when they're available.

Many people miss chances to improve their financial positions because they don't know what's available to help them do so. By reading this book, you've shown that you're interested in your personal finances and are willing to take the initiative to learn how to get, and keep, your finances healthy.

We'll look closer at these areas of financial opportunity later in the book, but it's important that you know what opportunities to look for. The sooner you start making the most of your money, the more money you'll have later.

◆ **401(k) plans.** We'll get into more detail about these little gold mines in Chapter 13, but suffice it to say that 401(k)s are a great way to save money. If you're eligible to participate at work, make sure you do. IRAs, the new Roth IRAs, and other retirement plans also are good vehicles for saving.

◆ **Compounding interest.** Starting to save even a little bit of money when you're young will pay off big time because of time. The longer money is invested, the faster it grows. That's called compounding, and it's a great way to see your money grow. We'll cover more about this in Chapter 10.

◆ **Lower interest rates.** If you're paying 18 or 20 percent interest on your credit card, you might be able to get a significantly lower rate just by shopping around and asking. A couple of points can make a big difference. Check out Chapter 4 for more on credit cards.

◆ **The best possible bank accounts.** If you're paying big bucks in bank fees, you're not making the most of your money. It takes some work, but it's worth it to look around and compare what's available. We'll get into this in more detail in Chapter 3.

◆ **A budget.** Most people wouldn't consider a budget a financial opportunity, but it definitely is. Preparing and using a budget gives you a chance to see where your money goes and an opportunity to cut back and save. There is more about budgets in Chapter 9.

◆ **Learning opportunities.** There is a wealth of financial information around for anyone willing to take the time to find and study it. Books, magazines, pamphlets, seminars, and the Internet are full of financial advice and learning opportunities. Many of the most informative resources will be mentioned throughout this book, and Appendix A lists additional resources.

If you resist credit card debt and take advantage of financial opportunities, you'll be taking a giant step toward your financial goals. Ask for help if you're confused about a financial matter. Many issues concerning money, investments, and so on can be confusing, even to people who study them on a daily basis, so don't be discouraged if some financial issues seem confusing at first. They'll become clearer as you learn more.

> **Money Pit** _____
>
> We have a tendency to believe that what we read is true simply because it's been printed. Don't fall into the trap of thinking all printed financial information and advice is correct. Some of it is not, and you could be at risk financially if you don't distinguish between true and untrue. The more you learn and understand about personal finance, the better you'll be able to sort out information and misinformation. Be sure to get your information from reliable sources, and remember: If it sounds too good to be true—it probably is.

But be sure you take all the financial advice you'll get with a large grain of salt. If you follow the advice of every financial guru who comes along, promising on one talk show or another to quadruple your investment in six months or less, you're likely to end up losing some serious money along the way.

Remember that if you seek advice from a friend or family member, you're likely to hear what's worked best for him. What worked best for him, however, just might not be what will work best for you. Nobody wants to sound like a dummy (or a complete idiot), so you're likely to hear about the good financial move your brother made back in '99, while he completely skips over the bonehead deal he struck in '02.

The Least You Need to Know

- ◆ If you're finding that managing your own finances and living on your own is challenging, remember that the longer you do these things, the easier they'll be.

- ◆ Many young people are postponing living on their own and are staying at their parents' home longer.

- ◆ It's important to balance your lifestyle with your finances.

- ◆ Your early financial picture might not be exactly what you had hoped, but hang in there. It will get better.

- ◆ You need to keep believing that you're headed for success, both financially and personally.

Taking a Look at Your Bank Accounts

In This Chapter

◆ Shopping around for the best bank bargains

◆ The big three: banks, credit unions, and savings and loans

◆ Considering online banking

◆ Balancing interest rates with bank fees

◆ Cutting costs when using the ATM

It's tough to keep up with banks these days, even your own. You just get used to dealing with the First Bank of Smithsville, when it merges with a bigger bank and changes its name to the First National Smithsville Bank. Just when you adjust to *that*, it merges again and changes its name to the National Smithsville Bank of Jonesburg. It's a full-time job just keeping up with all the changes.

You may be intimidated by the recent rash of bank mega-mergers or all the restrictions and conditions under which banks seem to operate. You might be downright confused about the type of financial institution with which you want to be associated. You may have to look around a bit to find a place that feels right for you, but don't be discouraged. It can be done.

Do You Have the Accounts You Need?

Chances are pretty good that you already have savings and checking accounts. You've probably been writing checks for years for things such as books and rent, or maybe by now you're paying all your bills online. You probably use a *debit card*, too.

> ### Show Me the Money
>
> You use **debit cards,** which look like credit cards, to pay for purchases, but the money comes out of your checking account. Debit cards give you the best of both worlds: You get the convenience of a credit card without putting yourself in debt. An ATM card may or may not be a debit card. An ATM card accesses your account through an ATM machine. A debit card accesses your account from almost anywhere.

Of course, there's the possibility that you've managed to get through life so far *without* checking and savings accounts. If that's the case, it's time to get them established. If you already have accounts, it's time to take a good look at them to see if you're getting the best deal that you can.

Checking Accounts

The concept of a checking account is simple. You keep money in an account and write checks (or use a debit card) from that account instead of paying with cash. Using checks eliminates the need to carry large amounts of cash or send cash through the mail to pay bills.

There are various kinds of checking accounts. A few pay interest (although none pay very much), while nearly all banks impose various fees and conditions. Some charge you a monthly fee if your balance falls below a minimum amount. Some charge you fees to open the account. Some charge you for each check you write, and others charge you if you write more than a certain number of checks each month. You get the idea.

It pays to look at some different banks when you're considering opening or changing a checking account, because the difference in fees and conditions imposed can be significant. According to Bankrate.com, which studies and reports on what's happening in banking around the country, fees keep going up, while interest rates (on the accounts that still offer them) are practically nonexistent.

If you're just getting around to opening a checking account, take a few minutes to think about how you'll use it. For instance, if you write only three checks a month—one to your landlord, one to pay your Visa bill, and one for your college loan—you may do well to consider an account that includes a charge for each check written. Your fee would be minimal, and there could be benefits elsewhere that offset the per-check fee. Many financial institutions provide extra services or waive the fee for minimum deposits in several accounts. On the other hand, if for some reason you carry your checkbook with you and write checks for everything from groceries to haircuts and shoes, then you want to avoid at all costs a bank that charges for every check you write.

> **Money Pit**
>
> Just like lunch, there is no free checking. Be careful when you see a bank that offers "free checking" when you open several accounts there. You could end up paying more fees on the other accounts or losing out on higher interest rates you could get from another bank.

If you always have a lot of money in your checking account or a corresponding savings account, the bank might waive monthly fees. But if your account balance varies, or you don't keep much money in it, look out. You could end up getting hit with a big charge for going below your minimum balance requirement.

> **Pocket Change**
>
> The average interest paid on checking accounts these days is way below 1 percent. In fact, it's way below half a percent, according to www.bankrate.com.

Be sure you find out some basic information about checking accounts from every bank you query. Ask about fees, minimum balances, interest rates, overdraft protection, and anything else you can think of that might be helpful to know.

After you've opened a checking account, or changed your account to a bank that offers a better deal, there are a few other things to keep in mind. One simple but important rule is to keep your checkbook in a safe place and report it immediately if it's lost or stolen.

You also must keep track of how much money you have in your account. If you don't, you risk bouncing a check. The average fee for bouncing a check these days is almost $30 per check, making it a very expensive mistake. Record every transaction immediately, or sooner or later you'll forget about one. Record the checks you write as well as ATM and debit card transactions. Always look over your statement each month and confirm all deposits, ATM transactions, and withdrawals. If you notice something that doesn't look right, call your bank right away. Banks do make mistakes, and they're not always in your favor.

Savings Accounts

A lot of the same points we discussed about checking accounts apply when you're looking for a place to open a savings account. You'll need to figure out your savings habits and find a bank that has a deal that will best suit your habits.

Most banks will charge a monthly or quarterly maintenance fee and maybe an additional fee if your balance falls below a required minimum. In addition, you might be required to keep a savings account active for a specified time or face penalties.

When you're looking for a place to set up your account, review the list of questions suggested in the section on checking accounts, and ask those that apply to savings. You'll also need to ask a few other questions that apply to savings accounts:

◆ Does the bank use a *tiered account system?*

◆ Will I be penalized if I close the account before a certain time?

◆ Is the account federally insured?

◆ How much interest will I get on my savings?

Show Me the Money

A **tiered account system** means you'll earn higher interest if your account balance is consistently over an amount as set by the bank, usually at least $1,000, but many times higher. There are exceptions, but generally it's better to have your money somewhere other than in a savings account if you have a large amount. Still, it's nice to know what you'll be earning on the money in your savings account.

Although many banks don't pay interest on checking accounts, all banks pay interest on savings accounts. Banks used to pay 5 percent interest on all savings accounts because it was a federal regulation. Then along came banking deregulation in 1986, and interest rates haven't been the same since. Deregulation allowed banks to offer different kinds of accounts, which became competitive with each other and earned substantial interest. The higher interest on those accounts resulted in savings account interest rates being lowered.

Still, it pays to shop around because the amount of interest varies from bank to bank. In addition to www.bankrate.com, financial magazines such as *Money* publish lists of the highest-paying bank accounts each month.

Pocket Change
These days, the average savings account is earning 1.22 percent. Better than nothing, but not much to get excited about, is it?

Other Useful Accounts

Money market accounts (MMAs), which are considered to be a type of savings account, generally pay a bit more interest than regular savings accounts, although these days the difference is minimal. You can write a minimum number of checks (usually three) on the account each month.

If your savings account balance becomes substantial, that is, containing more money than you think you'll need anytime really soon, consider putting some of it in a certificate of deposit (CD). With a CD, you deposit money for a specified amount of time, usually from three months to a number of years. The longer you leave your money in the account, the more interest you should get on it. Interest rates on CDs are higher than those on savings accounts and money market accounts, but there's usually a penalty if you need to get the money out of the account before the agreed-upon time. Although there are variable (changeable) rate CDs, CD rates are usually set for the term of the certificate, while money market rates are changeable at any time.

Dollars and Sense
If you write only a couple of checks a month, a money market account might be worth considering. But there's usually a hefty fee if you write more than the number of checks permitted. Any additional interest will quickly be chewed up if you have to pay for extra checks.

All Banks Are Not Created Equal

Take a look around the area where you live sometime and notice the difference in the financial institutions. There are probably quite a few, ranging in size from something as large as the Bank of America to a small, local bank. When you look a little closer, you'll even find some places other than banks that will handle your money for you. In addition to the options available in your neighborhood, a whole new world of banking is unfolding before us in the form of Internet banks.

Traditionally, there are three types of financial institutions: banks, credit unions, and thrifts. Commercial banks handle about three quarters of the total amount of assets within the entire financial system, but many people prefer thrifts or credit unions. Let's take a look at each type of institution and some of the differences between them.

> ### Pocket Change
> The U.S. banking system is federally operated, but it has 50 state jurisdictions, each with its own regulatory and operating procedures.

> ### Dollars and Sense
> The name of a bank can help you figure out whether it's state-regulated or federally regulated. If it's federally regulated, its name will include "National" or "N.A."

> ### Pocket Change
> Credit union membership has extended far beyond people who work for a particular business or industry. There are credit unions organized by ethnicity, such as the Polish-American Credit Union, and even by family name. There are seven Lee Credit Unions, supported by the approximately 100,000 people in the United States with the last name Lee.

- **Commercial Banks.** Sometimes called full-service banks, these are the most widely used financial institutions in the United States, with about 8,000 operating. Commercial banks are permitted to take deposits, loan money, and provide other banking services. They can have either a federal or state charter and are regulated accordingly. Commercial banks vary greatly. They can be huge mega-banks that have sprung up during the past several years or small, community banks. The 300 or so foreign banks that operate in the United States are technically commercial banks. They must comply with federal regulations, but many of them do not offer the banking services that the average customer requires.

- **Credit Unions.** These offer many of the same services as commercial banks: checking accounts, savings accounts, vacation clubs, ATM services, and calendars at the holidays. They generally can offer better rates on loans and savings, however, because, as nonprofit organizations, they don't pay federal taxes. It used to be that only people with common occupation, association, or geographical area could form and join credit unions. These days, however, practically everyone can join a credit union in one capacity or another. Before joining a credit union, make sure it's a member of the FDIC, which guarantees deposits. Not all credit unions are FDIC members.

◆ **Thrifts.** These are the financial institutions commonly known as savings and loans (S&Ls). Savings and loans have had a tarnished reputation since the late 1980s, when many of them failed and had to be bailed out by Uncle Sam (that is, taxpayer dollars). Recent legislative changes have greatly improved the quality of *thrifts*, making them good options for depositors once again. Make sure your deposits are insured by the State Life Insurance Corporation (SLIC).

◆ **Internet Banks and Online Banking.** Many banks today offer online banking, allowing you to access your accounts online to check balances and transactions, pay bills online, and transfer money from one account to another. You may be able to access stock quotes and trade stocks and mutual funds. In addition to online banking offered by traditional banks, there's a new guy on the block—*Internet banks*, also called *virtual banks* or *e-banks*. They offer most of the same services as traditional banks and are subject to the same federal regulations. They're convenient, open all the time, and, because they have a much lower overhead than traditional banks, they can offer some big financial advantages to customers in the form of higher interest rates and lower fees.

> **Show Me the Money**
>
> **Thrifts** are the collective name for savings banks and savings and loan associations. They generally accept deposits from, and extend credit primarily to individuals.

> **Show Me the Money**
>
> Traditional banks are known as **brick and mortar** banks. Traditional banks that offer online banking are being called **brick-to-click** banks, and, Internet-only banks are called **virtual banks** or **e-banks**.

A disadvantage of virtual banks is that they have no ATM machines of their own, meaning you end up paying service charges to conduct ATM transactions at all ATMs. Also, many e-banks won't let you deposit money to your account via an ATM, meaning you have to mail a check or transfer money online from another account.

Internet banks are aware of this problem, however, and are taking steps to resolve it. Some virtual banks allow you to drop off deposits at Mail Boxes Etc., and others are working out deals with regional ATM networks to allow their customers to use those machines for deposits.

Dollars and Sense

Some of the most well-known virtual banks include Juniper Bank (www.juniper.com), National Interbank (www.nationalinterbank.com), First Internet Bank of Indiana (firstib.com), and NetBank (www.netbank.com).

Pocket Change

It used to be that most of the profits financial institutions realized came from the spread between the interest they'd pay on deposits and the interest they charged on loans. But now more than 50 percent of the average bank's earnings comes from fees.

No matter how you decide to conduct your banking, interest rates probably will be a factor in deciding what financial institution you choose. These days, interest rates are pretty much low across the board. Still, you should look around and see where you can get the most interest on your money. Even a fraction of a percentage point adds up. And, as you get more money, it makes even more of a difference.

Another New Bank Fee?

We've already discussed in this chapter fees imposed by banks, credit unions, and thrifts. It might seem like every time your monthly statement comes, there's an additional fee. Some banks even charge customers for phone calls to the bank.

The best thing to do concerning fees is to go to your bank and get a copy of its fee disclosure statement. Look it over carefully, and see how many of the fees apply to you. If it seems like too many, you might want to think about finding a new bank.

Stop at the ATM, I Need More Cash

If you're like most people, you can't imagine life without automated teller machines (ATMs). They're so convenient and easy to use. According to an online group called The ATM Connection, 60 percent of Americans ages 25–34 use ATMs eight times a month, withdrawing an average of $55 each time. Some people, however, use ATMs with much greater frequency—visiting the machines as many as 160 times a year. The online group also reports that people who use ATMs spend 20 to 25 percent more money overall than people who don't use the machines.

Automated Teller Machines or Automated Theft Machines?

First introduced in the late 1960s, ATMs have been around for more than 30 years now, but they've proliferated during the past 15 years or so. ATMs are now found anywhere you might need some cash: restaurants, bars, coffee shops, department stores, movie theaters, and gas stations.

As convenient as ATMs can be, they can be expensive. Some cynics have stated that, considering the fees levied at cash machines, ATM should not stand for automated teller machine, but for automated theft machine. Some banks charge as much as $4.50 for you to withdraw money (keep in mind that it's *your* money), transfer funds, or get an account balance. If one of those heavy users who checks into the ATM 160 times a year pays $4.50 for every transaction, he could end up paying more than $700 a year just to access his own money!

The banking industry tells us that ATMs are wonderful because they're accessible 24 hours a day and are more convenient than having to go to a bank and wait in line for a teller. The truth is, the banking industry loves ATMs because they save the industry a lot of payroll costs and generate a lot of cash through fees.

> **Pocket Change**
>
> A group of state Public Interest Research Groups are gaining public support in their efforts to call attention to high ATM fees and have the fees reduced or eliminated. Public Interest Research Groups are nonprofit, nonpartisan consumer and environmental advocacy groups located around the country. You can check out the movement online at www. StopATMFees.com.

Tips to Cut ATM Fees

If you use ATMs—and who doesn't?—follow these tips to save yourself some money on fees. And don't forget to retrieve your card before leaving the machine!

- ◆ Use your own bank's ATMs whenever possible. Most banks still don't charge a fee for customers to use their machines.

- ◆ If your bank's ATM is "down" when you try to use it, note the time and place and call your bank the next business day to report it. It should credit your account for the amount you had to pay to use another bank's machine. If it doesn't, find another bank!

◆ If your bank or credit union doesn't have a machine that's convenient for you, shop around to find a machine with the least-expensive fee. Fees vary as much as $2 per transaction.

◆ Use your debit card at the check-out line of the grocery store and get cash back. Many stores will let you get extra money, usually a maximum of about $50, when you use your card to buy groceries. This strategy makes more sense than paying $3 to withdraw $50 from an ATM. Watch it, however, some merchants are jumping on the ATM bandwagon and charge a fee for this service. Even if they don't, your bank may.

◆ If you have to withdraw money at an ATM, think ahead and get enough so you won't be back in a day or two. It doesn't make sense to pay $2 to get $10 out of your checking account. Limit your visits to the ATM to once a week, or maybe even twice a month.

We're not saying that ATMs don't have lots of advantages. But be aware of the differences in fees from machine to machine, and try to find yourself the best deal available.

The Least You Need to Know

◆ Understanding your options in financial institutions will help you make a good choice when deciding where to put your money.

◆ Banks, credit unions, and thrifts (savings and loans) are the three most common types of financial institutions.

◆ Online banking and Internet banks are changing the way many people are conducting their financial business.

◆ You've got to know the questions to ask when trying to find the best checking and savings accounts.

◆ Being aware of the fees associated with ATMs can save you some money.

Chapter 4

Credit Cards and Debt

In This Chapter

- ◆ The history of the credit revolution
- ◆ The perils of credit cards
- ◆ Getting a credit card if you don't have one
- ◆ When using a credit card makes sense, and when it doesn't
- ◆ Using debit cards and prepaid credit cards
- ◆ Protecting your cards against loss and theft
- ◆ Understanding credit card fees

What a wonderful invention credit cards are. With credit cards, there's no need to carry cash, and they're much more convenient to use than checks. They're easy to get, and you can use them almost everywhere. Nearly every place, from doctors' offices to convenience stores, will gladly take your credit card instead of cash. So what's the problem?

There is no problem, as long as you can use your card wisely and pay back what you owe each month. Credit cards are convenient, no question about it. But they also can be very dangerous and have been the tool for financial ruin for millions of people.

Everybody Wants a Credit Card—Until They Have One

By this point in your life, you probably have at least one credit card. And you can be sure if you have one, or even if you don't, you'll be offered more.

Credit card companies in this country send out almost 2.5 billion offers for cards a year. That's 10 offers for every man, woman, and child in America. And then there are the companies that will find credit cards for those who have had serious credit problems and can't get conventional cards. There are more than one billion credit cards in circulation in the United States, according to the popular financial gurus, the Motley Fools. That comes out to four apiece for every person.

Credit cards are a huge business in this country, to say the least. It wasn't too long ago, however, that credit cards didn't even exist.

All that changed in the 1960s, when, at the tail end of the baby boom, the Bank of America introduced the first bank credit card. The idea caught on quickly, and Americans were soon charging up a storm. Unlike now, however, nearly everyone paid off the balance each month in those days. It was considered almost a disgrace to owe on a credit card. Cards were fun and convenient, but the balance on them was rarely carried over to the next month.

Somewhere along the line, the stigma of owing money on them lessened and eventually disappeared. Today, it's estimated that about 70 percent of cardholders carry a balance from one month to another. This balance is called *revolving consumer debt*, and it's on the rise. At the end of June 2003, the total revolving consumer debt in America had risen to $726.9 billion, according to Federal Reserve statistics. Credit card debt accounted for the great majority of that total.

This revolving debt can quickly cause trouble for credit card holders. When you don't pay off your balance, the bank or credit card company starts charging interest on what you owe—a lot of interest. The interest rate can vary greatly, depending on who

> **Pocket Change**
>
> Credit card companies began hitting on young people in the 1980s, when they realized they'd completely saturated the baby boomer market. Even high school students who have just turned 18 are, in many cases, offered credit cards.

> **Show Me the Money**
>
> **Revolving consumer debt** is the balance on a credit card that is carried over from one month to the next, incurring interest and fees as it does.

issued the card, but the average credit card interest rate as of June 23, 2004 was around 13.3 percent, according to bankrate.com. That's a lower rate than it was several years ago, attributed to an overall decrease in interest rates. Still, if you carry over a $2,000 balance at that interest rate, you'll pay $266 in interest charges per year, more than $22 for one month. Analysts are predicting that all interest rates will climb again soon.

> **Pocket Change**
>
> Among Americans who have one or more credit cards, the average debt being carried over from month to month is nearly $4,000, according to a 2004 Gallup Poll. The only way to avoid mounting debt like this is to pay off any debt you have now and not incur anymore.

Getting a Card If You Don't Have One

Now that you know about the history, advantages, and potential pitfalls of credit cards, you probably still want one if you don't already have one. And you probably should have one. As mentioned earlier, credit cards often are necessary. Some banks won't even let you open an account if you don't have a credit card, and it's important that you acquire credit in your name for use later on.

If you don't have a card, you can find applications at your local bank. You also can find them in magazines or by accessing a bank that offers credit cards, such as Citibank or Chase, on the Internet.

Normally, if you have no credit history, but are at least 18 years old with a job, you'll be able to get a card with a limited amount of credit, usually $500 to $1,000. If you don't have a job, but you have a parent who is willing to be a co-signer or guarantor (see the next section), you can still get a credit card.

> **CAUTION**
>
> **Money Pit**
>
> We know people who will spend hours, even days, shopping around for bargains. They'll never buy anything that's not on sale, yet they'll let their credit card debt accumulate and pay close to 17 percent interest on it. Even if they find a bargain purchase, they'll still lose money by having to pay those high interest rates on their credit cards.

If you are diligent with your payments, you'll probably be able to have your credit limit upped after 6 to 12 months. The amount of the increase is dependent on your income or your ability to repay the line of credit.

Co-Signers and Secured Cards

If you have no credit history and your earnings are low, or if you already have a bad credit history, you might not be able to get a card in your name alone. You may need to apply for a secured card or get someone to act as a *co-signer* or *guarantor*. A co-signer, or guarantor, is someone who agrees to assume responsibility if you can't, or don't, pay off credit card debt.

If you need a guarantor to get a credit card, the person must be an adult with a good credit history. Usually, a parent will take this role, although it could be someone else, depending on the circumstances. Both you and the other person whose name appears on the card are responsible for missed payments and overspending.

> **Show Me the Money**
>
> A **co-signer** or **guarantor** is someone who assumes the responsibility if you can't pay off credit card debt.
>
> **Collateral** is something of value put up as security for a loan. It is to ensure that the lender will not lose the money loaned.

A secured card or credit account is when the bank or credit card company requires a deposit that serves as *collateral*. The deposit is equal to the amount of credit allowed on the card. So, if you got a card with a $500 credit limit, you'd have to make a $500 deposit. There are often other fees charged to open a secured account, although, as more companies begin to offer these types of cards, some are dropping the fees in order to get an edge on the competition.

Some companies will pay you a bit of interest on your deposit, but don't expect it to be very high. You, on the other hand, will pay between 17 percent and 21 percent interest on unpaid balances, because your credit risk is considered higher than someone's with a regular card. But if you want a card and want to begin a credit history, a secured card might be the way you'll need to go.

> **Money Pit**
>
> The old saying, "If it sounds too good to be true, it probably is," definitely applies to ads for credit cards. You can get yourself into a lot of trouble if you make the mistake of dealing with a disreputable company. Many of the cards have "initial balances" (really substantial fees) on which you pay interest with very minimal monthly payments.

A big word of warning here: Be very wary of companies that offer credit cards, either secured or unsecured, at fabulous rates or to people who haven't been able to get a card. There are a rapidly growing number of unscrupulous companies that target people with poor or nonexistent credit ratings, who can't get approved for credit cards through traditional issuers. The Internet is full of offers for people who previously couldn't get cards. Some of these offers are pretty unbelievable and should be avoided.

If you do get a secured card, be sure that you find out when your account can be converted to a standard account. At that point, you should get your full deposit back, provided you've made timely payments and don't owe any money on your credit card.

The following are a few of the institutions that offer secured credit cards:

- ◆ Amalgamated Bank of Chicago (1-800-723-0303)
- ◆ Household Bank (1-800-771-7339)
- ◆ Merrick Bank (1-801-545-6600)
- ◆ U.S. Bank (1-800-285-8585)

How Many Credit Cards Does One Person Need?

Once you get one credit card, it's easy to get more. Unless you screw up royally, your mailbox will be home to many credit card applications. You'll learn to recognize them right away. Fancy envelopes, often gold or silver, stamped with words such as "low annual percentage rate," "no annual fee," or "pre-approved." You'd do well to toss those envelopes into the trash unopened, unless there's a good reason that you need more than one or two credit cards.

There's no reason to have a separate credit card for every department store, gas station, and electronics store in town. Having multiple cards in your wallet merely encourages you to use them and run up more debt. Nearly all retailers that accept credit cards take Visa and MasterCard. It's a lot easier to keep track of one credit limit (or two, if you really feel that you need a backup) than a dozen cards from all over the place.

Be aware that there are different kinds of credit cards. Some distinctions include the following:

- ◆ **Charge cards.** These are not really credit cards because you're required to pay off your balance at the end of each billing period. Charge cards are good because you have no interest charges, but they may come with an annual fee, and if you charge more than you can pay all at once when the bill comes, you're in trouble, because you'll be assessed a late fee.

◆ **Fixed-rate cards.** These credit cards have a fixed rate of interest. Some people like knowing exactly what interest they're paying at any given time, but these cards typically have the highest interest rates and have fallen out of favor in the past few years.

◆ **Variable-rate cards.** The interest rate on these cards changes periodically based on the rate charged by the lending institution holding the card. The rate is often tied in to the bank's prime rate, with six percentage points added on. These cards became popular a few years ago when the interest rates on them became lower than on fixed-rate cards. More than half of all cards in circulation today are variable-rate cards.

◆ **Gold, Platinum, and Titanium cards.** These status cards offer some advantages, such as buyer protection plans or cash back after you spend a certain (high) amount. They also can offer perks like emergency roadside service and insurance on newly purchased merchandise. They offer high credit limits, but they sometimes carry high annual fees. They generally are available only to people with established credit reports.

◆ **Rewards cards.** Increasing numbers of credit card companies are offering rewards cards, which give you something back. You might get cash back, as with a Discover Card; airline miles; a rebate on gas; rental car or hotel discounts; or discounted shopping at a particular store. Credit card companies do this in order to be competitive. The more you charge to the credit card, the bigger your reward will be. However, there usually is a fee involved with getting one of these cards, so think carefully about whether it's a worthwhile venture. Also, don't be tempted to overspend in order to increase your reward.

Keep It (Your Credit Card) in Your Pants

An important thing to remember about credit cards is that just because you have them, you don't have to use them to rack up a lot of debt for stuff you don't need. As gratifying as it might be to throw a bunch of bags onto the back seat as you leave the mall, your spending will catch up with you at the end of the billing period. And you know what they say about payback.

Knowing When to Use Your Credit Card

Say you're driving four hours to visit an old college buddy for the weekend. You're about two thirds of the way there when you notice your car's temperature gauge is on the rise. The needle keeps nosing up, and pretty soon you notice little wisps of steam coming from under the hood. You pull over; you know when you're beat. Somebody stops and gives you the name of a gas station down the road that does repairs. He says he'll stop by the station and have a tow truck sent up for you. Great, you say, because by now your car won't even start.

It doesn't take the mechanic long to figure out that there's a hole in your radiator the size of Iowa, and when he starts muttering about hoses, you see the dollar signs mounting up in your mind. You finally get the bill for the tow and the repairs, only to learn that you're out $247.93. You have just $60 in your wallet, and you're still hoping to get to your friend's house for the weekend. This definitely is a situation in which you should use your credit card and be grateful that you have it. Emergencies such as this are when credit cards are at their finest.

Dollars and Sense

Credit cards are necessary if you run into an unexpected emergency expense, so don't leave home without one if you're traveling.

They're great when you order something from a catalog or go shopping online. It's also good to have a card number when you call to make a hotel reservation and the front desk person says, "Would you like to secure that with your credit card?" Ditto for renting a car or reserving a plane ticket.

Sometimes Cash Is King

There are times and places, though, where you should forget you even have a credit card. Many financial advisers will tell you to never use a credit card to buy anything that depreciates. This includes clothing, shoes, gas, meals in restaurants, groceries, and so on.

That's good advice, but it's pretty tough to follow. Of course, there are exceptions to this rule. For example, what if you're on vacation and you see a cool pair of sandals that you just love. And they're on sale! If you pay cash for the sandals, however, you won't have enough cash for the rest of the vacation, so you buy the sandals and put the charge on your credit card. That's fine, as long as you'll be able to pay off the charge when the bill comes in.

Generally, however, there is a rule that should be followed carefully: don't use a credit card to pay for something that will be gone when the bill comes.

Advantages of Debit Cards or Prepaid Credit Cards

If you don't like the idea of carrying around cash, and many people do not, you can get a debit card. A *debit card* works like a check. When you use it to pay for a purchase, the money is deducted from your checking account. Available from your bank or credit union, debit cards have become extremely common and widely used. They are a great way to avoid carrying around a lot of cash, yet they won't get you into debt problems since the card won't work if the money isn't in your checking or savings account.

In addition to using your debit card for purchases, most can be used to obtain cash from an automated teller machine (ATM). As discussed in Chapter 3, if the ATM is not affiliated with your bank, there is likely a fee for a cash withdrawal. A better idea, when possible, is to get cash back when you use your debit card for a purchase. Treat debit card purchases like those for which you use a check. Be sure to record the transaction and the amount of the purchase in your checkbook, and remember to include any extra cash you get back. Keep track of how much money is available in your account. If you have $500 in your checking account and just wrote checks totaling $450 to cover monthly bills, you'll be able to access $500 with your debit card until the checks clear. The problem is, if you use your debit card to pay for $90 worth of groceries before those checks clear, you'll come up $40 short.

> **CAUTION**
>
> **Money Pit**
>
> You should be aware that a debit card may not offer the protection that a credit card does for items you purchase that are never delivered or defective. If you pay for something with your debit card and you have a problem with the item, try to resolve it with the merchant. If you can't, contact your debit card issuer for advice.

Another way to avoid credit card debt, or to obtain a credit card if for some reason you're having trouble doing so, is to use a prepaid card.

A *prepaid credit card* is just what its name implies. You pay up front, and then use the card until you've spent the money. At that point, you need to put more money into your prepaid account or the card won't work. The advantage is that you never incur interest fees because you've already paid for your card purchases. Disadvantages, however, are that you often must pay a fee to set up an account and each time you "load" your card. And, of course, you need to have money available in order to get a prepaid card.

Still, prepaid credit cards are useful for people who can't get a traditional card or are working hard to avoid high credit card interest fees.

Dollars and Sense

To learn more about the types of prepaid credit cards that are available, check out the online credit card center at www.credit-card-applications-center.com.

Keeping Your Credit and Debit Cards Safe

Regardless of how many or what types of credit and debit cards you have, it's extremely important to protect them. Credit card fraud and theft is very common, and debit cards can also provide opportunity to thieves. Fortunately, there are steps you can take to make sure your cards are safe.

Dollars and Sense

If you report a lost or stolen credit card before it's used by someone else, you're not held responsible for charges incurred to your account. If the card has already been used by the time you report it, you could be charged up to $50. If your debit card is lost or stolen, the amount you might be charged depends on how quickly you report the loss.

Most trouble occurs with credit cards that have been lost or stolen, so you need to keep close tabs on your cards. This is especially important if you're traveling. Thieves stole the wallet of a friend visiting Paris a few years ago. By the time she realized that her wallet was gone, which was only about 15 minutes after the theft occurred, the thieves had charged thousands of dollars worth of electronic goods to her account.

Someone looking to use your card doesn't even need the actual piece of plastic in order to do so. A sales slip with your card number

CAUTION

Money Pit

Be aware of who is standing near you while you enter your PIN when using a debit card, and be careful not to let anyone see the number you enter. Thieves have been known to observe a customer using a debit card so as to obtain the PIN, then steal the card and flee, cleaning out the customer's account before the card can be reported stolen.

and expiration date is all that a wily thief needs. Protecting your credit cards is mostly common sense. Don't ever give your account number to someone over the phone or internet unless you're absolutely sure it's legitimate. Make sure you get it back from the sales clerk after using it, and sign it—in ink—as soon as you receive it. For a list of tips on protecting your credit cards, check out Consumer Action's website at www.consumer-action.org.

Most credit and debit card fraud is preventable, and you can avoid a lot of trouble by being diligent with your cards and using common sense. Credit and debit cards can quickly change from a convenience to a huge hassle if they're lost or stolen, so be aware of where you keep them and how you use them.

Finding a Better Deal on Your Credit Cards

If you're going to use credit cards—and it's a very rare person who isn't—you might as well get the best deal on them that you can. Credit cards cost you money, make no mistake about it. But there are ways to minimize those costs.

Annual Fees

Intense competition among card companies has forced most of them to lower, or even drop, their *annual fees*. A research company in Maryland reports that more than half of all credit cards are available without an annual fee or that the fee will be waived if you ask.

Dollars and Sense _____

If your credit record is good and you're paying an annual fee on your credit card, write to the company or bank (the address should be on your bill) and ask to have the fee waived. If the bank won't waive it, write again (or call, but it's better to have a written record of everything) and say you're going to switch to another company. Betcha the bank will drop the fee rather than lose a customer.

If you are paying an annual fee, it shouldn't be more than about $20, unless, for some reason, you happen to have a gold card. Those fees usually run about $35 a year or more. If you do have a gold card, ask yourself why. At this stage of your life, do you really need it, or is it an ego thing?

Interest Rates

Interest rates do make credit cards interesting, that's for sure. The *interest rate* is what the bank charges you to use its money to finance what you buy with your credit card.

When you charge a new area rug for your living room for $300, for instance, the store from which you got them collects its money from the bank that issued your credit card. The bank, in turn, gets its money back from you along with interest if you don't pay the $300 back within a specified time. You usually have a *grace period*, which is a certain amount of time you have to pay off your purchases before you start getting charged interest.

If you pay off your credit card every month, which is the best way to do it, you won't incur any interest charges. Then your credit card is simply a convenient alternative to paying with cash. If you're like most people, however, you won't pay off your bill in full each month. That's where the trouble starts.

If you owe $1,000 on your credit card, and you make only the minimum payment each month, it will take you years to pay off the money you owe, and you'll end up paying nearly as much in interest as you owe on the loan. In plain language, it's a really bad idea to let the interest keep building up on your credit card debt. That rug could end up costing more than twice that amount if you pay them off $10 a month, plus interest.

Show Me the Money

An **annual fee** is a charge you pay to the bank or credit card company for the privilege of holding its card. An **interest rate** is the amount the bank charges you to use its money to finance what you buy with your credit card.

Dollars and Sense

Be sure you know what the grace period on your card is. The traditional grace period used to be 30 days, but it's getting shorter and shorter. The average grace period is now about 18 days.

Fierce competition among card companies and overall low interest rates have forced down credit card interest rates in recent years. Some banks offer credit cards at rates as low as 8.25 or 8.5 percent. You might even see one now and then for as low as 6.5 percent interest, or get a special starting rate of just 2.95 percent or even lower. Be careful, though. Usually those rates only apply for six months, after which time they go up. If you apply for a card with a special starting rate, be sure that you know the ongoing terms of the agreement.

There are cards available for 10 or 12 percent for cardholders with great credit, so if you're paying more than 13 or 14 percent, now is the time to look around for a better rate. For a list of comparative credit card rates, try one of these organizations:

◆ CardTrak.com has credit card information and interest rates.

◆ Bankrate.com's credit card page provides interest rate comparisons and advice on finding a better card.

When you locate a card with a good rate, go ahead and apply. If you've had a card for a while and you've maintained a good credit record, you should qualify for a better rate. If you've only had a card for a short time, though, it might be harder to get approved for a low interest rate. Still, it can't hurt to try. There's a lot of competition for cardholders, and some places are willing to give you a lower interest rate to keep your business. All you have to do, in some cases, is ask. If you haven't had much time to build up a credit record, and you're not approved for a lower interest rate, be diligent about keeping up with your payments and try again in a year to get a better rate.

Fees and More Fees

As bad as the annual fees and interest rates are on credit cards, it's the other, lesser-known fees that can really add up. No matter how boring and complicated it may seem, make sure you read all the fine print that comes along with your credit card policy. If you don't understand it, call the card company and ask for customer service. Insist that someone answer all your questions. Many people don't fully understand their policies, and they end up paying all kinds of hidden charges as a result.

Some other fees to look for on your own credit card, or when you're checking out an offer for a card, include the following:

◆ **Late fees.** You'll be charged a fee if your payment is late. That's in addition to the interest charges for not paying off your balance by a specified time. Not all banks charge the late fee, so make sure you find out when you apply for the card.

◆ **Cash advance fees.** These are nasty fees, and because they are, you should try to never take a cash advance. When you borrow cash against your credit card, most cards forget about the grace period and start charging you interest right away. About 50 percent of the card companies out there will charge you 2 to 6 percent more interest on a cash advance than on other charges not paid off by the end of the billing period. There's also usually a one-time fee of between 2 and 5 percent for cash advances.

◆ **Discretionary fees.** These fees, imposed on you to pay for things such as credit life insurance or a shopping service that you never ordered, are at the discretion of the card company, not you. Be sure to read your bill carefully, and don't pay for anything you didn't order.

◆ **Two-cycle billing.** Two-cycle billing is extremely unpopular among consumers, and rightly so. This billing method penalizes people who pay off their cards every month for a while, but then get behind and carry a balance. The bank will charge you an extra month's interest every time you begin a balance. This could result in you paying as much as four extra months' interest for a year.

◆ **Penalty interest rates.** If your payment is late, if you exceed your credit limit, or if you do anything else to annoy your card issuer, you could be slapped with penalty interest rates, which could add 3 to 10 percent to what you're already paying.

Make sure you read each bill carefully when you get it, and look for any charges you can't account for. If you feel you've been charged for something to which you didn't agree in advance, by all means pick up the phone and talk with someone in customer service. The intense competition between credit card issuers is forcing them to be responsive to consumers' needs and complaints. Make sure you take advantage of it!

Timeliness Is Next to Godliness: Paying Off Your Debt

You've already learned about late fees, but you might be surprised to know that your payment only has to be one day late in order for that fee to be issued. The typical late fee is $15, but some issuers are charging over $25. That means you could end up paying a good piece of change because you forgot to drop your envelope in the mailbox on your way to work.

If you're ever charged a late fee and your payment was only one day overdue, give customer service a call and ask to have the charge revoked. It might not work, but then again it might. The best thing to do, though, is to make sure you pay your charge card bills on time. If you're running late, send your payment by priority mail. It will get your check to the card company in two days, and at less than $5, it will cost you a lot less than paying the late fee on your bill. You could significantly hurt your chances of getting a lower interest rate or having your annual fee dropped if you have a history of late payments. And such a history could make it more difficult to get a different card.

The Least You Need to Know

- ◆ Credit cards have been around for a while, but their use has greatly increased, along with the debt people carry on them.

- ◆ Credit cards are great when used responsibly, but they can cause financial nightmares when they're used to buy things you can't afford.

- ◆ A person with a poor credit history or no credit history can get a secured credit card or have a co-signer or guarantor for a credit card.

- ◆ Regardless of how many or what types of credit cards you have, be sure to safeguard them to the greatest extent possible.

- ◆ It makes sense to use a credit card in certain situations, but not in every situation. Debit cards often are a good alternative to cash or credit cards.

- ◆ If you're paying high fees and interest rates on your credit cards, it's time to look around for another card.

- ◆ Paying off your credit card bill in full and on time each month is the best way to go. If you can't, then paying as much as you can, on time, is the next best plan.

Finding a Place with the Right Zip Code

In This Chapter

◆ Establishing your criteria for the perfect place to live

◆ The best ways to look for an apartment

◆ How much up-front money do you need?

◆ The pros and cons of living with roommates

◆ What about renter's insurance?

◆ Tightening the reins on living expenses

There are many, many financial implications associated with renting, leasing, or buying any form of housing, whether it's a studio apartment or a four-bedroom home. So, before you sign on the dotted line, take a little time to read and think about how renting or leasing will affect your financial future.

Doing the Apartment Thing

Many people find that renting an apartment is the way to go when they first move out on their own. There are usually plenty available (unless you get caught up in a housing crunch, as happens sometimes, especially in cities), and they come in a wide range of prices. You can get a studio or one-bedroom apartment if you'll be living on your own, or get an apartment with two or more bedrooms if you'll be sharing it with one or more roommates.

There are nearly as many kinds of apartments as there are people to fill them. With all those options and more to choose from, how do you find an apartment that …

♦ Is enjoyable and comfortable?

♦ Is affordable?

♦ Is in a safe area?

♦ Is convenient to work, shopping, and your friends?

Apartment hunting can be confusing, but if you get organized and follow some basic rules, you'll do just fine.

Scouting Locations

If you've got to live in the 90210 zip code (or any other particular zip code), you're really narrowing your choice of apartments that you like and can afford. Location, however, *is* important. Maybe you want to live in a certain area because it's close to your work and not too close to your parents. Maybe you've got some good friends who live there and have told you how great it is. There are all kinds of reasons you might want to live in a particular area, and if you do, that's where you should begin your apartment search.

Dollars and Sense

Be sure to consider the cost of getting to work or to other places you go frequently if you choose to live in an area that's not close to those places. The cost of gas or public transportation can add up quickly.

There are several good ways to find an apartment. Traditional methods include word of mouth, classified ads, and the phone book. As you know, however, more and more people are finding places to live on the Internet. A real estate agent can also help you locate an apartment, or you can simply drive to the area in which you're interested in living and see what's available. If you're still in college or still living in a college town, the university housing office will be able to give you some suggestions.

Signing Your Life Away

When you've found an apartment you like, there are still more factors to consider before you sign the lease. To start with, the landlord will want some information about you. He or she will probably do a credit check and verify your employment. You may also be asked to give some references.

You have to figure out whether you can afford the apartment and whether it includes the things you need. Is there a washer and dryer in the apartment or somewhere on the premises, or will you have to lug your stuff to the laundromat? Is there a grocery store nearby, or will shopping entail a trip across town? Will your landlord get someone to repaint the purple bedroom, or will he or she let you paint it? Can you have pets? Don't take anything for granted. If you're not sure about something, or if it's not specified in the *lease*, ask.

Show Me the Money

A **lease** is a legally binding agreement between a landlord and tenant. It contains the names of the landlord and the renter(s), the cost of rent and payment schedule, and other pertinent rules and regulations.

Never take an apartment without seeing and signing a contract between you and the landlord. Make sure the landlord signs it in your presence. If a landlord tries to tell you that you don't need a contract, get out fast. He or she could change all the conditions you agree upon verbally, and you'd have no way of proving it.

If the lease seems overly complicated or confusing, you may want to get a lawyer or real estate agent to check it for you before you sign. Experts say that rent agreements are becoming increasingly complicated, with all sorts of obscure conditions that you might easily overlook.

Some things to look for in the lease, or ask your prospective landlord about, include the following:

◆ What is the term of the lease?

◆ What are the provisions for renewing the lease?

◆ How much security deposit will be required, and what are the terms for recovering the deposit when you move?

◆ Who pays the utilities (such as heat and hot water)?

◆ Who's responsible for removing snow and ice in the winter or garbage all year round?

◆ Can you sublet the apartment if you move?

◆ How much notice must you give the landlord before you move?

◆ What rules apply to the rental?

◆ Are any appliances included (refrigerator, stove, and so on), and what happens if they break?

◆ What's the parking situation? Do you have a designated space that's close to your apartment?

◆ Does the owner provide security within the building or complex?

◆ Is a discount available if you do maintenance yourself? If there's any existing damage to the apartment, make sure you document it.

◆ When is the rent due?

◆ What happens if you're late paying the rent?

Don't ever let a landlord pressure you into signing a lease before you're ready to. If he or she tells you there's someone else ready to sign and you'll lose the apartment if you don't put your name on the dotted line, take a chance on losing it, even if you love it. The landlord may be trying to rush through with the deal before you notice that the lease doesn't work in your best interests. Be sure you ask the landlord for a copy of his rental policy, if he has one. Such a policy would list all rules that apply.

Knowing What You Can Spend

You should spend no more than 25 to 30 percent of your monthly *gross income* (your income before taxes are deducted) for rent. So if you're making $30,000 a year ($2,500 a month), you shouldn't be paying more than $700 a month for your rent, using the 28 percent calculation. The following table will help you figure out approximately how much you should be spending for rent.

Amount You Would Spend for Housing (at 28% of Income)

Annual Income*	Annual Housing Cost	Monthly Housing Cost
$ 20,000	$ 5,600	$ 466.67
25,000	7,000	583.33
30,000	8,400	700.00
35,000	9,800	816.67
40,000	11,200	933.33
45,000	12,600	1,050.00
50,000	14,000	1,166.67
60,000	16,800	1,400.00
70,000	19,600	1,633.33
80,000	22,400	1,866.67
90,000	25,200	2,100.00
100,000	28,000	2,333.33

Gross Income

Another thing to keep in mind is that you're free to negotiate with an owner concerning the rent he or she is charging. You'll probably be more successful trying this with a private rental, as opposed to an apartment complex where rents are established. If you've found a place you like that's a little out of your price range, go ahead and ask the landlord to drop the rent by $25 or $50 a month. Depending on the rental market in the area, you may or may not get the results you want. Saving $50 a month in rent adds up to $600 a year. It's worth asking about, don't you think?

Up-Front Costs

When you find an apartment you can afford, it's not quite as easy as handing over your first month's rent and moving in. Your landlord also may require the following:

◆ An extra month's rent (usually used to cover your last month)

◆ A *security deposit* equivalent to one or two months' rent

So if you find an apartment for $700 a month, you could end up having to pay out nearly $3,000 before you even move in.

Show Me the Money

A **security deposit** is the amount of money you pay to the landlord to protect against damages that occur to the apartment while you're renting it. He or she should give you an itemized list of deductions to your security deposit. If you fulfill the terms of your lease and leave your apartment in good repair, your money should be refunded.

The extra month's rent and your security deposit should be kept in an escrow account, which is an account specified for the purpose of holding your money until it is either used or returned to you. Some states, but not all, require that security deposits be kept in interest-bearing accounts for the tenant.

All that up-front money can be pretty discouraging news, to be sure, and it is one reason Gen Xers are hanging out longer with Mom and Dad. It's also why many people choose to rent with another person or a group of people.

Three's Company—Or a Crowd

If you decide to go with a roommate, you can cut your up-front costs by splitting them. Instead of $2,000, you'd need only $1,000. You can cut costs even further by renting with more than one person, but make sure you find out about any restrictions the landlord or neighborhood might have concerning the number of tenants per unit.

Money Pit

If you find out your prospective roommate smokes two packs of cigarettes a day and likes to have wild parties every weekend, and you can't stand smoke and like to relax with a good book on a Saturday night, call off the deal before it's made. If you sign a lease, you're legally obligated and will be held financially responsible for your share of expenses.

In addition to helping out financially, a roommate can be great company and make you feel more secure if you're a bit uncomfortable living by yourself. Be sure, however, that you consider any potential disadvantages before moving in with a roomy.

Once you sign a lease, thus agreeing to pay up-front costs and rent for a specified amount of time, you are legally obligated to do so. If you find out you can't live with your roommate and you've already signed the lease, it could be very difficult for you to resolve the legal aspects of the situation.

Look for other people who know your prospective roommate and try to get a feeling for what the person is like. Don't be afraid to ask the potential roommate any questions you feel are applicable, either. Some people conduct extensive interviews with prospective roommates and have the roommate agree to certain conditions before moving in. Even if it's someone you know, be sure you agree on basic rules for living together and get all financial matters in writing. For instance:

- How will the rent be split up?

- At what time of the month must the rent be paid?

- What if someone wants to move out?

- How much will each person contribute to the security deposit?

- How will costs like food and utilities be paid?

- Will one person write a check and be reimbursed by the other(s)?

- When will the reimbursement occur?

Dollars and Sense

If you get into legal trouble with a roommate, your best bet is to consult an attorney. If your roommate walks out on the lease, talk to your landlord and explain what has happened. He or she may be sympathetic and try to work with you. Meanwhile, an attorney can best advise you on what to do.

Leave nothing to chance. Remember that renting an apartment is a legally binding agreement. If you default on the agreement, or get caught in the middle of a problem with a roommate who defaults, it can negatively affect your credit rating and cause you problems for years to come.

Full House

Renting an apartment is great in many cases, but sometimes it makes more sense to rent a house. A house gives you more space and, probably, more bedrooms. If you live with a group of people, or you have a child or two, you know how important that can be. And houses often come with yards, which is a definite plus if you have kids. Of course, a house—even one you rent—requires more upkeep than an apartment. Be sure you know what's expected. Will you have to mow the lawn? Shovel the driveway when it snows? If you decide to rent a house, remember that the same rules apply as when you rent an apartment.

The definition of "family" has undergone great changes in America in recent years. While not too long ago a family consisted of mom, dad, and a couple of kids, we now have blended families, gay families, and groups of unrelated people living together as families. Regardless of where you fall on the family continuum, you should be aware that many communities have zoning laws that regulate the number of unrelated people who live in a single-family home. If you're thinking of renting a house with a group of roommates, be sure to check on the municipal regulations.

Another option for renters is a condominium. Condos often are available for rent, and can offer more space and privacy than an apartment in a complex. The same rules concerning a lease for an apartment or a house also apply to renting a condo. Be sure that everything is in writing and that you understand everything before you sign.

Dollars and Sense

If you buy renter's insurance to protect your belongings, then be sure you know what you have in case anything ever needs to be replaced. Make an inventory of your belongings, including brief descriptions, values, and serial numbers. Save receipts for major purchases and photograph each room of your house, condo or apartment, including closets.

Pocket Change

Some reputable insurance companies that offer renter's policies include Nationwide Mutual, Prudential, Allstate, Liberty Mutual, Erie Insurance, and State Farm. Check your phone book for agents who sell these brands.

Renter's Insurance

Once you've found an apartment and bought some stuff to put in it, you might want to consider buying renter's insurance. Although you're not responsible for damages to the building in which you're living (unless you directly cause the damage), you have personal property to protect in case of fire, theft, or water damage. Renter's insurance also protects you against liability in the event that someone is injured in your rented house, condo, or apartment. It can even protect you from personal liability if you rent a boat or Jet Ski.

If you have a lot of expensive electronic equipment, or anything else that's especially valuable, you really should consider renter's insurance. Be sure to get *replacement cost coverage*, which, for about 13 percent more in premiums, will give you 100 percent of the replacement cost on items that are damaged or stolen. If your policy is written for *actual cash value*, you'll only get what the items were worth at the time of purchase—not what it will cost to replace them.

Some landlords will require that you have renter's insurance, especially if you have a waterbed or aquarium that could cause serious water damage if it were to leak. Make sure your policy would cover those sorts of accidents. Be sure that your agent knows of any valuable items you own.

If you do decide to purchase renter's insurance, make sure you shop around at reputable companies to get the best rates. Every insurance company has its own rate system, so the company that gave your friend the best rate might not be the best outfit for you. Renter's insurance isn't terribly expensive, and can be well worth the money spent when you consider how much you'd need to pay to replace damaged or stolen belongings.

What Am I Gonna Sleep On?

You're finally out on your own. You've got your own apartment or house, and you can't wait to move in. You pack up your stuff, get somebody to help you move, and you're all set, right? But wait a minute. Where are you going to sleep tonight? A sleeping bag is great for camping trips, but seven nights a week on the bedroom floor can get a little rough.

Anybody who's been in a furniture store or browsed a catalogue lately will tell you that it's an expensive venture to furnish an apartment. Basic furniture for a living room, dining room, and bedroom can cost upward of $6,000 or $7,000, and that's without leather couches or big-screen TVs. If you're not prepared or able to spend that kind of money on sofas, chairs, and accessories, don't worry. There are other ways to do it.

Maybe your older sister has moved on to bigger and better things and will donate the couch from her first apartment. Your parents might let you take the desk or the bookcase from your old bedroom. Even Aunt Kay might have some treasures in her basement. If not, check your phone book for second-hand stores in your neighborhood. You might get lucky and find some high-quality furniture in these places at great prices. Or maybe you'll at least find something affordable that you can live with for a while.

Dollars and Sense

Don't overlook the shopper newspapers distributed in your area or the classified ads of your local daily or Sunday paper. Lots of people use these vehicles to sell unwanted household items and furniture—often at terrific prices.

Going to private auctions or auction centers can be fun ways to find used furniture at good prices, too. If you're not crazy about having furniture that belonged to someone else, you can check out outlets or discount furniture stores in your area. Or jump on the Internet and look at places such as Ikea (www.ikea.com) or Pier 1 Imports (www.pier1.com) for neat stuff at moderate (not cheap) prices. Just remember that much of that furniture comes unassembled.

I Gotta Pay for That, Too?

Just when you think you've got your financial situation pretty well under control, you start getting these pesky little bills. Nothing too big—$30 here, $19 there. When you add them up, though, you've got some significant expenses.

We're talking utilities: heat, electricity, cable TV, water, telephone, and gas. Make sure you have a clear understanding of what your rent includes before you move into an apartment. Some landlords include heat, water, and electricity with the rent; others don't. You don't want to work out a budget and then be surprised when un-expected bills start coming in each month.

Electricity

Ever since Thomas Edison invented electricity, people have been paying for it. Electric bills can be pretty daunting, especially if you're paying your own electric heat and/or air conditioning.

If you pay your electric bill, ask your landlord to show you the meter. Check the con-nections to make sure you're paying for only your electricity, not for you and your landlord who lives on the first floor.

Dollars and Sense

When ordering phone serv-ice, consider carefully whether you really need call waiting, caller I.D., and other extras that the tele-phone representative will try to talk you into buying. These costs can add up fast on your monthly bill.

Telephone

We could write a chapter comparing the qualities of various phone companies. But you no doubt hear more than you need to about various plans every time you turn on your TV or radio and perhaps sev-eral times a week from phone solicitors. Every com-pany will offer you a deal to come on board, but when you're tempted, try to look at the big picture as far as your phone bill is concerned.

Compare the costs for basic service and get the lowest one. A great way to get started is to check out SmartPrice.com, which offers a comparison of plans from various phone companies. Then control your costs by limiting long-distance calls and other extras. If you have a cell phone, and chances are very good that you do, consider whether you really need an additional phone. A growing trend is all cell all the time, with no traditional "land line." If you have a good cell phone plan, you might want to think about whether your cell might be the only phone you need. However, consumer advocates warn that, as cell phone use continues to increase, the demand for service might outweigh suppliers' ability to provide service, causing the quality of service to deteriorate.

I Want My MTV and CNN

People can spend hours debating the pros and cons of TV, but there's no arguing about one thing—watching TV has gotten expensive. Even basic cable service can cost upward of $40 a month. Throw in a couple of premium channels, and your bill can be well over $50. If you're looking to cut expenses, cut out a premium channel and you'll save about $100 a year. If you're looking to really cut expenses and have a lot more reading time, opt to go without cable.

The Cost of Staying In Touch

Charges or utilities can add up, there's no question about it. In addition to the basic electric, phone, and cable, keep an eye on what you're spending in some other areas:

- **Internet connection.** Whether you're using a dial-up, ADSL, or cable connection, you're no doubt paying for your Internet connection. Different Internet service providers offer various plans and rates, so shop around to make sure you're not buying more than you need. If you only spend a couple of hours a month online, it makes no sense to buy an unlimited plan.

- **Cell phones.** There are as many plans as there are types of phones, so look around carefully to make sure you have what you need, and not more. And if you plan to use the phone while you're driving, consider getting a system that allows your hands to remain free.

- **Pagers.** Unless you're a brain surgeon or have a job that keeps you away from the office, this expense is probably one you could do without.

The fewer bills you have to pay each month, the more money you'll have to put in a mutual fund, use for a vacation, or pay off your college loans. It's easy to overlook these monthly charges, but when you add them all up, you might be surprised at how much you're spending.

The Least You Need to Know

- You need to consider a variety of factors when looking for an apartment, house, or condominium that's right for you.

- Your rent isn't the only cost you'll have when you first move into an apartment or house.

- Having a roommate can cut costs, but beware of potential pitfalls.

- Buying furniture doesn't have to put you in the poorhouse.

- Your utility bills might be costing more than you realize, but there are ways to cut down.

Chapter 6

Road Rules

In This Chapter

- The ups and downs of the automobile industry
- Getting around without a car
- The difference between buying and leasing a car
- Buying new versus buying used
- The added expenses of car ownership

Cars, trucks, sport utility vehicles, vans—Americans have had a great love affair with automobiles since Henry Ford cranked out that first Model T in the early 1900s. We talk about cars extensively. Traditionally, we've admired them, spent hours washing and polishing them, and, up to a point, we've identified with the cars we drive. Let's face it, many of us would feel better about ourselves while driving a new Saab than a rusty old Ford. Cars are a source of status, and a person's car can provide some interesting insights into his or her personality.

This chapter takes a look at cars, and the advantages and disadvantages of buying, leasing, or doing without. Your car probably eats up more money than you realize, and you can save a lot of money by changing your car expectations. So park yourself somewhere and get ready to learn some interesting stuff about vehicles and driving.

Cruising the Auto Industry Landscape

We've always taken our cars pretty seriously in this country. For teenagers, getting a car is a rite of passage—a symbol of emerging adulthood. Adults, both young and old, need cars to get around. Gotta get to work. Gotta get the kids to school, soccer, and piano lessons. Gotta drive to the next state to visit the grandkids.

The minivan, first introduced by Chrysler in the 1980s, along with the modern sport utility vehicle, first launched by Jeep at around the same time, gave consumers more choices in what they could drive and created huge excitement. Since then, SUVs and vans have gotten bigger and fancier, with more and more people jumping onto the bandwagon to buy them. Trucks, especially very large trucks, also have captured the imaginations (and wallets) of many Americans, many of whom have little or no need for the power of a Hemi engine.

Although auto sales might not be at record highs, a lot of people are buying cars, trucks, and SUVs. Dealer incentives offered during the summer of 2004 gave buyers up to $5,000 back on some jumbo-sized SUVs, and some cars were discounted as well. And, while the costs of some major expenses (think college education) have increased disproportionately to the general cost of living, cars were more affordable that summer than they'd been in the previous 25 years, according to Comerica Bank in Detroit.

Auto manufacturers have been extremely successful over the past decades at getting us to think we have to have the latest models, that bigger and fancier is better, and that the cars we drive are indicators and extensions of who we are and how much money we make. And they sure as heck want to keep us thinking that way.

If Americans stop buying cars or start keeping their old cars for longer periods of time, car manufacturers and other industries will be in big trouble, and they know it. The American economy depends heavily on Americans buying new cars every three or four years. That habit greatly influences industries such as steel, rubber, and electronics. If the habit changes, those industries and others will suffer. As you can see, it's in the best interests of the auto manufacturers to keep consumers excited about the cars they drive, although it may not be in the best financial interests of consumers.

Planes, Trains, and Automobiles

The best thing about having a car at your disposal is the freedom it gives you. You can go wherever you want. Just pick a destination, hop in the car, and you're off.

Other than that, there's really not that much about having a car that's so great. They're expensive to buy and to maintain. They break down occasionally, leaving you sitting by the side of the road in a thunderstorm. They require time and attention, and by the time you pay for them, they're hardly worth the metal they're made of. But most of us still can't imagine life without our wheels. Our lifestyles would change dramatically if we were to go carless.

Yet plenty of people get along perfectly fine without a vehicle of their own—no car, no truck, not even a scooter to hop on and ride across town. Some of these folks hitch a ride with somebody else when they need one, or they walk. Others use something collectively known as *public transportation*, which includes the buses, trains, subways, and trolleys that carry people across town and across the country every day.

Taxicabs are available for those without vehicles, as are bicycles, in-line skates, and nifty scooters for trips around town. Need to travel farther? Buses, trains and airplanes are available for longer trips. Our country is fairly unique in its "a car for every driver" attitude. In other countries, cars are still pretty much seen as luxuries, and a family would never aspire to have more than one.

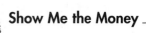

Show Me the Money

Public transportation is the collective name for the system of buses, trains, subways, and the like that carry people to and from their intended destinations.

Not Everybody Needs a Car

If you live out on a farm in Iowa, you probably need a car or truck to get you from one place to another. The nearest store might be 15 miles down the road, and you'll have a long, long wait for the transit system bus to come along.

On the other hand, if you live in the middle of New York City, you probably don't need a car.

Dollars and Sense

If you use public transportation regularly, be sure you check out commuter passes, which enable you to buy quantities of bus, train, or subway tickets at reduced prices.

Keeping a car in the city is terribly expensive, and it's a hassle. With abundant public transportation, you can easily get where you want to go without your own vehicle.

If you live in the suburbs, you probably think you need a car, and you're probably used to having a car. If you don't have one, though, you no doubt could get along without it. It would be an adjustment, but most suburbanites have access to public transportation, which could transport you to work and the other places you need to go.

Renting a Car When You Need One

Still, taking a bus when you leave New York City to go to visit your college room-mate in Washington, D.C. can be a hassle. It can turn a 225-mile, less-than-four-hour car trip into an all-day adventure, depending on how many stops you make along the way. And sometimes you're just not in the mood to chat with the person in the next seat, who just found out that her husband is having an affair and is going home to her mother.

The thing to do in that case is to rent a car. Extravagant, you say? Not really. Rental rates vary tremendously, and they change depending on availability and other factors. To rent a car in New York City would cost about $70 a day, or $210 for a three-day weekend, plus gas. More than Greyhound? Yeah. More than Amtrak? No. And if you're traveling with somebody else, renting a car becomes an even more viable option.

> ### Pocket Change
>
> You can pick up a car at a Budget rental car location in New York City on Friday and return it on Sunday for about $205, plus fuel charges. A round-trip Amtrak ticket from New York to Washington, D.C will cost you $249. Greyhound will take you from New York to D.C. and back for about $70, but it will take you six hours each way and you never know whom you'll end up sitting next to.

Some people live in the city without a car and rent one when they need it for business purposes. Hopefully, your employer will reimburse you for that expense if you find yourself in that situation. The point is, it's not always necessary to own a car.

The Great Debate: Buying or Leasing

Although it might not be necessary for everyone to own a car, facts are facts; most of us do. Owning a car means paying out a lot of money to get one, and then more money to keep it running.

Cars are expensive. Even if you're not looking for anything fancy, you'll pay a lot of money for a new car. If you're going to buy a car, there are several ways to do it. You can walk into the dealership, plunk down $26,435 on the counter, and drive off in your brand spankin' new Explorer. Yeah, right. Or, if you're like most people, you can finance your car.

Financing Your Car

Most dealerships offer car financing. However, unless you get a special deal like the 0 percent financing offered a few years back to boost lagging car sales after the 9/11 attacks, dealer financing normally costs at least one or two percentage points more than a bank or credit union, although dealers have been making an effort to compete, and, in some cases, are able to.

Also, if the car dealers control your loan, they could try to talk you into buying a more expensive car than you would normally, by assuring you that they'll give you the extra money you need to cover it. Even if a dealer offers what sounds like a terrific financing deal, make sure you consider all the facts and know what the actual cost of the car will be once the financing kicks in. And don't let a dealer persuade you that it's okay to drive the car off the lot before the financing is approved. Car dealers are out to make money one way or another, whether it's from the cost of the car or through finance charges.

Generally, a better way to finance your car is to get a loan from a bank or credit union. You'll probably get a lower interest rate and you won't be at the mercy of the dealership. In fact, if you walk into a car dealership with a pre-approved car loan, it puts you in a great position. Here's why:

Money Pit

Stay away from finance companies that offer guaranteed, same-day loans and other ploys to get your business. The rates these companies give you are virtually always higher than what you'd get from a bank or credit union. Most of these companies cater to people with bad credit, who would have trouble getting a bank loan.

◆ You know how much money you have, and you buy within that amount.

◆ The car salesperson knows you're serious about buying, and he'll do everything he can to make sure you buy from him.

◆ You're not at the mercy of the dealership to get your loan. Instead, the dealership has to work on your terms.

Shop around for interest rates when you're looking for a car loan. Traditionally, credit unions offer the best rates on car loans—more than $1\frac{1}{2}$ percent less on average than a bank loan. That difference can save you a lot of money over the length of the loan.

Consider the following when getting a car loan:

◆ Instead of an installment loan, go for a simple interest loan, which lets you pay interest only on the remaining amount of your loan. The bank will figure out the total interest on your loan and set up a plan where you'll pay the same amount each month for the life of your loan. That's better than a front-end installment loan, which requires you to pay interest each month on the full amount of the loan.

◆ Put down as much money as you can. The more you put down toward your car, the lower your interest rate will probably be. Plus, you'll be financing less, thereby paying less interest overall.

CAUTION

Money Pit

Some dealers offer new cars for no money down. The catch there, however, is that if for some reason you end up keeping the car for only a short time, you could find yourself in big trouble when you go to sell it. The value of a car depreciates dramatically in its first year. If you made no down payment, you actually could end up owing more than the car is worth at the end of a year or so.

◆ Use rebates (money the car manufacturer offers you as an incentive to buy its cars) to make your down payment bigger. If you're offered a rebate on a new car, by all means take advantage of it. But don't buy a more expensive car just because you get a rebate.

◆ Take the shortest loan term you can manage. Don't pay back a loan over five years if you can do it in three. Even though your monthly payment will be smaller on the five-year loan, you'll be paying interest for a longer time and will end up paying more in the long run.

◆ Pay off your loan early if you can. Some lenders let you pay off a loan early, but others will penalize you. Be sure to find out about that before you sign on for the loan. Don't take out a loan that won't permit you to pay it off early.

◆ The interest you pay on a car loan is not tax-deductible, but the interest on a home equity loan is. If you own a home and need to borrow money for a car, look into getting a home equity loan to use instead of a car loan.

Leasing

Leasing, the practice of paying a specified amount of money for a specified time for the use of a product, has been gaining in popularity over the past several years, and many people swear by it. It's a little tricky, though, because determining whether it's a better deal than buying is difficult. Basically, when you lease a car, you pay for the estimated depreciation that's occurring to the car while you're driving it. You pay only for the part of the car's value that you use, plus interest.

When you begin a lease agreement, the dealer estimates what the car's *residual value* will be at the end of your lease. If you have a *closed-end lease*, you simply come to the end of your lease agreement and turn in your car.

If you have an *open-end lease*, you may not be able to walk away at the end of the lease, you may owe the difference between the residual value of the car and the actual market value at the end of the lease. This might be the way to go, as long as the street value of the car has remained above the residual value determined by the dealer. You would then be buying the car for less than you could anywhere else. If the dealer overestimated the car's residual value,

Show Me the Money _____

Leasing is the practice of paying a specified amount of money over a specified time for the use of a product.

Residual value is what your car will be worth at the end of the lease. It's what it would cost to buy the car, used, at that time.

however, you'd be paying more for it than you would somewhere else. See what we mean about leasing being a tricky business?

There are some good reasons to lease a car, but there are some good reasons not to, as well. One major consideration is that you'll never pay less overall for leasing than you do for buying, because you'll always be paying, but never own the car. It's sort of like renting a car for an extended period of time.

Still, many people like leasing for one reason or another, such as those who have a special need for a particular vehicle for a limited amount of time.

Before you decide to lease, consider some of the pros and cons.

Pros of Leasing

There are some good reasons why people like leasing vehicles. Some of them are listed here:

- Many leases don't require a down payment or at least not a very high down payment.
- You probably can lease a more expensive car than you'd be able to buy.
- When your lease ends, you don't have to worry about getting rid of your car. You simply give it back.

Cons of Leasing

There are, however, some not-so-good aspects of leasing a car:

- The total cost of leasing is almost always more expensive than buying a car with cash and is also usually more expensive than financing a car.
- When your lease ends, you're out of a car.
- If you decide to buy the car at the end of the lease, you will owe sales tax.
- Most lease agreements impose mileage limits. If you go over the number of miles allowed, you'll have to pay a big penalty.
- Leasing doesn't cover insurance or maintenance, so you don't save costs.
- You might have to pay for the dealer's cost of auctioning the car when your lease expires. These fees are called *disposition charges*.

If, after considering the pros and cons, you decide to lease a car, there are some things that will be important to remember. The number one rule is to do your homework. There are as many lease deals as there are kinds of cars. Check out websites such as carpoint.msn.com or intellichoice.com, or visit your local bookstore for more information about leasing.

Show Me the Money

Disposition charges are just a fancy name for the dealer's costs to auction your car.

When you feel that you're sufficiently prepared to negotiate a lease, keep these tips in mind:

1. Always get a closed-end agreement. This type of agreement enables you to turn in your car and say adios. If you fall in love with your leased vehicle, you can negotiate for it, but you won't be obligated to buy it.

2. You're still responsible for repairs when you lease a car. Make sure you know in what condition you're expected to return the car.

3. Negotiate the highest residual value on the vehicle that you can. If you decide to buy it, you can renegotiate. If you don't buy it, you'll end up paying less for the part of the car's value that you've used.

4. Be up front with the dealer about how many miles you plan to put on the car each year. If you exceed the dealer's limit (usually around 15,000 miles a year), you'll be fined, big time.

5. If you drive 10,000 miles a year or less, ask whether there is a low-mileage discount available. Be persistent if the dealer is reluctant to give it to you.

6. Check out the *manufacturer's warranty* on the car. This is a written guarantee for the condition and performance of the car that makes the manufacturer responsible for repairs or replacement, and is a good guide as to how long your lease should be. You don't want to end up paying for costly repairs.

7. Don't sign a lease for longer than you'll want the car. For instance, if there's a possibility you'll be transferred to Singapore for work in two years, don't sign a three-year lease. You'll be penalized for breaking the lease.

8. Find out what happens if you lease a lemon. Cars you buy are covered by lemon laws. Make sure there's a similar provision if you lease.

9. Make sure the lease has gap insurance. Ask to have it included in the agreement with no additional charge. *Gap insurance* pays the difference between the value your insurance will pay if your leased car is stolen or totaled and the amount you're obligated to pay to terminate the lease.

Show Me the Money

A **warranty** is a written guarantee for the condition and performance of the car. It makes the manufacturer responsible for the repair or replacement of defective parts.

Gap insurance can be included in your lease agreement. It pays the difference between the value your insurance will pay if your leased car is stolen or wrecked and the amount you owe when you terminate the lease.

10. Don't let a dealer talk you into a lease agreement that's shorter than what you want. The dealer is anxious to get you back into the show room to look at another car. Some dealers will push for very short leases for that reason, and it could end up costing you more than necessary.

Lease agreements are notorious for being complicated pieces of confusing legalese, decipherable only by a Harvard Business School Ph.D. But if you know what to look out for, you can approach the whole process with a lot less aggravation.

The more you know about leasing and lease agreements going into the showroom, the less likely a salesperson will be to take advantage of you and give you something you don't need or want that will cost extra money. Remember these definitions:

♦ **Capitalized cost**   The price you pay for the car.

♦ **Finance charge**   The interest you pay on the car.

♦ **Residual value**   According to the dealer, the amount the car is worth when the lease is over.

Compare these numbers in every agreement you look at. Read up on leasing, be prepared with questions, and don't be pressured into getting something you don't want. If you decide to lease and follow those guidelines, you'll do just fine.

New or Used, Big or Small?

Regardless of whether you decide to buy or lease a car, you need to consider the value of the car you're getting and what you can realistically afford. Sure, you might be able to borrow $20,000 or $25,000 to buy that Toyota Camry, complete with all the options, but why would you? If you want a new car, look at everything available.

Consider this. If you borrow $25,000 at 8 percent interest for a Camry and pay it back over four years, you'll pay about $610 a month. If you borrow $15,000 at 8 percent interest for the same four years, for a Honda Civic, you'll pay about $366 a month. That's a difference of $244 a month. If you put that $244 into an investment that averages an 8 percent annual interest every month for 35 years, guess how much money you'd have? More than half a million dollars! No kidding—you'd have $560,000.

To get a better idea of how much specific cars cost, check out Intellichoice (www.intellichoice.com), a website loaded with all kinds of car stuff. It lists best over-all values for cars of various sizes, and its categories are divided into price ranges.

You're probably going to buy several cars before you hang up the keys for the last time. Money you save now and invest will buy you more cars and other extras you might want later on.

And who says you need a new car? Yeah, you're taking a chance if you buy a used car out of some guy's front yard, but many reputable car dealerships offer a good selection of used cars—known these days as certified pre-owned vehicles—complete with extended warranties and other perks. These cars can be had for a fraction of what they'd cost new, and if you take good care of yours, it should give you years of service.

If you buy a used car for half of what a new one costs, you can afford to pay a greater percentage of the cost up front and have to borrow less. Your monthly payments will be less, giving you more money for other things. If for some reason you think you must have a new car instead of one that's been used, consider that the minute you drive the new car off the lot, it's lost a percentage of its value. It's already a used car, and you haven't even gotten it home yet!

Car Buying and Social Responsibility

Along with nearly everything else in this country, there are politics built into car buying. Despite calls to decrease our dependence on foreign oil, small businesses are offered incentives that seem nearly too good to pass up to buy gas-guzzling SUVs.

Patriotism is somehow connected to buying a big Ford or Dodge pickup, despite constant warnings of declining air quality and global warming.

Regardless of your views on vehicles, foreign oil, politics, and environmental issues, we all could benefit by taking a hard look at what we really need in a car or truck. Sure, if you've got three kids who have lots of friends, a boat to tow, and live in a snowy region of the country, then an SUV probably makes sense. If you're a single person who drives a Hummer because you like the way you feel when you're in it, you might want to examine your motives.

Statistics in May 2004 showed that the average American driver is logging up 12,000 miles a year, up nearly 2,000 miles from two decades ago. And, the vehicles we're driving are bigger and heavier and use more gas. With increasing concerns about global security, ongoing war in the Middle East, and our environment in the balance, perhaps we all should take a look at our cars and driving habits.

Taking a Look at Hybrid Cars

The first *hybrid car*—a car that uses a combination of gasoline and an electric motor powered by a rechargeable battery for fuel—was released in the United States in 1999. Since then, consumer interest in hybrids has skyrocketed, probably largely in response to rising gas prices.

Hybrid cars contain smaller engines than traditional vehicles and use the battery to get extra power when going up a hill or accelerating quickly. They're lighter and more aerodynamic than traditional cars as well. Although the car's motor gets power from a rechargeable battery, the car owner doesn't have to remove the battery or plug it into anything to charge it.

Show Me the Money

A **hybrid car** is one that uses more than one source of fuel to power it. A combination of gasoline and a rechargeable battery are used as power sources.

Gas mileage varies among hybrids. The Honda Insight is rated at 60 miles to the gallon for city driving and 66 for the highway. The Toyota Prius gets 51 mpg in the city and 60 mpg on the highway, and the Honda Civic hybrid gets 48 mpg for the city and 51 mpg for highway driving. The first SUV hybrid—the Ford Escape—was released in the United States in August 2004. The Escape gets about 36 mpg for city driving and 31 for the highway.

Analysts say we'll see a lot more hybrids on the road, especially if gas prices continue to increase. Environmentalists praise hybrid cars as being socially responsible, and many drivers are enthusiastic about and interested in the vehicles.

Remembering That Safety Counts

Regardless of the type or size of car you buy, remember that some vehicles are safer than others. Sure, any car can be safe or unsafe depending on how it's driven, but some cars hold up better in crashes than others, giving you and your passengers a better chance of surviving. You also can get better insurance rates if you drive a car that's rated as safe.

How can you find out which cars are safer? One source is Consumer Reports. Each year, they publish a list of the 25 safest vehicles, based on how well they're designed to avoid a crash and how they hold up in the event that a crash can't be avoided.

Safety counts, especially once you start hauling kids in your cars. Remember, though, that no vehicle is safe if you're trying to talk on your cell phone, eat your lunch, and listen to your favorite CD while you're driving.

Best Places—Online and Off—To Shop for a Car

Car shopping is a big deal because it involves spending a lot of money, so it's important to know the best places to shop. The face of car buying has changed over the past decade or so, due to Internet car sales. While cars once were primarily sold at car dealerships, on used car lots, or even on somebody's front lawn, you now can buy a car on eBay.

The most traditional way to buy a car is still to go to a car dealership, haggle with the salesperson, and strike a deal on the vehicle you want.

If you're contemplating buying a car from a dealer, be sure to get online at www. Edmunds.com or www.kbb.com (Kelly Blue Book) to get all the information you'll need about the car you're thinking about. You'll be able to compare dealer costs and incentives, contact dealers to determine inventory and bargaining potential, and compare transaction prices.

Or you can actually buy your car online, without ever having to leave your home. Check out sites such as CarsDirect.com, AutoVantage.com, or Automotive.com. These sites allow you to order the car you want for a price that the site has already negotiated with a dealer for. You order the car online, and the site finds a dealer near you that has it.

If you're willing to go the extra mile, you might be able to get a great deal on a car that's for sale on the Internet at a site like eBay's Motor Auction. But you'll need to do your homework and find out the value of the car, whether there are any complaints posted on the site about the person selling the car, and so forth. If the car happens to be located near where you live, it's easier than if you need to travel to see the car. If you have to buy a plane ticket to check out the car, add the cost of your ticket to the cost of the car.

Don't forget about classified ads and car shopper publications that list cars for sale in your area. Just be sure to do your homework, regardless of how you decide to car shop.

Your Car Costs More Than You Think

The initial purchase of a car is a big expense. Adding insult to injury, the car keeps on costing you money once you own it! Cars are expensive, there's no getting around it. You'll need to think about maintenance costs—both routine and nonroutine. You'll also need to have insurance on your car, and with gasoline going for more than $2 a gallon in many parts of the country, you can expect high fuel costs as well.

Then there are tolls, parking fees, finance charges, inspections, and cleanings. When you add it all up, the cost of having a car is more than $6,000 a year.

> **Dollars and Sense**
>
> Don't feel obligated to have your car maintained by the dealer from whom you bought it. It might be more expensive than having it done by an independent mechanic. Ask some people who have the same kind of car where they go for maintenance. A good mechanic whom you can trust might not be the easiest thing to find, but it's worth it to spend some time locating one.

Cars cost a lot of money. In many cases, it costs more to buy a car today than it did to buy a house 30 years ago. Maybe Gen Xers will be the ones to stop the my-car-is-an-extension-of-who-I-am mentality and get society grounded when it comes to vehicles. Until then, do your homework and know what to look for when getting a car, regardless of whether you buy or lease and whether you get a new or used vehicle.

The Least You Need to Know

♦ Americans have always loved their automobiles, and car manufacturers have worked hard to keep that love affair alive and well.

♦ For many people, a car is not essential; other modes of transportation can get you where you want to go.

♦ There are advantages and disadvantages to both buying and leasing vehicles. Be sure to do your homework before doing either one.

♦ Buying a less expensive car can yield huge savings for your future.

♦ Buying the car is the first expense, but car expenses don't end there. It costs thousands of dollars a year to operate a vehicle.

Part 2

On Your Own and Loving It

So things are looking up, are they? You have a job that you like (most days), a car that runs, and a place to live with some pretty good friends. Sure, there are some rough spots along the way. Your salary is not what you think it should be, and the car is not exactly a BMW.

You're trying to stick to your new budget, but it's such a drag! Even though you know you should have saved that extra $20 last week, the opportunity for a night out with your pals was too good to resist. As long as you're confessing, there's that little balance you've been carrying over from month to month on your credit card, too.

All in all, though, life is pretty good. This is a time when you're establishing habits that will affect your personal finances for the rest of your life. This section gives you lots of ideas and suggestions for getting into good habits, which, hopefully, you'll carry with you.

Chapter 7

What Do You Have?

In This Chapter

- Dealing with a salary that's lower than you'd like
- Remembering other benefits of working
- Understanding your net worth
- Looking past the obvious for financial assets

Starting out on your own is an exciting time, but it is generally not the easiest time financially. In this chapter, we're going to take a look at what you have, which may be more than you realize. We'll talk about your income, which, incidentally, includes more than your salary. We'll also talk about other less tangible assets you have in connection with your job.

Living With the Job You've Got

The American economy is cyclical. It experiences highs, then lows, and then rebounds back again. The public's confidence in the economy— called *consumer confidence*—dips and rises along with the movement of the economy.

The early 1980s and the early 1990s were periods of recession in the United States, and consumer confidence was very low. Then, with the booming stock market fueling the economy during the mid and late 1990s and into the new century, consumer confidence rose sharply. It slipped again, however, after the first half of 2000, when the economy began to slow down and hundreds of thousands of jobs were eliminated.

Show Me the Money

Consumer confidence is a measure of how consumers feel at a given time about the current state of the economy.

The 9/11 terrorist attacks caused the already faltering U.S. economy to slow down even more—taking consumer confidence down along with it. Three years later, the economy is still uncertain. Some say we are well on our way to economic recovery. Others claim that we are nowhere near recovery, citing lagging job growth, record-high world oil prices, and a faltering stock market.

This economic uncertainty has made many people, including those in their 20s and 30s, understandably nervous. Baby boomers nearing retirement age are wondering if they'll be able to retire. Many people are out of jobs, or are working jobs for which they're overqualified because they can't find anything else.

For many reasons, many people who have jobs are sticking with them, even if they don't consider them to be ideal. That's not to say there isn't room in the job market to move around within many areas of employment, and many economists are hopeful that our country's financial situation will turn upward and remain there in the middle part of this decade.

If you find yourself in a situation where you're thinking that maybe you're lucky to have your job—even if it isn't that great—try not to be discouraged. Remember that the market is cyclical and has always rebounded from the dips it's taken in the past.

Looking at Your Options

Let's say that you graduated from college three years ago, and after a year, you landed a job with a medium-sized advertising agency. You're currently earning $30,000 a year.

Although $30,000 sounds like a lot of money—and it is—we all know that money goes fast, and there are an awful lot of things to spend it on. Hardly anyone who works thinks that he or she makes enough money, even if you are grateful for the job you have in an uncertain job market. It's no surprise that the most frequent complaints about jobs are not about bosses (although those probably run a close second), but about salaries.

> **Pocket Change**
>
> Talk about a Gen X success story! Jerry Yang and David Filo started the Yahoo! Internet site in 1994 when they were engineering graduate students at Stanford University. Ten years later, Yahoo! is a publicly held company worth billions.

If you have a job you like, but not the salary you'd like, there are several things you can do:

- You can (gulp) ask for a raise.

- You can look for a higher-paying job.

- You can stay in the job you have and hope you'll advance or be able to move on when the economy and job market opportunities improve.

Of these choices, the first two are definitely more proactive and require more courage than sticking it out and seeing what happens—especially in a faltering economy. It takes a fair amount of guts to march (or tiptoe) into your boss's office to ask for a raise. And it takes a lot of energy to start a job hunt, especially if it hasn't been too long since you've been through one. If there's an indication that there's room for advancement in your current job, the best thing to do might be to hang out, do your very best, and see what happens. But if your salary is so low that you can't get by, or if you're forced to live paycheck to paycheck without being able to save a cent, then you might have to take some action.

Asking for a Raise

If your plan is to ask for a raise, make sure you're in a position to do so. Obviously, if you've only been working for the company you're with for a few weeks or months, you won't endear yourself to anyone by asking for more money. Or if the company is teetering on the verge of bankruptcy, your boss isn't going to be at all happy when you saunter in and ask for a raise. Another thing to consider is your market value. Never go to your boss and complain that the guy in the next cubicle is making more than you are for doing the same job. Bosses hate knowing that employees talk about their salaries, and opening that kind of conversation definitely will not put you in her good graces. Instead, if you know you're underpaid, point out what other people doing your job on the open market are making.

Trade publications and some professional associations do regular salary surveys and can be good sources of information. Or scan the Sunday classified ads for jobs similar to yours and their salaries. You also can check out JobSmart, a website with links to 150 salary surveys. Access it on the Internet at www.jobsmart.org.

Looking for Another Job

If you're really unhappy with your salary and you know there's no chance for a raise anytime soon, you might be tempted to go out and look for another job. Some people would advise against that in an unsteady economy, but sometimes shopping around for another job seems like the only viable option. If that's the case, what kind of job should you look for?

Employers over the last decade or so have become less likely to insist on a particular degree for a particular job. They're more likely to look for someone who is smart, versatile, willing to work, and able to work independently. If that description sounds like you, it may give you a lot more flexibility if you decide to job-hunt. Don't feel that you're stuck in a particular field just because that's what your degree or certification is in. You may be able to go from one career to another that interests you without much difficulty. In fact, it's estimated that the average worker will have about 11 jobs and three careers over his or her working life.

Although there are other factors besides growth potential to consider when you think about a job you'd like to have, it's an important consideration. It makes no sense to get into a career that won't be around much longer. The U.S. Bureau of Labor Statistics has identified 10 job areas as those that will be the fastest growing—both in terms of jobs added and salary increases—between the years of 2000 and 2010. You can find the list on the Bureau of Labor's web site at www.bls.gov.

Although we once looked to big corporations for good jobs and job security, predictions are that small businesses, which can act quickly to implement new ideas and technology, will become increasingly important as employers. And guess who is starting up many of these small businesses that are going to be so important? Right! Gen Xers see owning their own business as a sign of success, and many are making the dream a reality. A recent report by IBM showed that today one out of five small businesses is owned by someone under 35 years old. So don't neglect the small businesses when conducting your job search. Who knows? You may get inspired to create your own business.

If you're thinking about changing jobs, consider using the Internet to help. It's becoming increasingly important as a tool for job-hunting. If you're ready to hop online, try some of these sites:

- ◆ CareerBuilder.com is the largest online job search site. It contains a job board and the classified ads of several major newspapers. Access it at www.careerbuilder.com.

- ◆ Monster.com is one of the oldest job-search sites and is still considered one of the best. It contains many job opportunities and other career-related subjects. Access it at www.monster.com.

- ◆ HotJobs.com is a popular site that's owned and run by Yahoo! It's regarded as effective and easy to use. It's on the web at http://my.hotjobs.yahoo.com.

If you can't reconcile your salary problem, looking for another job might be the answer. Just be careful of inadvertently putting yourself into a worse situation than you are in currently.

Considering a Career Counselor

If you've decided that you can't stay in the job you have, but you're not quite sure where you'd like to be headed, you might consider seeking the services of a career counselor. A career counselor is a certified individual who can help you to clarify your career goals, assess your abilities and aptitudes, provide information about different careers, develop an individualized career plan, help create a resume, and teach skills and strategies for job hunting.

While a career counselor does not go out and find you a job, he or she can help you evaluate where you are, where you've been, and where you'd like to go.

What About a Headhunter?

A headhunter is a person who matches you with a company that is looking for someone to fill a particular position. Normally, the company hires and pays the headhunter. A headhunter also will handle negotiations between a prospective employee and the company.

If you seek the services of a headhunter, be aware that the headhunter's first loyalty is to the company seeking an employee—not you. If you decide to try a headhunter, be sure to ask around and find one who is reliable and reputable.

Sticking It Out

If you can't get a raise in your current job and you're not inclined to go looking for a new one, your only choice is to stick it out, and there are several reasons why you might choose to do that.

Maybe you have a job you love that just doesn't happen to pay very much. Certain professions, social work and childcare for instance, are notoriously low paying. Nobody going into these fields expects to get rich, but thankfully, there are dedicated people willing to do these kinds of very important, but underpaid, jobs. If you have a low-paying job that you love, you'll have to decide whether to stay where you are. If you decide to keep it, you'll have to adjust your standard of living to mesh with your earnings.

> **Dollars and Sense**
>
> It's easy to overspend when you're around people who have more money than you do. Resist spending more than you should in order to keep up, and leave your credit card at home when you're out with your friends.

If, on the other hand, you're staying in a low-paying job because you're too scared or unmotivated to go after a better one, you're dealing with a different issue. Reread the previous section about the job market and give it a shot. You've got nothing to lose but a low-paying job.

There's More to a Job Than the Money

Regardless of how much your salary is, there's more to a job than the money you make. Jobs hold many opportunities, which savvy employees will learn to recognize and take advantage of. Did you ever wonder why some people seem to get ahead at work so much more easily than others? It might be that they're smarter or better workers, but often it's just that they're better at taking advantage of opportunities. Make the most of your job, even if it's a low-paying, entry-level position, and consider the potential benefits of your job, as suggested below.

- ◆ **Contacts.** Use your job contacts to help you advance in your job or find a different one. Consider everyone you meet a potential contact.

◆ **Experience.** There is experience to be gained from every job, and whatever experience you gain can be used to advance you to a different position or job.

◆ **Benefits.** If you receive health insurance, a 401(k) plan, paid vacation and sick time, dental coverage and other benefits, you're making more from your job than you might realize. The average employer pays a 25 percent supplement in benefits for every employee.

◆ **Personal satisfaction.** Regardless of the salary, it's important to feel personally satisfied with the work you do, and that satisfaction should count when you consider your job.

Dollars and Sense _____

Think about the people you know who seem to move ahead, have lots of opportunities to be with interesting people, and know what's going on in their jobs and communities. Chances are they keep up with contacts they make, and use those contacts to expand their career networks. Try it—it really works!

Dollars and Sense _____

If you had to buy your own health insurance, it could cost you hundreds of dollars a month, depending on the plan you choose. And that's just for one person! If you need to buy your own health insurance, be sure you shop around; rates vary greatly. A good place to start for an idea about rates and different policies is HealthcareShopper. com. It's on the web at www. healthcareshopper.com.

There are many great jobs that don't pay very much, but provide immense personal satisfaction. Jobs in the tourism field tend to be lower-paying jobs, but, if you love to travel and learn about foreign lands, you might be very satisfied in that field.

Or maybe you love working with kids and would be perfectly happy as a preschool teacher. Perhaps you enjoy being with elderly people and would like to work in a nursing home or assisted living facility. Perhaps you're working in, or feel pulled toward, the ministry, or a job in social services.

Assessing Your Assets

If you've got a job, you're probably bringing home a paycheck. Very few people show up at the office every morning just because they love to be there. The paycheck at the end of the week (or every two weeks) might not be the only thing you like about your job, but it's pretty high on the list, right?

Even if your salary isn't as much as you'd like it to be, it's probably still your primary source of income. When you begin to consider your *net worth*, or financial situation, your salary is very important. For most of us, the salary pays the bills, boosts savings accounts, and sets up emergency funds.

When you examine your financial situation, however, you might be pleasantly surprised to find out you have more than you realize. There could be money you've overlooked. To determine your net worth, you have to know exactly what you have and exactly what your expenses are. After you've thought carefully about any and all funds you might have in the form of savings, bonds, mutual funds, or whatever, take a minute to fill out this net worth worksheet (using the value of the asset as of the valuation date). It should help you to get a better understanding of exactly what you have and what you're worth. Who knows, you might be pleasantly surprised!

Show Me the Money

Your **net worth** is what you get when you add up all your financial assets and then subtract all your financial liabilities.

NET WORTH WORKSHEET

ASSETS

Bonds	$
Cash accounts	$
Certificates of deposit	$
Mutual funds	$
Savings bonds	$
Stocks	$
Tax refunds	$
Treasury bills	$
Cash-value life insurance	$
Subtotal	$

Personal Property

Businesses	$
Cars	$

| Personal property | $ |
| Subtotal | $ |

Real Estate

Mortgages owned	$
Residence	$
Income property	$
Vacation home	$
Subtotal	$

Retirement

Annuities	$
IRAs	$
Keogh accounts	$
Pensions	$
Subtotal	$
TOTAL	$

LIABILITIES

Current Liabilities

Alimony	$
Child support	$
Personal loans	$
Subtotal	$

Installment Liabilities

Bank loans	$
Car loans	$
College loans	$
Credit card bills	$

Furniture loans	$
Home improvement	$
Life insurance loans	$
Pension plan loans	$
Subtotal	$

Real Estate Liabilities

Residence (include second mortgage/line of credit)	$
Income property	$
Vacation home	$
Subtotal	$

Taxes

Capital gains tax	$
Income tax	$
Property tax	$
Subtotal	$

Other Liabilities

_____

_____

_____

TOTAL ASSETS	**$**
TOTAL LIABILITIES	**-$**
TOTAL NET WORTH	**$**

Think carefully about what you might have. Are there any savings accounts that were set up for you when you were a kid? What about savings bonds? Some families are great at buying U.S. savings bonds for birthdays. Have you put aside money some-place for emergencies? Do you have money saved for a car or a house?

The interest you earn on a savings account counts as income (and is taxed as income), although you probably don't regard it as such. If you have any bonds, the interest on them also counts as income. Your income tax refund, bonuses, and any monetary gifts you receive also count as assets and must be counted when considering what you have. If you have a *cash value life insurance* policy, the amount of cash value is counted toward your net worth. Generally, though, when we talk about income, we're primarily talking about your salary.

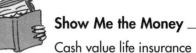

Show Me the Money

Cash value life insurance is a type of insurance policy, purchased for the long term, which sets aside funds within the policy for future payment of premium. The accumulated funds can be borrowed by the policyholder and, thus, count as an asset for net worth purposes.

Your Secret Stash

Most people start working pretty much from the ground up when it comes to accruing money. When you first start out on your own, it usually isn't very hard to figure out what you have. Sometimes, though, you might overlook money you've accumulated or that other people have accumulated for you. Hardly anybody has a long-lost rich uncle who dies and leaves behind a fortune, but many people do have well-meaning relatives who try to help them along by setting up bank accounts or buying bonds in their name. Consider whether you may have any of the assets listed below. If you do, they'll affect your net worth.

- ◆ **Accounts.** Relatives often set up bank accounts in a child's name, which, for one reason or another, sometimes get forgotten and overlooked.

- ◆ **Mutual funds.** *Mutual funds*, including stock funds, bond funds, hybrid funds, U.S. funds, money market funds, and so forth should be included when figuring your net worth. If you get statements from a company such as the Vanguard Group, Charles Schwab & Company, Jack White & Company, or Fidelity Investments, you have mutual funds to consider when figuring out what you have.

Show Me the Money

Mutual funds enable you to pool your money with that of a large group of investors. Professionals invest the pool of money in stocks, bonds, and other securities, and you own shares that represent the investments. We'll go more in depth about mutual funds in Chapter 13.

◆ **Stocks (Equities).** Some families give shares of certain stock, such as Disney, to kids in order to introduce them to the stock market or as gifts.

Dollars and Sense _____

Financial experts recommend keeping an emergency fund of three to six months' salary. The money would be used if you lost your job, or got sick and couldn't work, or faced any other emergency circumstances.

◆ **Bonds.** Bonds are often given as contest prizes, birthday presents, or as part of scholarship packages in schools. If you know of any bonds you have, or think you might have, track them down and include them in the "what you have" category of your personal finances.

◆ **Emergency money.** If you have emergency money, it should be included among your assets. If you don't have any set aside, you should.

As you take inventory of what you have, a personal finance software program can be useful to help you track and tally your assets. After you've carefully considered all your sources of income and other financial assets, add them up, and you'll determine what you have. Only when you've fully explored what you have will you have a better idea of how you might address your wants and needs, as discussed in the next chapter.

The Least You Need to Know

◆ People almost always think they should be paid more for their jobs than they are.

◆ If you're dissatisfied with your salary, you need to decide what you're going to do about it.

◆ If your salary isn't what you'd like, it helps to remember that your job is giving you experience, contacts, and benefits.

◆ Your net worth is all your financial assets, less all your financial liabilities.

◆ When you think and research carefully, you might discover overlooked financial assets.

Chapter 8

What Do You Need?

In This Chapter

- Wanting and needing are two very different things
- Looking at your lifestyle
- Evaluating your expectations
- Determining what you really need
- Thinking about what you can do without

Now that you've got a better understanding of what you have in terms of your personal finances, it's time to take a look at what you need. If you're the kind of person who must have every cool thing you see advertised, or buy everything that your best friend buys, this chapter may make you decidedly uncomfortable. Why? Because we're going to tell you that you don't need to buy the $500 digital camera. And unless you're going to use it as a substitute for a car, you don't need the $900 racing bike, either.

You should, however, keep reading, because recognizing the difference between what you want and need and learning to postpone immediate gratification are two of the best things you can do for your financial health.

Your Financial Lifestyle

Take a few minutes and think about your financial lifestyle. This lifestyle has nothing to do with whether you're single or married, gay or straight, or into the bar scene or the church scene. Your financial lifestyle is everything you do that affects your pocketbook.

To help you get started, we've prepared a simple quiz. Answer these questions honestly by checking Yes or No, and you'll be better able to evaluate your financial lifestyle:

1. Do you go out to dinner often? ❏ Yes ❏ No

2. Do you spend a significant amount of money—maybe 10 percent or more of your income—on movies, at happy hours, dinners at restaurants, or other leisure activities? ❏ Yes ❏ No

3. Do you love to shop for new clothes, even when you don't need them? ❏ Yes ❏ No

4. Do you wear only certain name brands, such as J. Crew or Polo? ❏ Yes ❏ No

5. Are you intrigued by all the latest electronic stuff, and do you own more of it than you need? ❏ Yes ❏ No

6. Do you look at cars as status symbols, making the kind of car you drive very important to you? ❏ Yes ❏ No

7. Are your vacations usually trips to trendy, "in" spots? ❏ Yes ❏ No

8. Do you have a closet full of gear you've bought (and barely used) for various activities such as skiing, hiking, rock climbing, or biking? ❏ Yes ❏ No

9. Do you regularly buy new CDs, DVDs, or computer software? ❏ Yes ❏ No

10. Do you spend a lot of money in a short time and then are you unable to recall what you bought once the money is gone? ❏ Yes ❏ No

Here's what your answers mean:

♦ If you answered yes to seven or more questions, you've got a financial lifestyle that will land you in the poorhouse when you're 65. Don't worry, though. You can change it.

♦ If you answered yes to between four and seven questions, your financial lifestyle is on shaky ground, but it's fixable.

♦ If you answered yes to three or fewer questions, you can just skim the rest of this chapter. Your financial lifestyle is in good shape.

If your financial lifestyle needs some work, don't worry. That's what we're here to do. Let's first take a look at why you might have adopted your particular financial lifestyle. Then we'll look at some ways to change it, if it needs changing.

Evaluating Your Expectations

If this is starting to read like a self-help book for breaking bad habits and changing the way you live, stay with us. We're about to get to the financial point. If you have an unhealthy financial lifestyle, it's important to realize what causes it. Although there are exceptions, the most likely reason your financial lifestyle is not where it should be is because you have unrealistic expectations.

If you expect that your first apartment is going to look like it was just redone by the cast of *Extreme Makeover*, you've got unrealistic expectations (unless you've got a rich uncle or somebody else who's just looking for ways to spend his money on you). If you expect that your first car is going to be a new BMW convertible, again, your expectations are unrealistic.

It's time to evaluate your expectations and, if they're too high, adjust them to what is realistic. That's not to say you shouldn't set lofty goals for the future. Maybe it's realistic to expect that in seven years you'll be driving a new BMW, and in 20 years, you'll be living in a 15-room house in Malibu. For now, though, a used Chevy and a two-room

CAUTION

Money Pit _____

Advertising has taken on a new dimension, now that companies use the Internet to showcase their products. Sexy websites that serve as advertising forums can be hard to resist, especially because manufacturers make it so easy to order their products right away. Beware of this high-tech advertising—it's mighty tempting stuff.

walk-up with extremely small (make that practically nonexistent) closet space might just have to be your reality.

Pocket Change

Psychologists tell us there are all kinds of reasons we spend money. Some people spend to boost their self-esteem, to make other people like them, or to make up for what they perceive as deprived childhoods.

Pocket Change

Research has repeatedly shown that people who have the basic necessities of life—shelter, food, clean water, breathable air, and adequate clothing—are happier than those who don't. Once those needs have been met, however, people with more aren't necessarily any happier than those with less.

Dollars and Sense

When you find yourself wanting something and the credit card is in your hand, do yourself a favor. Put the card away, go home, and sleep on it. Think about what you're going to buy and how it will affect your more long-term dreams and expectations. The mountain bike or digital camera might not seem so important in the morning.

Why, as a society, do we have such high expectations of what we should have? That's a no-brainer. From the time we're kids watching cartoons in the living room on Saturday mornings, we're sent a clear message that we need stuff—lots and lots of stuff. If you believe that you should have everything you want and have it now, you've fallen right into the trap that advertisers have set for you. They have you exactly where they want you.

By the time you've moved past wanting sugary breakfast cereals, action figures, and skateboards, and are old enough to start looking at cars, cameras, and computers, Mom and Dad aren't footing the bill anymore. Still, you think you should get exactly what you want because you always have. The ads are still pretty convincing, even though you're not a kid anymore. So you figure if Mom won't buy you the new Compaq, you'll get it yourself. Next thing you know, you've got a great computer, but you've run up a $3,000 credit card bill because you expected to get that computer as soon as you decided you needed (read *wanted*) it.

Looking at What You Need and What You Don't

Most of us have too much stuff, but there are certain things that we all need: a place to live, food to eat, clothes and shoes to wear. Many of us need cars to get where we need to be. Some of us need things such as medicine on a regular basis, glasses, or contacts. We need a telephone, a heater, and a fan. Some things are simply necessary.

Nobody is going to argue that you shouldn't buy the things you need. It makes no sense to put money in the bank that you should have used to buy yourself a pair of glasses. Our argument is with thinking, as so many of us do, that you need everything you see, or everything that someone else has, and then buying it. All that does is make you have too much stuff and jeopardize your financial future.

The Bare Necessities

There are some expenses you simply can't avoid. These include taxes, shelter, utilities, food, and some form of transportation. If you have college debt or owe on a credit card or car loan, repayment of those debts is a necessary expenditure. You'll also need to pay for insurance, health care costs that aren't covered by insurance, clothing, and education costs if you're still in school.

In addition to these nonavoidable expenses, there is another financial necessity: regular contributions to a savings account, retirement fund, or other vehicle, to assure your future financial health. This is the most overlooked, neglected necessity there is, and a huge source of regret among people who didn't do it.

The temptation to skip this last necessity is great. You think you're doing just fine. You're paying your bills and paying back some of the money you owe for college loans and credit cards. But what about the future? What about the house you want to buy someday? How about expenses you'll have if and when you get around to having kids? What about the Master's degree you're thinking about?

If you can foresee expenses down the road, money to pay for them should be included in your "what you need" category. They won't pay for themselves, and the sooner you can put some money away for specific goals in the future, the better off you'll be.

Dollars and Sense

When you start thinking about how you'll spend your paycheck, deduct the amount you plan to save first. If you want to save 10 percent of your paycheck, for instance, don't even consider that money as part of your income. Deduct it automatically and budget with the remaining 90 percent. Remember, it's important to pay yourself first!

It's hard to defer buying now in order to save for a future goal. It defies our society's mindset of getting what we want when we want it. But if you pass on the leather jacket and invest the $250, you're on your way to sending a child to college someday or getting out of the apartment and into your own house.

Niceties or Necessities?

Now that we've covered the necessities, we'll have a look at some things that are often thought of as necessities, but might not be:

◆ **Household furnishings.** Nobody wants to live in an empty house or apartment. Some furnishings are nice, but are the curtains that match the bedspread necessary, or is that *need* really a *want*? Expensive artwork, decorative rugs, the state-of-the-art microwave, and the solid cherry entertainment center that houses the big-screen TV are not essential to your existence.

◆ **Cable TV.** Many people claim they couldn't live without TV, but we'll go out on a limb here and assert that they can live quite nicely without HBO. Cable TV is expensive, and the extras can send your bill through the roof. Look at this area carefully when determining what you need.

◆ **Restaurants and bars.** Food is necessary, but eating in restaurants is not. Although it's nice to get together with friends after work or on weekends, you can spend a lot of money on a few drinks in the bar. If everyone agrees, maybe a rotating happy hour at someone's apartment makes better financial sense than the bar.

Pocket Change
A college-age friend was horrified recently when her boyfriend, who had too many beers while hanging out in the local bar, threw his American Express card down and told the bartender to get a round for everybody. Had she not grabbed the card and escorted her boyfriend out, he could have been looking at a large and completely unnecessary expense at the end of the month.

◆ **Wheels**   If you need a car to get back and forth to work and to the other places you go, it's a necessity. But there are many cars to choose from, and some cost a whole lot more than others.

◆ **Bad debt**   Some kinds of debt are worse than others. A mortgage, college loans, and even a car payment are understandable, necessary debt that you'll have to repay. But if you're paying 18 percent interest on a fancy dinner at a restaurant that you charged to your credit card three months ago, that's really bad debt.

◆ **Drugs and personal items**   There is a lot of gray area in this category when it comes to want versus need. You need vision care and glasses, but do you need designer frames? You need skin-care products, but do you need a basketful of cosmetics in every color produced? You need medicine for your headache, but doesn't the store brand work just as well as the higher-priced Tylenol?

◆ **Classes and instruction**   Financing an education is one of the best expenses you'll ever have. There may be a time, though, when you'll have to defer on classes and instruction until you're better financially equipped to pay for them. If you need a Master's degree to advance in your job, then by all means go ahead and work toward the degree. But the philosophy course that you thought sounded interesting will be offered again next year, and it might be a good idea to wait until then to take it. You might also want to hold off on the flower-arranging course, the personal trainer at the gym, and the bassoon for beginners program.

◆ **Fashion**   You need clothes. You don't need Nautica. You need shoes, but you don't need more pairs than you can fit into your closet. If you can get away with not wearing a suit to work, you probably don't need clothes that have to be dry cleaned. Many people have closets full of clothes they don't wear, on which they've spent hundreds, even thousands, of dollars.

◆ **Entertainment**   Some people will disagree, but we say with conviction that leisure and recreation are necessities. Regardless of what you do, you need leisure time and fun activities with which to fill it. The problem is, leisure can be very expensive. Although you need entertainment, you don't need the fancy cruise you booked to the Bahamas or tickets for two to *Mamma Mia!*.

◆ **Extras**   You say you need exercise, and you're right. You could get sufficient exercise by running and working out with some weights at home, but you want to take the Pilates class at the gym where everybody goes after work. And the leggings that you love to wear because they make your legs look longer? That's a want, not a need. The expensive salon haircut, the gift you got for your girl-friend last week, the watch that cost a third of your weekly salary, the daily cappuccinos, and the you-name-your-favorite weakness are wants as well.

When you separate your needs from your wants, you'll have a much clearer picture of how to pay for both of those categories. You'll know exactly where your money needs to go. You wouldn't think of skipping your rent payment to go on vacation, would you? That's because you recognize that the rent is a need, but the vacation is a want. Some spending decisions aren't so obvious, however.

A good thing to do is to make a list of your needs and make another list of your wants. Be honest with yourself, but not indulgent. Don't underestimate your needs, because you must know what they are to determine how much money you'll need to pay for them. On the other hand, if you confuse wants with needs and think you need more than you actually do, you'll become frustrated that your paycheck can't stretch that far.

If it gets to the point where you can't finance your needs, you need to make some pretty drastic lifestyle changes. If you live by yourself, maybe you need to get a room-mate to cut housing costs. After all, living alone, by choice, is a luxury. Or maybe you need to trade in that new Honda for a used one. As long as it gets you where you need to go, does it really matter if it's a 2003 or a 2001? The next two chapters go into detail about budgets and saving money, so read on for lots of suggestions about how to better handle your money.

The Least You Need to Know

- ◆ It's easy to confuse needs with wants, but they're two very different things and must be treated differently as far as your money is concerned.

- ◆ If your financial lifestyle is not healthy, it's time to change it.

- ◆ It might be necessary to lower your expectations if you want to improve your financial lifestyle.

- ◆ There are some things that everybody needs; among these needs are shelter, food, clothing, and money for taxes.

- ◆ As a society, we're encouraged to think that we need much more than we really do and that we need it immediately.

- ◆ When you understand what you need, as opposed to what you want, you'll be able to prioritize your finances.

Chapter 9

The B Word: Budgets

In This Chapter

- ◆ Why nobody likes a budget
- ◆ Accepting that a budget is the way to go
- ◆ Knowing what to include in your budget
- ◆ Deciding whether you need to earn more or spend less
- ◆ Using software to help prepare and maintain a budget

Mention the word budget when you're with a group of people, and you're likely to hear a collective groan. Used as either a noun or a verb, the B word is not a favorite in most people's vocabularies. Making a budget or sticking to one probably ranks right up there among life experiences such as going to the dentist or buying a new transmission for your car.

Why is that? Why do we hate budgets so much, and why do so many of us refuse or neglect to use one? Businesses use budgets. Can you imagine Microsoft spending millions of dollars and not keeping track of where it was going? Schools use budgets. Governments use budgets (or at least claim to). It's clear that budgets are sensible, necessary things to have. We'll even go a step further here, and say that budgets are desirable because they keep us out of trouble, if used properly.

Why Budgets Have Such a Bad Rep

A *budget* is simply a schedule of income and expenses. It's a way of keeping track of the money you earn and planning how you spend your money. See, that's not so bad, is it?

If budgets are sensible, necessary, and even desirable, then why do they have such a bad reputation? Why do your friends groan and roll their eyes when the word comes up in conversation? The reason is that making a budget, or working within a budget, implies having to use restraint or, worse yet, having to do without. As a society, restraint and denial are things that we have a lot of trouble dealing with.

If you have a certain amount of money budgeted for clothes, for instance, and you've already spent it for the month, you won't be able to buy that cute sweater you saw at the mall, at least not this month. You'll have to pass on the movies Friday night if you want to have enough money left to go out to dinner Saturday. You might even have to say "no, thanks" to the weekend at the beach that your friends are planning.

Show Me the Money

A **budget** is a schedule of income and expenses, usually broken into monthly intervals and covering a one-year period.

Pocket Change

About 110,000 people age 25 and under filed for bankruptcy in 2003, according to an ABC News report. Most cases were attributed to credit card debt and student loans.

To deny yourself something that you want flies right in the face of all the advertising with which you're constantly bombarded. Credit card companies, too, tell you to go ahead and get what you want. Buy it now and worry about it later is a pervasive attitude in our society.

If you're working within a budget, you can't do that. A budget forces you to look at what you make and to pay attention to what you spend. A good budget will tell you to the dollar how much you can spend on things such as food, restaurants, clothes, makeup, drinks with friends, and movies.

Most of us don't like the restrictions a budget imposes. We'd rather buy that great coat and figure out how to pay for it later. Well, prepare for a change in attitude.

Everybody Needs a Budget

Presumably, because you're reading this book, you want to avoid the traps that so many people fall into: too much debt, too little savings, too much spending. To do that, you've got to have a budget. Unless you've got a photographic memory and a calculator for a brain, you can't possibly keep track of your income and expenditures in your head.

It will take a little time to set up a good budget that's comfortable for you to use, but it's well worth it to get a clear picture of your financial situation. You can use the sample budget we've included in this chapter as a guide, or adapt it for your own purposes, but know that there's no one way to set up a perfect budget. It depends on your needs and how detailed you want your budget to be.

What Your Budget Should Include

You can start your budget simply by identifying spending categories and listing all the money, either estimated or exact, that you spend in each category each month. Try to include everything you spend money on, right down to toothpaste and Juicy Fruit. Take a look at this sample budget to see just where your money goes. Feel free to revise it to best suit your needs.

Where Your Money Goes: A Sample Budget Worksheet

Item	Estimated	Amount/Worth
Housing		
Mortgage/Rent		
Phone		
Cable		
Furniture		
Appliances		
Maintenance		
Total:		
Transportation		
Gas/Maintenance		
Tolls		
License/taxes		
Public transportation		
Total:		

continues

Where Your Money Goes: A Sample Budget Worksheet (continued)

Item	Estimated	Amount/Worth
Taxes		
Federal		
State		
Local		
Social Security		
Luxury		
Total:		
Debt		
Credit card		
Car loans		
Student loans		
Personal loans		
Line of credit		
Total:		
Entertainment		
Movies, concerts, and theater		
Vacation		
Hobbies		
Pets		
Magazines and books		
Videos and music tapes		
Restaurants		
Total:		
Personal		
Food		
Gifts		
Clothes		
Shoes		

Item	Estimated	Amount/Worth
Jewelry		
Dry cleaning/laundry		
Hair/makeup		
Health club		
Other		
	Total:	

Health Care

Co-payments		
Drugs		
	Total:	

Insurance

Car		
Home		
Disability		
Life		
Health		
	Total:	

Children

Day care		
Babysitters		
Toys		
Clothes		
Other		
	Total:	

Charity

Donations		
	Grand Total:	

Nonroutine Expenses

Although certain things, such as your rent, groceries, and clothes, will be obvious expenditures as you start preparing your budget, make sure you include a category of less-obvious expenses. Things such as Christmas or Hanukkah gifts, the birthday party you want to give your boyfriend in May, the $100 you contributed to the Red Cross to aid hurricane disaster victims, and wedding and baby gifts, are all known as *nonroutine expenses.* They aren't exactly unexpected—I mean, Christmas and Hanukkah do roll around every year—but they're not expenditures that come up each month, so you're more apt to overlook them.

Car repairs also are nonroutine expenses. If you don't budget for them, they can be devastating financial news. It's hard to anticipate when your muffler is going to drop off onto the highway, but you must have some money budgeted for a new one when it does.

Show Me the Money

Routine expenses include the more obvious expenditures, such as rent, insurance, food, and entertainment. **Nonroutine expenses** are expenditures that people often overlook because they don't have to pay them regularly. They include car repairs or medical expenses.

Or what if you've budgeted money for routine checkups with the dentist, but learn during one of those checkups that you have a loose filling in your back tooth that needs to be taken out and replaced? A little procedure like that could set you back more than $100 and wreck your monthly budget.

The way to anticipate nonroutine expenses is to figure out all that you've had in the past year. Include car repair bills, big gifts, unexpected medical bills, the weekend at the ski resort that came up unexpectedly, and any others you can think of. Add up the cost of all those things, and then divide the total by 12. That's how much you should set aside each month for nonroutine expenses.

If you're just out of college and starting out, estimating your nonroutine expenses will be difficult because you probably won't have much of a history of these types of expenses to work from. If that's the case, ask someone to help you. Maybe you have a friend who's been on his own for a few years and can give you an idea about these types of expenses. Or perhaps a family member can advise you on car repairs and other expenses.

Routine Expenses

The first items to list are known as *routine expenses*. You'll need to have the following in your budget:

◆ **Housing.** Your rent or mortgage will make up the biggest chunk of your housing expenses, but don't forget the other things that you pay for, too. How about your phone bill, your utilities bill, and the sofa and loveseat you bought? Consider the set of dishes you got at Ikea, and the washer and dryer. How about your cable bill? If you're paying costs for upkeep, such as having the carpets cleaned, windows washed, or painting done, be sure to include that, too.

◆ **Debt.** This is probably another big expense category, unless you've been very frugal or very lucky. Include in the debt category everything for which you owe money: your car, your student loans, your credit cards, and so on. Do you have a line of credit opened anywhere? What about personal loans? If your dad loaned you $1,500 for a security deposit and the first month's rent on your apartment, include that in your debt category. Include both principal and interest payments.

> **Dollars and Sense**
>
> When you put together a budget, you can set aside your savings in one of two ways. Either include the money you'll save each month in your routine expenses, or deduct it from your income before you start making your budget. Paying yourself first will pay off greatly down the road.

◆ **Insurance.** Include any insurance you pay for in this category: auto, health (don't forget your co-payment if you're partially insured by your employer), renter's, and so on.

◆ **Taxes.** If you don't own property, you probably don't pay many taxes other than sales taxes and those deducted from your paycheck. If you do own property, you'll need to include the local property taxes, even if you put money in escrow and your mortgage company makes the payment for you. Also include the taxes that are deducted from your paycheck: federal, state, social security, occupational privilege, and any others.

◆ **Transportation.** If you don't own a car, your expenses in this category will be what you spend on public transportation. If you own a car, include routine maintenance costs (such as oil changes) and what you spend on gas and car insurance. Don't forget those pesky little expenses for your license and car registration. If you pay tolls regularly when driving, include those, too.

- ◆ **Health care.** Hopefully, these costs are minimal. But don't forget to budget for dental costs if your insurance doesn't cover them, eye exams, glasses, prescriptions, and routine doctor visits.

- ◆ **Entertainment and Vacations.** If you're like most people in their 20s and 30s, this category will contain considerable expenses. Make sure you include everything, for this is one of the first areas we'll be looking at in which to cut costs. This category covers a variety of expenses, such as vacations, restaurants (even fast food), and the cost of drinks if you go to bars, clubs, or coffee houses. Think about movies, concerts, museums, cover charges, and any costs associated with hobbies (golf, bowling, skiing, or whatever). Don't forget pet costs, magazines and books, video rentals, the money you spend on DVDs, CDs, DVD and CD players, and any other expenses related to entertainment. Don't forget the money you spend in the office football pool and on the trip to the casino. Be honest when you list expenses in this category. Many people don't realize how much money they spend on entertainment until they sit down and add it all up.

- ◆ **Personal.** This category includes food, clothing, shoes, jewelry, laundry and dry-cleaning costs, your health club fees, all fitness expenses, and money spent on hair stylists, manicures, makeup, and toiletries.

- ◆ **Children.** If you have kids, you already know they're expensive. If you don't have kids, but plan to someday, it doesn't hurt to know what costs are involved. Include expenses incurred for baby-sitters and day care, toys, clothes, food, diapers, and shoes.

- ◆ **Giving.** List money you contribute to your church, synagogue, or charities.

After you've listed your expenses, add them all up. Think about any categories you might have to include that aren't listed here, and don't forget to include the nonroutine expenses we talked about earlier.

Trimming the Fat: Analyzing Your Expenses

You already have your expenses organized into spending categories; you now can break them down further into *fixed expenses* and *variable expenses*, and *nondiscretionary expenses* and *discretionary expenses*. When you have all your expenses categorized, it will be easier to see how you can control your budget. Analyzing different ratios within your budget will also help you determine where you should be cutting back your expenses.

Some of your expenses are fixed and others are variable. Fixed expenses include the following:

- Rent

- Car payments

- Any other payments that don't vary in amount, such as dues or club membership fees

- Your mortgage, if you have one

Show Me the Money

Talk about picky! You can break down your expenses into **fixed expenses,** such as rent and car payments, and **variable expenses,** such as food and entertainment. Don't stop yet! These categories can be further broken down into **nondiscretionary expenses,** which are things you can't do without, such as food and rent, and **discretionary expenses,** which you can do without (vacations and entertainment).

While these expenses may be necessary, like rent or mortgage payments, they often can be scaled down. If your rent is more than you can afford, you might have to move to a smaller place or get a roommate. Or perhaps you could refinance your mortgage for a lower interest rate (be sure to consider the expenses involved in refinancing before deciding to go ahead). You may really like the club you've joined, but if the membership fees are too high, you may have to consider dropping out. And, we've already discussed the varying expenses of car ownership in Chapter 6. Still, fixed expenses are not the easiest ones to scrimp on. Let's take a look at the variable expenses.

Variable expenses include the following:

- Food

- Utilities

- Entertainment

- Vacations

It's probably easier to cut back on variable expenses such as these than on fixed expenses. Utilities can be adjusted to save money, and you can pass up the lobster tails and eat chicken instead. After you break down your expenses into variable or fixed, you can add another category: discretionary or nondiscretionary. *Nondiscretionary expenses* are things you must pay for or buy, including the following:

- Food

- Rent or mortgage

- Car payments

- Utilities

Nondiscretionary expenses can't be avoided, but you might be able to control them, as discussed earlier. *Discretionary expenses*, on the other hand, are those that aren't necessary, including the following:

- Vacations

- Entertainment

- Club memberships

These discretionary expenses are the most obvious ones to curtail if you're trying to cut back on expenses.

Now you can organize your expenses by how they fit into both sets of categories. The following are fixed, nondiscretionary expenses:

- Rent or mortgage

- Car payments

Variable, nondiscretionary expenses are as follows:

- Food

- Utilities

Your fixed, discretionary expenses include the following:

- Club dues

- Membership fees

Your variable, discretionary expenses include the following:

- Vacations

- Entertainment

Basically, there are two ways to use this information to save money: You can control your discretionary expenses (skip the vacation this year), or limit your nondiscretionary expenses (find a roommate or move into a smaller apartment).

Spending Ratios

When it comes to figuring out where you need to cut expenses, you'll find spending ratios to be useful tools. A *spending ratio* is simply the percentage of money, as it relates to your gross income, that you use for a particular area, such as housing or entertainment. If one area of expense becomes too great, you'll see that ratio is too high and begin to cut back.

To figure out your housing payment ratio, which is one kind of spending ratio, add up all your housing costs (rent or mortgage, insurance, property taxes, and so on). Compare that number to your total income. If your housing costs are more than 28 percent of your gross income, you're paying too much for housing and should look for ways to cut your costs.

To figure your total debt ratio, add up all your monthly payments, including car, credit card, rent, and so on. Compare that number to your total income. If it's more than 36 percent of your income, these expenses are too high, and you should look for ways to cut them.

Finally, you can figure out your *savings ratio*, which is the percentage of your gross income that you save. Compare the amount of money you save each week or month to your income for that period. You should be aiming for 8 percent a year. If you're not saving that much, you should look for ways to cut expenses and save more.

Show Me the Money

Spending ratios are used to determine the amount of your gross income that goes toward a particular expenditure area. They can be used as tools in cutting expenses. Your savings ratio is the opposite of your spending ratio. It is the percentage of your gross income that you are able to save within a given time.

There are other ratios, too, but these are good ones with which to start. Don't get too hung up on these ratios. If your housing costs are 29 or 30 percent instead of 28 percent, it doesn't mean you should immediately sublet your apartment and move back home with Mom and Dad. But if you find your ratio is up to 35 or 40 percent, you ought to think about downsizing.

One Job, Two Jobs, Three Jobs, Four

After you've figured out how much you're spending, you'll know exactly how much money you need to pay for that spending. You'll also have a clear picture of what you spend your money on. You might be surprised at the amount you're spending unnecessarily.

Pocket Change

According to the U.S. Department of Labor, one out of 17 Americans was working more than one job in 2003. That was between 7 and 8 million, or a little over 5 percent of all workers. Of all those holding a second job, 24 percent were between 25 and 34 years old and 30 percent were between 35 and 44 years old.

After you've figured out what you have, and the amount of money you need to spend, take a good, hard look at how you're doing. If you're able to meet all your expenses, make regular payments on any debt you have, save a portion of your income, and have some money left over for discretionary purposes, good for you. You're in good financial shape.

If, however, you're spending everything you earn and not saving anything, or you're spending *more* than you earn, you've got to change your ways. If you have credit card debt that never gets paid off, or you're in over your head with car loans or other debt, your financial condition is shaky.

There are two ways to handle that situation: You can either spend less or earn more. Those who are in a real financial bind may very well need to do both of those things. For many people, it's easier to change their mindset and cut down their spending. Some hard-core spenders, however, would rather try to earn more than spend less.

If you fall into the hard-core spender category, and you don't see a big raise in your future anytime soon, you need to figure out a way to get more money. You can do something illegal, but that's definitely *not* recommended. You can play the lottery every night, but statistically, your chances of getting ahead that way are pretty slim. You can hope for a big inheritance or some other windfall, but you'll probably wait for a long, long time. If you can't cut down on spending, you'll need to get another job; there's no getting around it.

Money Pit

Many relationships fail because one person becomes unavailable or unapproachable because he or she works too much. When working becomes (or appears to become) more important than the relationship, you can bet there will be trouble.

You'd probably be much better off if you cut your spending rather than get another job in order to pay for it, but working two jobs is better than racking up big debt with no way to pay for it. Many people take a second job when they're trying to earn money for a specific expense, such as a wedding or college tuition. That's fine, as long as they're careful to put the extra money in savings so they'll have it when the expense occurs. It's easy to lose sight of a long-term goal when you suddenly have extra money to spend.

Pocket Change

If you think you need a second job, look carefully at what you'll make and the possible expenses that you'll incur because of the job. If you'll be earning $8 an hour on a second job, but spending more money on transportation costs and clothes for the job and eating dinner out every night because you're too tired or don't have time to make something at home, it just might not be worth your time and effort.

If you do decide to take a second job, consider carefully what it will do to your life. What activities would you have to give up? How much less time would you have to spend with family and friends? It's a personal decision, but being able to buy a lot of things is less than ideal if you don't have time to enjoy them.

Sticking With It

After you have your budget written up, you need to keep track of how you're doing compared with the budget. Many people have drafted great budgets, only to give up on them after a few months. Your spending habits aren't the same every month, so you need to keep track of your expenses for several years to get an accurate picture of what you're spending over the long term.

Dollars and Sense _____

Some people use the jar or cigar box system to help them measure how well they're sticking to their budgets. This system simply entails collecting receipts for everything you buy and putting them in a box or jar earmarked for a particular category. At the end of the month, you tally all the receipts to determine your expenses. Low-tech? You bet. But this system has worked for lots of budgeters.

Many people who neglect to budget for nonroutine expenses get discouraged and quit using their budgets when they're hit with a car repair or other major expense. That's why it's important to include money for those types of expenses.

If you slip up one month and overspend, don't be too hard on yourself, and don't give up on the budget. It's like when you're trying to lose some weight. Just because you overeat one day doesn't mean you should quit the diet and eat whatever you want the next day, too. Go back to the plan, and you'll reach your goals.

Software and Websites for Budgeting

As you would expect, there are a number of software programs that can help you with a budget and other aspects of your personal finances. The following are some of the most widely used Windows-based programs for personal finance management:

◆ Microsoft Money 2004 Premium includes features that let you budget, track investments, bank and pay bills online, plan for taxes, and manage finances. There's an electronic checkbook, and you can track your expenses and print financial statements at the end of each month.

◆ Intuit's Quicken Deluxe 2004 includes many of the same features as Microsoft Money, plus a feature that tracks your expenses and shows you how they compare with what you've budgeted. And, Quicken information can be transferred into Turbo Tax software during tax time, saving you the trouble of entering data.

◆ Moneydance includes features that allow you to print checks, track expenditures, print reports, and reconcile bank accounts. It doesn't have as many features as Microsoft or Quicken, but is easy to use and recommended. Websites that offer advice on setting up budgets and handling other financial matters are plentiful. Check out these sites to start:

  ◆ The Household Budget Management site gives advice on how to prepare a practical, useable budget. You can access it at www.dacomp.com/ budget1.html.

  ◆ Right On The Money shows you how to plan a budget and provides tools for making one. You can find it at www.rightonthemoney.org.

  ◆ MoneyAdvise provides a budget worksheet and other tools to create a personalized spending plan. Access it at www.moneyadvise.com.

  ◆ The Bankrate.com budgeting calculator helps you to start your own budget and provides lots of tips and suggestions. You can access it at www.bankrate.com/brm/calc/Worksheet.

♦ The Financial Planning page on About.com has a lot of helpful ;
ning a budget, as well as information about personal finance softwa..
http://financialplan.about.com.

A computer and some fancy software might make budgeting easier and more fun, but
they aren't absolutely necessary. You can easily make a budget yourself with just a
pencil, paper, and maybe a cheap calculator. The most important ingredients of successful budgeting are a willingness to make a budget and to stick to it after it's made.

The Least You Need to Know

♦ Nobody likes to think about budgeting, much less do it, but you can and should
do it.

♦ You can use computer software or cigar boxes, but everyone should have a
budget to know exactly how they spend their money and how they are implementing their plan.

♦ After you have a handle on what you have and what you need, you can assess
your financial condition.

♦ If your earnings aren't greater than your expenditures, you've got to earn more
or spend less.

♦ If you're tempted to take a second job in order to earn more money so you can
spend more, consider cutting expenses instead.

Chapter 10

Getting Into the Swing of Savings

In This Chapter

- ◆ Determining your financial personality
- ◆ Saving and spending: Habits to learn or unlearn
- ◆ Saving a little can result in a lot
- ◆ A savings mindset is a good start
- ◆ Learning to save on just about everything

Basically, there are two kinds of people: savers and spenders. In this chapter, we'll take a look at these financial personalities and help you determine in which category you belong. Get ready—you might discover a few things about yourself.

Are You a Saver or a Spender?

If you know to the nickel how much money is in your wallet or purse at this moment, keep track of exactly how much you spend and where you spend it, buy only clothing that doesn't need to be dry cleaned, and eat pasta three times a week to stretch your food dollars, you're probably a saver.

If, on the other hand, you simply *must* eat at that little bistro with the great wine selection twice a week, can't imagine life without your $140 Nikes, haven't a clue as to where you might have spent that $50 you stashed in your wallet Saturday morning, and haven't had your Visa paid off for more than a year, chances are you're a spender.

Most of us probably fall somewhere in the middle of the saving/spending continuum, but plenty of people go to extremes.

Evaluating Your Financial Personality

When we talk about your financial personality, we're not making any value judgments. Whether you're a saver or a spender is part of your personality. It's sort of like whether you're outgoing or reserved, or whether you love Indian food or hate it. It's just something about you.

Being a saver or a spender isn't good or bad on its own, but either personality can cause problems if it's not managed properly. You probably won't need to look too closely at your own habits to determine whether you're a saver or a spender.

If you're a saver, good for you. It doesn't necessarily make you a better person, but you have a great start on managing your personal finances.

If you're a spender, don't despair. There's something to be said for living the good life. The only problem is, too much of the good life now is likely to mean less of the good life later. Your financial personality ties in directly to your financial situation, so spenders have to learn to exercise some self-control.

Savers Have It Made (Almost)

If you've determined that you're a saver, give yourself a pat on the back. Managing your personal finances probably will be a little easier for you. Now, get ready to assess your saving habits. Could you be saving more? Are you saving smart? Are you saving in the right places? Are you saving *too much*?

We've all heard the stories of elderly people who die in one-room apartments with few comforts, who, unknown to everyone, had savings and investments of a million dollars or more. They were saving their money to give to their children, or their church, or the local animal shelter. For whatever reasons, some people choose to forego comforts and even necessities (heat, air conditioning, even food) in order to save their money.

It makes no sense, of course, to save so much money that you don't have the things you need and some of the things you want. After all, that's why we work. It's a rare person who would continue to show up at the job every day if the paychecks stopped coming.

There are no guarantees in this life, and unfortunately, some of us won't even make it to retirement age. It would be tragic to deny yourself everything you want in order to save money for a day that never comes. It's important to strike a balance between extreme frugality in the name of saving money and a devil-may-care spending spree that compromises your financial future. You'll learn more about saving and investing for the future in the upcoming chapters on investments and retirement funds.

Spenders Have to Work a Little Harder

If you're a spender, you can console yourself with the fact that you're far from alone. Most people find it much easier to spend money than to save it. From the time we're children in America, we're sent a clear message: Go ahead—spend. Whenever we watch TV, pick up a magazine, or get on the Internet, we're bombarded with advertising telling us to spend. Buy cars! Buy beer! Buy shampoo! Buy jeans! Buy anything, but buy!

One hundred years ago, people made a lot less money than they make today. They spent a whole lot less, too. One reason was that there was simply less to buy. There were no malls, no television shopping clubs, no luxury vacation condos, and not many expectations.

Dollars and Sense _____

Try this exercise: Choose one room and identify all the things in it that are unnecessary and unused. Then, estimate the cost of each item and add them up. When you've finished, multiply the total by the number of rooms in your house. If you invested the total you just came up with, you'd no doubt enhance your retirement fund nicely. Think about that the next time you're in Pier One.

We are part of a society that pushes spending and consumerism, and we're bombarded every day with the message that spending money is good. Is it any wonder so many of us spend so much?

A Penny Saved Is More Than a Penny Earned

We've all heard the expression, "a penny saved is a penny earned." When it comes to saving money, we don't think much in pennies anymore, unless you're a kid with a piggy bank. We think in dollars, or tens of dollars, or hundreds of dollars. That's part of the problem for many people who have trouble saving money. They feel that it's not worth saving a few cents or a few dollars, so they don't. They spend a little here and a little there, not realizing how quickly those little bits of money add up.

> **Dollars and Sense**
>
> If you spend a dollar a day for a soda or coffee, think about this: Investing a dollar a day earning an average 8 percent return for 40 years would give you over $100,000 at the end of that period.

Think about the money you spend each day on incidentals: a cup of coffee and a bagel at the Dunkin' Donuts on your way to work, a sandwich and a Snapple at the deli at lunchtime, and a bottle of shampoo at the drugstore on your way back to work. Your friend calls after dinner, and you meet at Starbucks for a caffè latte. No big deal, it's just an ordinary day. When you add it all up, though, you'll see that this ordinary day cost you more than $15 in incidentals.

Multiply the expenses for a typical workday by five, and you're spending $75 a week on incidentals. By the end of the week, you have nothing to show for your spending but half a bottle of shampoo and a caffeine habit, and the weekend is just beginning.

Of course, nobody is telling you to cut out all incidental spending. You do need shampoo, and coffee drinkers might argue that even shampoo is secondary to the Starbucks blend. But what if you cut that incidental spending in half? For instance, you could make your coffee at home and carry a sandwich to work. Would saving $25 a week make a difference in your long-term savings? You bet it would! If you saved that $25 each week, at the end of a year you'd have $1,300.

Yeah, $1,300 is a lot of money, but maybe you're still not convinced to cut back at Starbucks. If you invested the money at a 10 percent return, you'd quickly see that a penny saved is much more than a penny earned:

♦ Investing $25 a week in a mutual fund with an average after-tax annual return of 10 percent (the historical stock market average) for 5 years would give you $8,400.

♦ Investing $25 a week in a mutual fund with an average after-tax annual return of 10 percent for 10 years would give you $22,300.

It's hard to imagine that cutting out a cup of coffee and a sandwich each day can make that much of a difference to your savings, but it does. Interest, especially compound interest, can give you big returns on small investments. What's the difference in types of interest, you ask? Let's have a look.

Simple interest, which is what we normally just refer to as interest, is a method of calculating what you earn on your money by applying the stated rate on only the actual balance on deposit for the exact period of deposit. For instance, if you invest $2,000 in an account for one year at 5 percent interest, the bank would pay you $100 at the end of the year. Not bad, huh? You get $100 just for letting your money sit there. But if you were earning compound interest on your $2,000, you'd be in even better shape.

Dollars and Sense

Some financial advisors suggest paying for every purchase with dollar bills, and saving all the change you get. At the end of the month, take all the change to the bank for deposit. You'll be surprised at how it will add up.

Compound interest is paid on an initial deposit plus any accumulated interest from period to period. Compound interest gives you interest on your interest. It's definitely the way to invest. Compounding interest at 5 percent over a year wouldn't make a great difference on a $2,000 deposit, but it still would give you a couple of dollars more for your money. When you get into big investments at higher interest rates, compounding interest really becomes significant.

Show Me the Money

Simple interest is a method of calculating what you earn on your money by applying the stated rate on only the balance on deposit for the exact period of deposit. **Compound interest** is paid on an initial deposit plus any accumulated interest from period to period.

Interest is generally compounded in one of several ways: continuously, daily, weekly, monthly, quarterly, or annually. The more often it's compounded, the better off you'll be. Look for banks that compound interest continuously or daily. When your money starts growing, you'll be pleasantly surprised.

Sounds pretty amazing, doesn't it? This is the power of compound interest and why a penny saved is a lot more than a penny earned.

Getting Into a Savings Mindset

Trading a spending habit for a savings habit isn't easy, but it can be done. Being aware of your spending habits is an important first step. You need to realize that you're spending close to $10 a day on coffee, bagels, and shampoo before you can decide to cut out the bagel and save a little money.

If you're a saver, you already realize the importance of putting money away for all the things you'll want or need in the future, such as a house, cars, college, and retirement. Even if you haven't started saving yet, knowing that it's important puts you on the right track.

Dollars and Sense

For two weeks, try keeping a list of everything—from a pack of gum to a new suit—that you buy. This will give you a better picture of where you're spending your money.

Dollars and Sense

Practice what we talked about in last chapter's discussion on budgeting, and find an area of nonessential spending. Examine it carefully and find expenditures that you can eliminate.

If you're a natural-born spender, don't despair. You have plenty of company. Don't think, though, that overspending is something you can't change, like being born short or tall. You can't change your height, but you can change your spending habits.

Nobody feels like they have much money if they compare their financial situations to the dynasties of Bill Gates or Malcolm Forbes.

If you're determined to keep up with your friends, and you buy more and more so that you'll have what they have, you trap yourself into the mindset of spending. If you don't concern yourself with what your friends are buying, and think about what you have and what you need, however, you can develop a savings mindset. If you can achieve the mindset that saving money is good and is something from which you'll benefit greatly in the future, you'll find it a lot easier to pass up things you want in order to keep your cash.

Of course, people spend money for many different reasons, not just to keep up in the great game of possessing. Some people spend because it makes them feel better if they're disappointed, hurt, or angry. Some people enjoy spending money so much that it becomes an addiction. "Shopaholic" is a word that many people use jokingly, but an addiction to spending is a real and serious problem for some people. Of course, other addictions, such as drugs or gambling, can also take huge tolls on your personal finances. Anyone with an addiction of any kind should seek help as soon as possible.

Pocket Change

If you think you have a spending addiction, help is available. Check your phone directory to see whether there's a chapter of Debtors Anonymous (DA) in your area. DA uses a 12-step program, similar to Alcoholics Anonymous, and has helped many people from all social and economic backgrounds overcome spending addictions. For more information about DA, go to www.debtorsanonymous.org.

Saving Money on Almost Everything

Many people have a perpetual plan to start saving money, but they never do. They swear they'll start saving 10 percent of their salary, just as soon as they've got the new car, computer, boots, mountain bike, Palm handheld, guitar, bracelet, or whatever. If you want to save money, you have to make a firm commitment and stick to it. That means you won't be able to buy the mountain bike this month or next month. You might not even be able to buy it this year. Besides deferring expenses, another good way to save money is to get the best deal on the purchases you do make.

Dollars and Sense

For ideas on how to save money when purchasing the things you need, consider reading "The Complete Tightwad Gazette" by Amy Dacyczyn, or "Living Well on a Shoestring: 1,501 Ingenious Ways to Spend Less for What You Need and Have More for What You Want" by the editors of Yankee Magazine. Of course, you'll want to exhibit your new frugality by purchasing used copies of these books.

There are entire books written on living frugally, and it just might be worth your while to invest in one for tips and advice about saving money on everything from food to vacations. Much of the advice you'll encounter is just plain old common sense, such as getting your food at a discount grocery store rather than the high-priced convenience store. Still, you're sure to find some useful information.

Little savings on food, clothes, energy bills, entertainment, and incidentals can add up to big savings over time. Keep a record of all the things you don't buy and the ways you figure out to save money. You'll be surprised at your total.

The Least You Need to Know

◆ Some people are more naturally attuned to saving money than others; however, saving can be learned.

◆ Natural savers have a head start when it comes to successfully managing their personal finances.

◆ You'll be surprised at how fast even little savings add up over time.

◆ Once you put yourself in the mindset to save money, you won't mind as much doing without some of the things you'd like to have.

◆ There are dozens of ways to save money on everything from food to exercise equipment.

Chapter 11

Your Credit: Use It, Don't Abuse It

In This Chapter

- How your credit history affects your life
- Avoiding problems with credit and debt
- A new worry—identity theft
- Getting help for credit and debt problems when you need it
- Fixing your credit and debt problems
- Learning about and accessing your credit report

Many people don't understand that their *credit history* is carefully documented in a *credit report*, which, by the way, usually contains some very personal and specific information. So let's start at the beginning and see exactly what a credit history is, how you build it, and what it's used for. Then you'll be able to understand why it's so important and how it can affect many areas of your life.

Building a Credit History

Your *credit history* is the record of everything pertaining to any credit you've ever had or applied for. If you want to borrow money for a car, a house, a vacation, debt consolidation, college, or a business, you'll need credit.

If you go to a bank to borrow money and there's no history of your ever having any credit, you don't stand a good chance of getting the loan. The bank will be reluctant to take a chance on you because it has no indication of whether you'll pay back the money or default on the loan.

Show Me the Money

Your **credit history** is a record of all the credit you've ever had or applied for. Details of your credit history are documented extensively in a **credit report.**

Establishing a credit history used to be, and in some cases still can be, a classic catch-22. If you can't get credit because you have no credit history, how will you establish a history so that you can get credit?

It used to be that you could go to your neighborhood bank, and the banker would lend you money because he'd known you and your family for 35 years. Today, you'd be hard-pressed to find a bank that has anything much left of the personal touch, although some try to lure you in on that pretense. Banking is big business, and there's not much room for taking risks by giving loans to guys and gals just starting out.

For better or worse, it's not hard to establish a credit history these days. Credit cards are plentiful and available for the taking. The trick is to develop and maintain a healthy credit history.

Knowing When Enough Is Enough

You want to establish a credit history because you're looking ahead and you know that you're going to need some loans. The old car you've had since your freshman year isn't going to last forever. You'd eventually like to trade in your apartment for your own house, and you think that somewhere down the road you'd even like to start your own graphics business.

Pleased with your forward-looking plan, you start collecting credit cards. Soon, you've got Visas, MasterCards, Discover cards, gas cards, and phone cards. You've got cards for Sears, J.C. Penney, Bloomingdale's, and Marshall's. You have more cards than you know what to do with, and pretty soon you have more bills than you know what to do with, too.

Well, you're establishing a credit history all right, but it's not the kind that's going to get you a loan to help start your own business. If you can't keep up with the payments on all your cards, your credit history will show you as high risk. When you go to apply for those loans, you won't be regarded as a good candidate, and you will have unnecessarily put your credit rating in jeopardy. Having too many open lines of credit (credit cards) can be harmful to you when you apply for a loan—let's say, a car loan. Lenders want to feel secure that your debt is under control—that you are managing your finances responsibly.

You're much more likely to be approved for a loan if you have a good record of paying off debt on a few credit cards, or even one card, than you would after you've been bogged down with a dozen cards that got away from you. Keep in control of your credit cards and your debt, and make sure your payments are on time. Know when enough is enough, and establish a good, responsible record of repaying debt.

> **Dollars and Sense**
>
> If you're getting more credit card applications than you know what to do with and want to stop them from showing up in your mailbox on a daily basis, you can remove your name from credit card company lists by calling 1-800-5-OPT-OUT.

Oops! I Think I'm in Trouble

Debt and credit card trouble can sneak up on you gradually or can suddenly appear, seemingly out of nowhere. You'll know trouble is coming when you can no longer pay off your debts at the end of the month with the money from your paycheck. If you have to dip into your savings to pay off your debts, sit up and take notice, because your spending habits just might be spiraling out of control.

If you overspend and exceed your credit limit, the credit card company will put a stop to your account. The general rule is that when you have exceeded your limit by 10 percent, your card will be frozen from further use until you make a payment to get the balance down below your limit, and you'll be charged a whopping fee as well. You could request an increase in your limit, but that's jumping from the frying pan into the fire, isn't it? Besides, most credit card companies are reluctant to increase your limit after you have exceeded it. If you need to increase your limit, do it before you max out your cards.

Recognizing Credit Trouble

Some people get so far into debt trouble that it's extremely difficult to fix. If you think you're having trouble managing your debt, it's very important to acknowledge the problem early and take immediate steps to fix it. Today, an increasingly common problem is identity theft, where thieves obtain your personal information and use it to establish credit card accounts in your name. This, as you can imagine, has the potential to cause huge credit problems, even though you weren't responsible for the spending. It's important to recognize the potential for identity theft and to take whatever steps possible to prevent it.

Preventing and Recognizing Identity Theft

Identity theft occurs when thieves compile enough information about you to acquire credit cards or purchase items online in your name. As far as the credit card company or online retailer is concerned, you are responsible for the purchases, even though you never ordered or received goods. Identity thieves usually set up new credit card accounts, changing the responsible address from your home to a post office box.

In 2003, the Federal Trade Commission (FTC) released a survey that provided the following information:

- 27.3 million Americans have been victims of identity theft during the past five years.

- The total cost to American financial institutions was $33 billion, and the direct cost to consumers was $5 billion.

- Identity theft is the fastest growing crime in the United States.

- In 2003, identity theft accounted for 42 percent of all complaints filed by consumers before the FTC.

- In 25 percent of all cases, the identity thief was someone the victim knew.

Unfortunately, you can be a victim of identity theft and not know it. You could attempt to make a credit card purchase, only to be turned down because your credit report shows you recently purchased a second home at the shore, a luxury car, and a diamond necklace for your wife. All without you having a clue. One way thieves obtain the personal information necessary to pull off identity theft is to scour residential and business trash. Documents such as cancelled checks, tax information, and bank statements can provide thieves with many of the numbers they need to establish accounts or make purchases in your name. These numbers include phone numbers, driver's license number, credit card numbers, personal identification, bank account numbers, social security numbers, and so on and so forth.

Make certain that when you use your computer to access private information, you're on a secured site. Be sure the lock icon is visible on the website, and that the site uses a 128-bit SSL to keep your data secure.

To minimize your chances of identity theft, shred all papers before disposing of them. Check all bank and credit card statements carefully, and immediately report any suspicious withdrawals or purchases. Close out any credit cards that you don't use, and don't ever give anyone information if you're not absolutely sure who they are and why they need the information. Never give personal information to someone who calls on the phone, and always be sure you take and secure credit card slips after making a purchase. Don't leave your mail in the mailbox over night, do not provide personal information in an e-mail, and keep track of all bills, receipts, and statements. And, check with your credit card provider to make sure it monitors and checks suspicious activity on your account.

Knowing When to Get Help

Even though identity theft is a growing problem, it still accounts for very few of all cases of credit trouble in America. We've discussed extensively how our society encourages us to spend. We're big-time consumers, doing just what advertisers and marketers want us to do.

Pocket Change

A rule of thumb is that your total debt service at the end of the month should not be more than 36 percent of your monthly gross income. Total debt service (the amount you are required to pay monthly to keep your debts/loans current) includes payments for rent or mortgage, car payments, college loans, and charge card (the kind you must pay off every month) payments. If your debt service is more than 36 percent of your income, you'd better take a closer look at what you're spending money on.

People buy things and spend a lot of money for many different reasons. Some are compulsive spenders, buying more and more because it fulfills some need within them. Studies show that many women try to gain affection by financially supporting men. They are trying, in effect, to buy love. People who were abandoned or ignored as children sometimes try to fill that emotional void with things, and will buy whatever they can.

Overspending has serious consequences and can be a true addiction, just like drinking or gambling. If you think you can't stop spending, and you're incurring more debt than you can handle, get some help. You can contact Debtors Anonymous at the General Services Office, PO Box 920888, Needham, MA 02492-0009. The phone number is 781-453-2743. Or access it on the Internet at www.debtorsanonymous.org. There are also counselors who specialize in financial recovery. Some of them work for nonprofit organizations, and their services can be obtained at no cost. Check your phone book for local listings.

Repairing the Damage

If you determine that you have a problem with your credit and debt, there are steps you can take on your own to fix it. The most immediate step is to stop incurring more debt. To do that, you might have to get rid of your credit cards completely. "What?!" you shriek. "Live without credit cards? Impossible!"

Guess what? It's not impossible. It won't be easy, but if you can't resist racking up debt on your credit cards, then you're better off without them. If you can trust yourself, then keep one to use when you want to rent a car or reserve a hotel room. Otherwise, cut them up and call the credit card companies to cancel your accounts. Then, plan carefully to pay for whatever you buy with cash, check, or a debit card.

When you stop piling up more and more debt, you can start working to get rid of what you already have:

Dollars and Sense

Try putting your credit card in a deep freeze to avoid using it when you shouldn't. Put it in a container of water in the freezer, and thaw it out when you want to use it. Waiting around while it thaws allows you time to consider the purchase and whether it's a good idea. If you do this, remember that it's against the rules to use the microwave to thaw it out!

- Take a close look at what you owe and to whom you owe it. Record all the information and pay special attention to any bills marked past due. If you're in the middle of a credit card billing cycle, call the provider and ask for your balance. You need to know exactly where you stand.

- Contact those creditors to whom your payment is overdue. Let them know that you acknowledge your debt, and you will work in good faith to pay it off. Ask if you can work together to come up with a plan that will enable you to pay off the debt in a manner that you can afford.

◆ Think about possible sources of money. As difficult as it might be to go to a family member or friend, confess your sins and ask for a loan; it may be the healthiest thing for you to do, financially.

◆ If you have any money in a savings account, break into it and pay off what you can. It's practically a sure bet that you're paying more interest on your debts than you're earning on your savings account.

◆ If your debt is serious, consider borrowing from your retirement account at work. Ask the benefits department at your company if you're permitted to borrow from your account balance. If you are, find out what the interest rate is. It's usually reasonable, and as you pay off the loan, the interest goes back into your account.

◆ Sell assets. Sell any stocks you may have, or sell a collection. Downsize your car from the one of your dreams to a Hyundai. Do whatever is necessary to get caught up.

◆ Consider getting a second job.

Be honest with yourself when assessing your debt. If you're afraid you might have a problem, you probably do. But unless you've had the problem for a long time and have ignored it, you probably can figure out a way to fix it before it gets completely out of hand.

Reputable and Not-So-Reputable Sources of Help

Credit counseling has been available for over a half century to advise, serve as an intermediary with creditors, lower interest rates, and consolidate monthly bills. While there are many reputable companies that provide these services, numerous scam companies have surfaced over the past decade or so. If you get involved with one, you may end up with even bigger problems than you started with.

If you're thinking of seeing a credit counselor or counseling firm, keep in mind the following tips when you're deciding where to go:

◆ Ask what the total monthly fee will be. You should never have to pay more than $50 a month for the services of a credit counselor. Some predatory firms charge as much as 10 percent of their customer's payments, totaling a couple of hundred dollars a month.

◆ Check with your local Better Business Bureau or Consumer Protection Agency to see if there are any complaints or current investigations about all firms you're considering.

◆ Never sign a contract at the first meeting. Make certain you have time to understand the agreement, the repayment schedule, and the fees. Never disclose your bank account number before you have signed a contract.

◆ Be wary if a counseling service doesn't suggest other options besides its debt management plan. Remember, it might be possible to sell some personal property or refinance your mortgage to lower your debt, rather than embarking on a debt management plan.

◆ Lack of affiliation with the National Foundation for Credit Counseling or the Association of Independent Credit Counseling Agencies may be a reason to avoid a firm. Such an affiliation doesn't guarantee that you're getting the best firm, but it does mean that the company obtains a majority of its income from grants and donations, rather than from fees alone.

◆ If it sounds too good to be true, it probably is. Credit card companies have minimum-payment guidelines they use to lower their interest rates, so there is minimal negotiation for most folks. Beware of the firm that promises to remove your unsecured debt, pay off debts with pennies on the dollar, or guarantee that you'll avoid bankruptcy.

◆ Also, beware of the firm that advertises its services during late-night movies or uses telemarketers to promote its services.

Your Credit Report and Credit Score

When you applied for your first credit card (probably back in high school or college), your name and a lot of personal information got zapped into a computer, and your personal credit report began. Since then, every time you applied for another credit card or a store card, took a vacation loan from your bank or credit union, or applied for a car loan, information was added to your credit report as well as to what is known as a credit score.

There are three big nationwide credit agency companies, and each of them probably has the same information about you and your credit history. They get it from banks, finance companies, credit card suppliers, department stores, mail order companies, and various other places that have had the pleasure of doing business with you. Smaller, regional credit bureaus supplement the information.

<table>
<tr><td>Pocket Change</td></tr>
<tr><td>The three largest credit agency companies are Equifax Credit Services, TransUnion Credit Information Services, and Experian.</td></tr>
</table>

All the information on file concerning you and your credit history is evaluated and used to determine your credit score. This score is distributed to lenders to help them decide whether or not you're low-risk. The best known and most widely used score is the FICO score, which is based on a system developed by Fair, Isaac and Co., Inc. It's based on a mathematical equation that takes into account many types of information from your credit report. Your credit score identifies you either as a low-risk or high-risk candidate for a lender.

A potential lender will look at your credit report and your credit score when deciding whether or not to give you a loan. The lower your score, the less likely it is that you will be offered a loan. If you are offered one, it will undoubtedly come with a higher interest rate or more restrictive terms.

FICO scores are regarded as providing the best guides to future risk based solely on credit report data. Most U.S. consumers score between 300 and 850. Lenders look most favorably to those whose scores are 650 or higher. The general rule of thumb is that the higher your score is, the less risk you pose to a lender. Historically, people with high FICO scores have repaid loans and credit cards more consistently than people with low FICO scores. Although there is no single "cutoff score" used by all lenders, it is important to know and understand your score.

Usually, the FICO score is given with four reason codes, in order from the strongest negative reason to impact your score, and then the second strongest factor, and so on. It is important to understand how you scored (review your credit agency report at least once a year and especially before making a large purchase, like a house or a car). Ask what you can do to improve your score over time.

Here are several major factors that affect your credit score:

♦ **Your level of revolving debt**   This is one of the most important factors considered for the FICO score. Even if you pay off your credit cards each month, your credit card may show the last billing statement in relation to your total available credit on revolving charges. If you think your FICO score should be higher, work to pay down your revolving account balances.

◆ **Shifting balances** Don't shift your credit card balances from one card to another to make it appear that you're being diligent about paying off debt. And don't open up new revolving accounts. These tactics will not improve your credit score.

◆ **The length of time your accounts have been established** This can hurt you when you're first starting out, but consumers with longer credit histories tend to be lower-risk than those with shorter credit histories.

Money Pit

When you understand how much credit information is floating around out there, it becomes easy to see how mistakes are made with that information. Human error is a big factor, and somebody who misreads some information about you can screw up your credit report royally.

◆ **Too many accounts with balances.** Too many credit card accounts with balances is a dangerous sign that you won't be able to make that many payments should your employment status change.

◆ **Too many credit inquiries within the last 12 months** Borrowers who are seeking several new credit accounts are riskier than persons who are not seeking credit, though these have only a small impact on your FICO score. These inquiries have much less impact than late payments, the amount you owe, and the length of time you have used credit.

Your personal credit report includes information such as your name, Social Security number, date of birth, your address from the time you first got a credit card until now, everywhere you've worked during that time, and how you pay your bills. Whenever you apply for a loan or for credit, the place at which you applied will check out your report with a credit agency. In turn, it will give the credit agency any additional information that it's picked up on you.

The Fair Credit Reporting Act limits who can see your credit report. Of course, the list is pretty long, but it does set some guidelines. Your credit report can be released by a reporting agency under the following circumstances:

◆ In response (God forbid!) to a court order or a federal grand jury subpoena.

◆ To anyone to whom you've given written permission.

◆ To anyone considering you for credit or collection of an account.

◆ To anyone who will use the report for insurance purposes.

◆ To determine your eligibility for a government license or benefits.

◆ To anyone with a legitimate business need for the report, in connection with a business transaction with which you're involved. This includes your landlord when you apply to rent an apartment.

When you realize how often your credit report can be accessed, then you can begin to see how important it is that you keep it clean. But even if your credit record is perfect, your report might not be, and that could affect your credit score. A study showed that one out of four people who took the time to thoroughly review their credit reports discovered a mistake that eventually was corrected. Be aware that every time an inquiry is made for your credit report, it is automatically logged into your report. Although this isn't necessarily bad, numerous inquiries may need to be explained to a potential lender.

You're going to learn more about why it's important to keep an eye on your credit report and exactly how to go about getting a copy of it.

Dollars and Sense _____

If you ever apply for a job in an area such as defense, banking, or the medical field, you can expect that your prospective employer will take a look at your credit report before deciding whether to hire you. If you're turned down for the job because of something in the report, you're required, under federal law, to be notified of your right to get a copy of the report at no charge.

Dollars and Sense _____

Experts recommend that you read your credit report carefully about once a year, especially before you apply for credit or when you know that the credit report will be checked (as when you rent an apartment). This is the only way to be sure that no mistakes have been made that will damage your credit record.

You have a legal right to submit a letter up to 100 words long to the credit agency, disputing something you've discovered on your credit report. The letter must be included in your file. If you do this, make sure your letter is clear, concise, and to the point.

How to Get a Copy of Your Credit Report

Even if you don't plan to apply for a car loan, a mortgage, or a credit card anytime soon, it's a good idea to take a look at your credit report once a year. You can get a copy of your report from any of the three largest credit agencies:

Equifax Credit Services
PO Box 740241
Atlanta, GA 30374
Toll-free: 1-800-685-1111
www.equifax.com

TransUnion Credit Information Services
Consumer Disclosure Center
PO Box 1000
Chester, PA 19022
Toll-free: 1-800-888-4213
www.transunion.com

Experian
PO Box 949
Allen, TX 75013
Toll-free: 1-888-397-3742
www.experian.com

If you've been turned down for a mortgage, loan, or credit card, you're entitled to get a copy of your credit report for free at your request from the credit reporting service. Otherwise, if you want to get a copy of your credit report to check it over, there will be a fee (about $8 in most states). Call one of the companies listed here, or contact them by mail with an enclosed check or money order. Be prepared to provide your name, address, Social Security number, and maybe your date-of-birth as ID. We recommend that you get your annual update from a different company each year to check for errors. When you have the report, look it over carefully. If you discover a mistake, take the following steps to correct it:

- ◆ Contact all three credit agencies by certified mail and inform them of the mistake you've discovered. Request that they investigate.

- ◆ If you don't get a reply within 60 days, send another letter. Remind the companies that they are required by law to investigate incorrect information or provide an updated credit report with the incorrect information removed.

If you see information you don't like on your credit report that, unfortunately, isn't a mistake, don't despair. The Fair Credit Reporting Act mandates that negative information on your report be removed after a certain period of time. Even if you (gasp!) declare bankruptcy, that information is supposed to be removed from your report after 10 years. The trick, of course, is keeping your credit report healthy and in good shape. In this case, preventive maintenance works best.

The Least You Need to Know

- ◆ It pays to be aware of your credit history because it affects so many areas of your life.

- ◆ It's not how much credit you have, but how you handle it, that affects your credit history.

- ◆ Recognizing and acknowledging credit and debt problems early can stop the situation from getting out of control.

- ◆ If your credit problems are more than you can handle, there are places that can help.

- ◆ You should know what your credit report contains and how you can get a copy of it, and correct mistakes when necessary.

Part 3

Coasting Along

"Wow! I'm making some pretty good money, here." Things get a little more comfortable after you get a few raises or maybe even a better, higher-paying job. You can think about doing some things that weren't in your vocabulary just a little while back—things such as vacations, investments, emergency funds, and your own apartment.

With this better financial position, however, come added decisions and responsibilities. Chapters 12 through 15 tell you all about things that influence your personal finances at this stage of your life—things such as investments, taxes, and insurance. But it's not all serious, grown-up stuff. You're earning money and getting ahead—it's a great time to have some fun, too. This part examines how to strike a balance between living well now and starting to look to the future.

Movin' On Up

In This Chapter

- ◆ Planning ahead while you're moving ahead
- ◆ Setting aside some emergency money
- ◆ When to keep your car and when to trade it in
- ◆ Is there a higher degree in your future?
- ◆ Taking vacations and other fun stuff
- ◆ Ditching the roomies for a place of your own

Getting started was pretty tough, but things are looking up for you now. You've gotten a couple of raises at work, and it seems that your future in the industry is looking pretty good. You even had people from that competing company calling a few months ago to see whether you might consider working for them.

You're feeling good that you're not in a paycheck-to-paycheck situation anymore, and you've managed to save some money. You're watching your credit card debt and trying to keep your balance down. Your car loan is paid off, and you're up to date with college loan payments. You think you're pretty much on track financially.

Congratulations! You've come a long way in a short time, and you're on your feet, financially speaking. But before you start patting yourself on the back, you still have a lot to learn, and many of the things we haven't talked about yet will cost you money. Now is the time for you to start setting financial goals. Think about what you'll need in the future and how much those things will cost.

Go ahead and enjoy your newfound financial comfort. Live a little. Don't get carried away, though. Remember that financial security for the future requires good planning and some self-control and sacrifices today.

Emergency Funds

Just when you think you have some fun money, we're going to tell you to stash it away in case of an emergency. Sorry to burst your bubble!

An emergency fund is essential. If you lose your job—a dilemma that too many people have had to face recently—or run into dire straits from another direction, you'll need some money to tide you over until you get reorganized.

Some people need to have an emergency fund to tap into because of the unsteady income provided by their jobs. If you're in a business where you earn a lot of money sometimes and very little or no money at other times, you might need emergency money to use during the lean periods. Of course, it's important to set up a budget so that you don't spend more than you should when you have money coming in.

Money Pit

Be careful to not use your emergency fund as a convenient source of money if you run a little short at the end of the pay period. The intent of an emergency fund is to keep you afloat if your income is interrupted. If you're not careful, you could easily deplete your emergency fund before an emergency occurs.

If you don't have an emergency fund and you lose your job or get into financial trouble, the temptation might be to use your credit card. You could live perfectly well on your credit cards for several months, depending on your credit limits. Nearly everyone, from your doctor to your grocery store, will take your plastic instead of your cash, and your credit card issuer will be delighted. But if you end up with $4,000 or $5,000 in credit card debt at the end of that time, you'll be the one who's sorry. It will take you a long time to get back on your feet again.

Dollars and Sense _____

Three to six months' salary is the rule of thumb for what you should have in an emergency fund. If you have other sources of emergency money, such as family or a 401(k) plan that you could call on for a short-term loan, you probably can get by with less. If you have no other sources of money, try to save a little more.

Establishing an emergency fund should be a priority in your personal finance plan. You can build the funds within a money-market fund, which will give you accessibility and liquidity, as needed. You'll learn more about money markets in Chapter 13. Even better, use a monthly or biweekly automatic debit from your checking or savings account to transfer money into your emergency fund. That way, you pay yourself first, before you're tempted to use the money for other purposes.

Finding Another Car

Just when you think you're sailing along financially, the odds are that you'll run into some rough seas. It's practically a rule, almost as certain as death and taxes. For many people, these financial setbacks pop up in the form of car problems. As long as you own a car, you're subject to the problems that go along with it.

Your car is eight years old, and you've been pretty hard on it. You've put well over 100,000 miles on it, and you're at the point where you don't feel like sinking any more money in it. Everybody says you won't get anything when you go to trade it in, but you're thinking it's time to get rid of it. What to do?

There's no set formula that can tell you exactly how long you should have a car before you trade it in for a new one. It would be helpful to your financial planning if you knew that every six years to the day you would need to trade in your present vehicle for another one. But there are far too many variables involved to come up with anything like that.

Money Pit _____

Unless you know and trust your mechanic, it's a good idea to get a second opinion. I once had a mechanic tell me I needed an entirely new exhaust system. When I took it to a garage that specialized in exhaust systems, the mechanic told me he could replace one section of pipe, and it would be as good as new. I would have been out big bucks without the second opinion.

If you're constantly shelling out money for repairs and your car has become undependable, it might be time to kiss it good-bye. If you do decide to trade in your car, be sure you know its value before you start negotiating with a salesperson. You can find out the value from the National Automobile Dealer Association guide, commonly known as "the blue book." And keep in mind that you often can do better financially if you sell your car privately, rather than use it to reduce the cost of the new car.

On the other hand, we know people who have a car for a few years and then get a wandering eye. Suddenly, nothing about their car is right anymore. Little rattles become huge annoyances. Just having the oil changed seems like a big imposition. They're ready to move on to something new. Remember, though, that having no car payment is better than having a car payment, and that money you don't have to pay each month on your car can be used for other things—an emergency fund, perhaps.

Back to School

If going back to school is part of your plans, now might be a good time to start thinking about it. If you're still paying off college loans, you might be reluctant to put yourself further into debt for more schooling. But if you think you need an advanced degree to get ahead in your career, you might as well get it as early as possible, to increase your chances of advancing earlier and earning more money before you retire.

Another thing to think about is your schedule. As busy as you think you are now, believe me when I tell you that it doesn't get any better. If you're still single, but planning to get married some day, you probably have more free time now than you will after the wedding bells have rung. If you're married and plan to have kids in the future, you'll have much less time for school or anything else when your house is filled with cribs and diapers.

> **Pocket Change**
>
> Graduate school is expensive. In 2002, according to the Nellie Mae National Student Loan Survey, the average amount of debt of graduate students was $31,700. That compares to $21,000 for graduate students in 1997. For law and medical students, the average debt was $91,700.

If you decide you need a graduate degree and that it makes sense to get it now, look into your options before committing yourself to a program. The fastest way to get a degree is to go back to school full time. Most people, though, can't afford to do that. School has to be something that's done in addition to and around the schedule of your work.

Colleges and universities anxious to fill their graduate schools have gone to great lengths to make their graduate programs appealing to working men and women. Classes are often scheduled at night and on weekends, catering to those with nine-to-five commitments.

M.B.As, Ph.Ds, M.C.Ps, M.Archs, and Sc.Ds

Titles for graduate degrees can appear to be so much alphabet soup, but the right degree can help you to advance in the workplace.

The U.S. Census Bureau reported in 2002 that men and women who hold graduate degrees can expect to earn about $2.5 million over the course of their working life, compared to about $2.1 million for those who hold only undergraduate degrees. The report, called "The Big Payoff," also states that a doctoral degree holder averages about $3.4 million work life earnings, while someone who holds a professional degree, such as a doctor or lawyer, has an average potential of $4.4 million.

Online Degrees—How Do They Measure Up?

An option experiencing explosive popularity is online learning. Also called distance learning, this virtual education gives students their courses electronically, via technologies such as the Internet, e-mail, satellite, and compressed video. Distance learning is becoming more widespread all the time and is employed by schools as traditional as Duke University and the University of Virginia. Peterson's Guide to U.S. Colleges in 1993 included only 93 schools offering online learning. The 2001 guide listed 1200 schools with an online option.

Show Me the Money

In case you're confused by the title of this section, **M.B.A.** stands for a Masters of Business Administration, **Ph.D.** is the abbreviation for Doctor of Philosophy, **M.C.P.** indicates a Master's of City Planning, **M.Arch.** signifies a Master's of Architecture, and **Sc.D.** is short for Doctor of Science.

Pocket Change

To access "The Big Payoff," a report by the U.S. Census Bureau that cites salaries based on educational attainment, go to the bureau's home page at www.census.gov and type "the big payoff" in the search box.

Dollars and Sense

Try to tailor your advanced degree to a particular career opportunity, if you can. For example, if you have a psychology degree and you're interested in working with industry, look for something such as a Master's program in industrial and organizational psychology.

The University of Phoenix was one of the first schools to adopt online learning, and its program is considered to be a model. At this university, more than 171,600 working students from around the world have earned online degrees since 1976.

The average online student at the University of Phoenix is 30-something, and most are working in full- or part-time jobs in addition to taking courses. Textbooks are mailed to students before the course begins, and they receive their instructors' lectures by e-mail, which they can download onto their computers. They communicate with the instructor and their classmates by e-mail, writing weekly summaries of what they've learned. Even exams are taken online.

Alas, however, the cost of online courses at a quality school is comparable to classroom learning. And, if you're not disciplined enough to work on your own to complete course requirements, online learning might not be the answer for you.

Money Pit _____

As online degrees have proliferated over the past decade, there has also been an increase in the number of bogus institutions and degrees being issued. While there are some decent colleges, such as Jones International and Capella, which were created solely as Internet schools, there also are some online schools of questionable (or worse) repute. Be sure to do your homework before enrolling in any online course that's not offered by a reputable, known college or university.

To find out what's available, access the website of the college in which you're interested, or call the school for more information. You can also learn more about distance learning and choosing a good online school at About Distance Learning at http://distancelearn.about.com.

Finding Loans to Help Finance Your Education

If you decide to go for an advanced degree, make sure you check with the school you'll be attending to see what financial aid programs might be available. You might have a better shot of getting some aid if you're doing your graduate work at the same school you received an undergraduate degree from. Many employers will reimburse you for educational expenses if you receive a grade of C or better for the course. Check with your company's human resources or benefits department to find out what might be available. Keep in mind that money spent on education that can help you to advance is a good way to spend money, even if it means you'll be incurring some more debt.

If you do decide to head back to the classroom or are just entering college for the first time, be sure to consider tax credits for which you may qualify. Two tax credits, the Hope Credit and the Lifetime Learning Credit, are targeted at taxpayers who are entering college for the first time and those who are taking job-related courses. There's also a new federal income tax deduction for educational tuition and fees.

The Hope Credit benefits taxpayers who pay for the first two years of post-secondary education, while the Lifetime Learning Credit is a tax benefit for those taking classes to learn new job skills or improve current skills.

The new tuition and fee deduction is not a tax credit, but a deduction from your income. Beginning in 2004, the deduction increased to $4,000. There are restrictions, of course, but this deduction allows many people to deduct educational expenses that they couldn't before.

To learn more about the tuition and fee deduction, go to the Internal Revenue Service website at www.irs.gov/publications/p970/ch06.

Dollars and Sense

In addition to loans, keep in mind that there may be grants, fellowships, and scholarships available to help finance your education. Be sure to talk to someone in the financial aid office of the school you're considering. Schools often have money available, but only make it available to students who specifically request or apply for it.

Life Is Better in the Tropics

When your financial situation improves a little bit, it's tempting to start thinking of all the fun things you want to do and all the places you'd love to visit. Vacations are great, but unfortunately, they can be very expensive.

If your tastes run to fancy resorts in tropical destinations in the middle of February, you'd better be prepared to drop a significant chunk of your income on your vacations. Just remember that when you come home, you'll still have to pay the rent and the electric bill.

Dollars and Sense

Remember that a driving vacation is almost always cheaper than if you have to buy airline tickets, especially if there's more than one person. Several people sharing the cost of gas and tolls can cut travel costs significantly.

There are lots of ways, though, to take vacations that won't wreck you financially. All you have to do is be creative. Think about it: If you're vacationing with a group of friends, won't you have a good time just about anywhere you go? There are plenty of vacations that won't cost you a month's salary. Consider camping or getting a bunch of people to split the cost of a house near the beach.

It's easier than ever to find bargain vacations. If you and your friends are flexible, you can get some great discounts by signing up for a trip midweek and going that weekend. Put the money you save into your emergency fund.

Some airlines will notify you by e-mail of bargain fares. Check out www.travelnavigator. com to sign up for notice of discount fares from some of the major airlines. For last-minute bargain airfares, try Cheap Tickets at 1-800-377-1000, or check out the airlines' websites for last-minute specials.

If cruises are your thing, you can find some discounted prices on well-known cruise lines by checking out the following sites:

- Cheap Cruises at www.cheap-cruises.com

- Cruise Web at www.cruiseweb.com

- Cruise Bargains at www.cruisebargains.com

For discounted rates at major hotel chains, check out the websites of the major chains.

For discounted information in general, check out these websites:

- www.orbitz.com

- ww.priceline.com

- www.expedia.com

- www.cheapfares.com

These websites permit you to bid on services at lower than standard costs if you are willing to travel at the last minute.

Aren't These Computers Cool?

People in their 20s and 30s have grown up with technology and embrace it more than any other age group. It's part of your lives and is integral to your work and your leisure. We all know that technology is advancing at a phenomenal rate, which makes it hard sometimes to keep up with everything new. Our TVs are changing, our cameras are changing, our means for communicating with one another are changing, and our computers never stop changing.

The market is full of tempting, high-tech gadgets, from iPods to camera phones, personal digital assistants to MP3 players. The problem with all these gadgets is that they're expensive, and it's very possible that you'll end up with more of them than you need—or can afford.

No matter what it is that you're going to buy, make sure you do some comparison-shopping. Look at ads in magazines to compare different brands, or check out a trade show where many items are displayed at once, and buy only when you've saved enough to buy. The expensive "toys" can be budget-busters. Plan, dream, and save for the day you'll have your very own large-screen digital TV.

> **Pocket Change**
>
> People 70 years old today have come from a world without TV to a world of amazing computers and other practically unimaginable technology. No wonder some people have trouble keeping up!

Getting Your Own Place

If you've been living with roommates, or are even still at home with Mom and Dad, you might be getting ready to look for your own place. You'd like a little more privacy, or maybe you have to bring work home at night and it's hard to get it done because of the noise.

For whatever reasons, if you move from a roommate situation to a nonroommate situation, you'll probably find that living expenses will cost you more. Even if you move to a smaller place, paying the full rent on an apartment by yourself will probably cost more than sharing rent. You'll also have to come up with the up-front costs of a security deposit and a couple of months' rent when you first get your own place. And even if you've accumulated some furniture and household items by now, it's likely you'll have to get more because you won't have other people's stuff to supplement your own.

Consider how living by yourself will affect your long-range plans. If the extra costs associated with living on your own are going to prevent you from realizing goals such as buying a house in five years or getting married in two years, perhaps you need to re-examine your priorities. The expenses discussed in this chapter are only some of the things on which you'll be spending your money. We're not going to tell you to invest every penny you make and never have any fun—what kind of life would that be? A word of advice, though: Weigh the value of things you spend money on today against the value of things you hope to acquire in the future.

Is an extra trip to the ski slopes this winter going to be worth having to wait six months longer to get a house when you're ready to buy? Will buying the new computer mean you'll have to delay starting a retirement fund? It's hard to postpone what we want today in exchange for the promise of financial security tomorrow. If you want that security, however, you have to be willing to do just that.

The Least You Need to Know

◆ It's tempting to spend more money when you're making more, but it's important to remember your future financial needs.

◆ As soon as you start earning money, establishing an emergency fund should be one of your first financial priorities.

◆ Cars are a recurring expense, but there are ways to keep the costs down.

◆ If you're going to go back to school, you'll need to figure out when it makes sense to do so.

◆ Vacations and grown-up toys are fun, but they can take a big bite out of your budget.

◆ Living by yourself might be appealing, but you have to evaluate whether the extra cost is worth it.

13

What's All This Talk About Investments?

In This Chapter

- ◆ Starting your investments without a ton of money
- ◆ The logic of dollar cost averaging
- ◆ Sorting out what investment vehicles are available
- ◆ Everybody's talking about 401(k)s
- ◆ Mutual funds and money markets
- ◆ Looking at certificates of deposit

If you're like most people, you believe that investments are a good thing. Having money to invest means that you have savings that you want to put to work for you. Everybody should have some investments so that their funds earn money. Good investments grow over time, which helps you keep up with inflation and helps to assure your financial security when you retire. Although most people see investments as desirable, the act of investing intimidates them. Investing implies taking action and moving money around to different places. Investing must be learned, and it sounds mighty complicated. Investing is a risky business that can result in losing money that you've been saving for years.

If you want to have investments but are reluctant to do much investing, you're in good company. A good portion of the general population has no clue about how or where to invest money. As a result, they keep money in low-interest accounts, effectively denying themselves the money they could be earning.

This chapter will not tell you everything you'll ever need to know about investments, but it will give you basic information about various kinds of investments and tell you which ones make sense for new investors. We can't guarantee that after you read this chapter you'll never make a mistake when it comes to investing your money, but you'll be better prepared to avoid mistakes that result from poor judgment or greed. You should be able to invest your money responsibly, and understand why you put it where you do.

Starting Small

Many people think they just don't have enough money to invest it anywhere. Or, they think they'll need to pay a financial advisor to direct them to where they should invest their money, and that will cost more than they have to invest in the first place. Neither of these ideas is true.

> **Money Pit**
>
> Don't even think about investing money if you owe credit card debt. Making 4 percent or 5 percent off an investment pales in comparison to paying out 17 percent or 18 percent on your Visa. Pay off the plastic first. You can't get ahead while you're carrying a load of debt.

You don't need a ton of money to start investing. You can begin investing with just $50 (we'll tell you how to do that a little later in the chapter). You don't necessarily need a financial advisor or a salesperson to tell you where to put your money, either. Many investments can be purchased without a salesperson, and if you do your homework carefully, you'll be able to figure out on your own the best places to put your money at this point in your life.

Almost everyone who starts investing starts small and builds up their investments over time. If you work carefully and patiently, you'll do the same. It's fun to watch the growth, particularly when you remember that you started small.

How Much Do You Have to Invest?

No, you don't have to be rich to invest, but you do need to know what money you have available to invest. Just because you have $10,000 sitting around in various accounts doesn't mean you have $10,000 to invest. Think carefully about the money you have and what your goals for that money are.

For instance, if you have the equivalent of three months' salary set aside for emergencies, that's not money that you want to tie up in a long-term investment. You need to be able to get it when you need it in case there *is* an emergency. It's the same with the money you've been saving for a down payment for a house. You sure can't afford to take much risk with that money, because you're going to need it in a couple of years.

As you learn more about investment vehicles, you'll find out which ones are good for short-term investments and which ones to go with for the long haul. That's important, because you don't want to tie up money for 20 years that you might need in two. How you invest your money depends largely on how long it can remain out of your reach. It also depends on how much of it you can afford to lose. Some investments are a lot riskier than others, and you need to know what you're getting into before you throw your money into the pot.

To figure out what kind of a risk-taker you can afford to be, think about having $1,000 invested for one year. If you think you can afford to lose no more than 6 percent of that money ($60), then you're a low-risk type of investor. If you could stand to lose up to 15 percent ($150), you're a moderate-risk type of investor. If you could stand to lose as much of a quarter of your money ($250), you're a high-risk type of investor.

> ### Pocket Change
>
> Investment clubs, which are simply groups of people who pool their money to buy investments they all agree on, may not be as much in vogue as they were five or six years ago, but there are still many around. According to financial gurus David and Tom Gardner, also known as The Motley Fools, investment clubs collectively have more than $175 billion worth of equities in their portfolios. That's "billion" with a B—a huge amount of investments.

Of course, this $1,000-invested-for-a-year scenario is terribly simplified. Your stakes would be a lot higher if you were talking about many thousands of dollars. It's easy to say you could afford to lose $150, but if you had $50,000 invested, you'd have to decide if you'd be willing to lose $7,500.

What's Out There?

It's important to know which types of investments will keep your money safe and sound while earning you a little bit of interest, and which have the potential to make you a lot of money while playing roulette with your investment. If you're just learning about investments and investing, there's no question that it can be intimidating. Stocks, international stocks, money markets, mutual funds, annuities, real estate, precious metals—there's a lot to swallow. It's almost enough to make you stick your money into a savings account and keep it there, earning its lowly 1 percent or less in interest a year.

Savings accounts are a form of investment, and a very safe form, but you can do better than that. The following sections discuss some good investment vehicles for people who are just starting: mutual funds, money-market funds, and certificates of deposit (CDs). We'll get into detail about a lot of other kinds of investments in Chapter 19. For now, though, we'll stick with the basics.

Mutual Funds

Mutual funds are the most common investment vehicle for individuals, because they don't require a lot of money to get started. They carry some other advantages, as well.

What are mutual funds? They're investments that pool the money of many people and place the cash into stocks, bonds, and other holdings. When you put your money into a mutual fund, you're throwing it into a pot with another couple hundred million dollars or so. Some mutual funds can go as high as a billion dollars or more.

> **Show Me the Money**
>
> **Mutual funds** are investments that pool the money of many investors and place it in stocks, bonds, and other holdings. Unless the mutual fund is a particular type known as an "index fund," the money is managed by a **portfolio manager** and a team of researchers. **Index funds** normally are not managed funds.

The money is managed by a *portfolio manager* and a team of researchers, who are responsible for finding the best places in which to invest the money. While a *portfolio* is a group of investments assembled to meet an investment goal, a portfolio manager is someone who is paid to supervise the investment decisions of others. The managers get paid for their services from a fee within the fund, usually a percentage of the value of the fund. Although you don't see this fee, you should remember that it exists. The terms "portfolio manager" and "money manager" are used interchangeably. Both handle the management of a portfolio, be it for individuals or for a mutual fund. They are paid a percentage of the assets under management.

In addition to the portfolio manager's fee, there are several other fees you need to be aware of when deciding which mutual fund is right for you:

> **CAUTION** **Money Pit**
>
> Be careful when you buy a no-load mutual fund. You won't pay any commission, but you could be charged fees for marketing and promotional costs (known as a 12(b)1 fee), fees for reinvesting your dividends, and other hidden fees. Make sure you know what fees will be charged before you agree to buy.

- No-load mutual funds let you avoid paying a sales commission on your transactions. No-load funds are shown by advisers who receive compensation otherwise, often by an hourly rate. The companies that offer no-load funds have toll-free phone numbers that you can call for recommendations of what funds to buy.

- Load funds pay sales commissions to a broker, financial adviser, insurance consultant, and so on. The load, or a portion of it, is paid to the adviser who recommends the mutual fund to you. If your mutual fund has a load, know how much it is and how you pay it. Fund loads/fees should be reviewed by the salesperson and stated in the prospectus (paperwork) sent from the company. Load funds have front-end loads, deferred sales charges, or back-end loads:

  - Front-end loads are fees paid up front. A 5.75 percent front load means you pay 5.75 percent of every dollar invested as a fee, and you invest the remaining funds. $100 invested means that $94.25 goes in the fund and $5.75 goes to the salesperson.

  - A deferred sales charge permits the load to be postponed, and it gradually declines over a period of years until the sales charge is 0. Thus, if you invest $1,000 in February in a mutual fund with a 5 percent deferred sales charge, you would pay 5 percent if you sell the fund the first year, 4 percent the second year, and so forth until the sixth year, when you could withdraw all the funds without a fee.

  - A back-end load means you pay a set fee upon the sale of the mutual fund. For example, if you purchase and then sell a fund within too short a time, certain funds will charge a back-end fee (often 1 to 2 percent).

Usually, how your financial adviser is paid determines the type of fund you're shown as a possible investment. (Chapter 19 discusses how to identify a mutual fund that is right for you in more detail.)

Mutual funds can offer you some great advantages:

♦ Money can be taken directly from your bank account each month and transferred into a mutual fund. This makes investing nearly painless.

♦ Mutual funds can offer *diversification*. If you are diversified, and one or more of your investments hits a slump, then you can rely on your other investments to boost your total portfolio. You could, for instance, divide your money among three or four different types of stock funds (we'll talk about the different types of mutual funds in Chapter 19), ensuring that you'd always have some money invested in a profitable area of the market. Part of diversification is also investing in bonds, as well as just different types of stocks. It can be difficult for you to plan that diversification on your own, which is why people look to mutual funds to diversify their portfolios.

♦ It doesn't cost much out-of-pocket to buy mutual fund shares. If you purchase a no-load fund, you do not pay a sales charge to buy the fund. *Brokerage* for the investments within the mutual fund, or the cost of buying or selling shares of the stocks or bonds, are generally far lower than standard brokerage, because the fund managers buy or sell so many shares of a security at one time and buy and sell frequently. Having this power enables them to negotiate trades for a lot less money than you could on your own. Many people assume that mutual funds do not pay to trade *securities*, but that's a false assumption. Fees occur whenever a security is traded; although the fees are usually lower inside a fund, due to the large number of shares traded.

♦ The Securities and Exchange Commission (SEC) oversees the records and expenses of all mutual funds.

♦ You can direct almost any amount of money to where you want it. If you're into a mutual fund for the long haul, you can direct your money to funds that invest more heavily in stocks instead of directing your money to the more conservative bond funds.

> **Show Me the Money**
>
> **Diversification** is investing your money in different securities in different industries, hoping to protect your investment against one or more companies undergoing financial disaster. **Securities** are investments that represent evidence of debt, ownership of a business, or the legal right to acquire or sell an ownership interest in a business.

If you're looking for mutual funds that don't require a lot of money to open or to be contributed to each month, consider the following options. They all were given high ratings by *Morningstar Mutual Funds*, a newsletter published twice a month by Morningstar, Inc. in Chicago:

American Funds: 1-800-421-0180   www.americanfunds.com

Fidelity Funds: 1-800-Fidelity   www.fidelity.com

Oakmark Funds: 1-800-Oakmark   www.oakmark.com

T. Rowe Price: 1-800-638-5660   www.troweprice.com

Vanguard: 1-877-662-7447   www.vanguard.com

One final advantage of mutual funds is that they carry almost no risk of going bankrupt. Due to diversification within a fund, a mutual fund is very unlikely to lose its entire value. You can invest $5,000 into XYZ Computer Company, and within 5 years, the value could drop to $0, but $5,000 invested a diversified general mutual fund should follow the ups and downs of the stock market, not just one stock.

Take a careful look at mutual funds as you begin to think about investing your money. They're a great place to start investing and are an excellent vehicle in which your money can grow.

Dollar Cost Averaging

You wouldn't be reading this book if you could figure out when interest rates were going to go up or when is the perfect time to invest in the stock market. You'd be selling all your stock the day before the market takes a dive, and buying it back the day before the market skyrockets. You'd spend the rest of your time trying to figure out how to spend your money.

But, since it's just about impossible to predict the markets accurately on a long-term basis, investors get the most out of their money by *dollar cost averaging* their investments. Dollar cost averaging is investing equal amounts of money at a regular interval, usually each month. Because you are investing the same

> **Show Me the Money**
>
> **Dollar cost averaging** is the practice of investing the same amount of money at regular intervals, such as monthly, in order to average out the fluctuating cost of the investments you're purchasing.

amount, you can buy more investments when the price is low, and fewer shares when the price is high. As a result, the average dollar amount you pay per share is usually lower than the average market price during the time you're investing.

Dollar cost averaging is an easy, controlled way to build a significant investment portfolio that has proven to reduce risk and to help build investments over time.

Let's say that you decide to have $75 automatically deducted from your checking account each month and invested into a mutual fund. The price of the fund the first month you invest is $23.17 per share, buying you 3.2369 shares with your $75. The next month the share value is $24.15 per share, and you get 3.1056 more shares, bringing your total up to 6.3425 shares worth $153.17. For your third investment, the fund drops to $19.65 per share, getting you 3.8168 shares and bringing your total up to 10.1593 shares worth $199.63. You see how it works? The number of shares your $75 bought you varied from month to month. The idea is to keep investing and let your money work over time, rather than trying to time the market.

Money Markets

A *money-market fund* (MMF) is a mutual fund with a nonfluctuating $1 investment value per share (that is, per unit that you purchase). Like a savings account, if you put $500 into an MMF, then you'll get $500, plus interest, out—"dollar in, dollar out." Although money-market funds aren't insured or guaranteed, most mutual fund companies try to keep them safe enough so that the fund value is never a problem. Your return on these investments is the *yield*, the amount your financial institution pays on your money.

> **Show Me the Money**
>
> A **money-market fund** is a mutual fund with a nonfluctuating $1 investment value per share. Your return on these investments is in the yield—what a bank or financial institution pays on your investment, including compounding.

Note that money-market funds are different from the money-market accounts we discussed in Chapter 3. Money-market accounts are accounts held with banks and insured within FDIC guidelines. Money-market funds are offered by mutual fund companies and are not insured. Their safety is dependent upon the safety of the investments within the funds. An example is a U.S. Treasury money-market fund, which is very safe because the Treasury bills and notes held in the fund are insured even though the fund itself is not. Some brokerage houses have insured money-market accounts, and these accounts are associated with banks. If the bank is FDIC-insured, then the money-market account is insured as well, unlike a money-market fund.

Money-market funds are good, safe choices for short-term investments. Your original investment is fairly secure while you earn competitive interest rates. They're not the most exciting investment vehicles, but if you have money that you need to keep at a constant value you might want to give them a look.

Money-market funds typically pay a bit more interest than savings or checking accounts, and like money-market accounts, most of them enable you to write up to three checks a month to a party other than yourself for free. The check usually has to be for at least a minimum amount (often $250).

There are various types of money-market funds. Some are invested in only U.S. Treasury obligations and are not subject to state income-tax liability. Some are invested in municipal bonds and similar investments, so they are known as tax-free investments. If you purchase a tax-free mutual fund that participates only in investments within your state, the fund is called a triple tax-free fund (no federal, state, or local income tax). If you are in one of the higher tax brackets, this kind of money-market fund might be a way for you to go.

CDs—We're Not Talking Compact Discs

In the world of music, CDs are compact discs. In the world of personal finance, they're *certificates of deposit*. CDs (the financial ones, not the music ones) require that you deposit your money for a certain amount of time. It could be days, months, or years, depending on the type of CD you choose. The financial institution that holds the CD agrees to pay you a certain interest rate and yield for the time that it has your money.

CDs are investments for security. If you pick an insured bank or a savings and loan, for example, then your investment is guaranteed to be there when the CD matures (comes due). The most popular CDs out there are the ones for six months, one year, two years, three years, four years, or five years. Normally, the longer you keep your money in a CD, the more interest you'll get. This increased interest rate

Show Me the Money

A **certificate of deposit** is an investment that pays a fixed interest rate on your money if you keep it in for a specified amount of time.

is the financial institution's way of rewarding you for allowing it to keep your money for that period of time.

If you don't hold up your end of the bargain and you take your money out of the account before the specified amount of time has expired, you'll be charged a penalty. The amount of the penalty varies, but it can be pretty hefty. If the circumstances are right, you could even end up with less money than you started with for pulling your money out early. You'd lose not only whatever interest you had earned, but part of your principal as well.

Interest rates vary, but most CDs pay more than savings accounts or money-market accounts. Most pay fixed rates, but some offer variable rates, meaning that the interest rate can change. The choices are as varied as the bank's imagination. The interest rates on CDs vary not only from bank to bank, but they change within a bank, as well. Rates are contingent on many factors (watch for CD specials), but they tend to mirror the interest rates in the general market. If you buy CDs with low interest rates, purchase those that are short-term and wait for rates to rise. This eliminates you tying up your funds for long periods of time. Some banks, however, might allow you to add money to a CD account at the interest rate of that particular day. That way, if you opened the account on a day when the rate was low, you can boost your earnings by adding money at a higher interest rate later.

> **Money Pit**
>
> Some CDs advertise no penalties, but they probably have many stipulations. CDs are required by law to charge a penalty if the money is withdrawn within the first seven days, so there really can be no such thing as a no-penalty CD. A CD that's advertised as having no penalty is probably a money-market account in disguise.

If you're going CD shopping, don't just start and stop at your local bank. Check out the rates at savings and loans, at credit unions, and online at www.bankrate.com. Credit unions typically pay up to half a percentage point higher interest on CDs. Savings and loans generally pay more than banks, but less than credit unions.

A CD isn't the most exciting investment you'll ever make. But if you have some money that you can afford to be without for a specified period, it might be worth your consideration. There are many different kinds of CDs, so be sure to do your homework before plunking down your money.

401(k)s

It's a weird name for a retirement plan, but *401(k)*s have arguably done more to get young people investing for their futures than anything else. The 401(k) savings plan was introduced in 1982 as a way for employers to save money they had been putting in *pension plans*.

There have always been retirement plans. Employers used to (some still do) provide pension plans for employees. Basically, a pension plan is an employer-sponsored retirement plan, in which the employer contributes money to a retirement fund set up on behalf of an employee. Pensions were—and still can be—good for workers, because they basically provide additional job benefits. They don't cost workers any-thing. The downside of pension plans, though, is that they can make it hard for employees to leave their companies. If employees want their full pensions, they have to stay with the company until they retire.

Although pension plans aren't as common as they used to be, some companies still offer them. If you're considering a job that offers a pension plan, don't take the plan lightly when considering it as a benefit. After all, who can argue with an employer putting money aside on your behalf, with the understanding that it will be distributed to you bit by bit when you retire?

> **Show Me the Money**
>
> A **401(k)** is a type of retirement savings plan that enables employees to contribute a portion of their paychecks to a company-sponsored investment plan. A **pension plan** is an employer-sponsored retirement plan in which a retiree receives a fixed, periodic payment.

In contrast, 401(k)s enable employees to contribute a portion of their paychecks to a company investment plan until they leave the firm or retire. At that time, the employee's money can be either left where it is, rolled over into another retirement account, or claimed by the individual, who usually will face some penalties and an income-tax liability for taking the money early. This *portability*, the ability to take your retirement plan with you to your next employer, is one of the major reasons these plans are so popular.

A Match Made in Heaven

The 401(k) accounts (if your employer is a nonprofit organization, you'll have a 403[b] plan instead of a 401[k]) have been criticized for putting too much of the responsibility for saving on the employee and leaving the employer off the hook. Still, employers are not obligated to provide a defined benefit plan pension, and if they don't, 401(k) plans are an effective way of ensuring you that you'll have money available when you retire.

In addition to providing flexibility, 401(k)s may offer a great savings incentive by way of an employer match. The amount of the match varies from company to company. If you're really lucky, your employer will match dollar for dollar your contribution up to a certain percentage of your paycheck. The most typical match is for every dollar an employee contributes up to 4 percent, the employer throws in 50 cents. By taking advantage of the match, you get an automatic 50 percent return on your money. It doesn't take a financial wizard to figure out that that's a good deal!

Many firms match an employee's contributions with company stock. We all know that company stock can be a good thing, but it isn't always a good thing (ever heard of Enron?). If you're with a company that is matching your 401(k) contributions with company stock, just be sure to keep a close eye on the value of your account. While there are risks associated with getting company stock, for many employees it's better than not having any match at all.

Dollars and Sense _____

If it gripes you to have money taken out of your check every pay period to put in your 401(k), think about this. If, between the ages of 25 and 35 you contribute $5,000 a year to your 401(k), and you average 8 percent yearly earnings on your money, you'll be really happy that you saved when you reach age 65. Why? Because you'll have accumulated nearly $900,000 from 10 years of savings.

Investing in Your 401(k)

What happens to your money once it goes into the 401(k)? You get to decide where your money should be invested by choosing from a list of various investment options provided by your employer through the plan. If your employer has the 401(k) account in various mutual funds or a family of funds (which provide a variety of fund choices within the same company), you could divide your money between stocks and bonds with perhaps some fixed-interest rate investments or money-market funds thrown in for good measure.

Understandably, selecting investments can be a daunting proposition for someone who knows next to nothing about investments. But experts say that the process of choosing these options has served as a crash course for a lot of young people who would otherwise know nothing about investing money. They say that selecting investments is not that complicated if you choose to keep it simple.

Employers have been reluctant to offer advice regarding their employees' 401(k)s because they're afraid that if their advice turns out to be wrong, they might be liable. Financial advisors, however, have come up with some guidelines to direct employees in investing their 401(k) plans. Most suggest that a conservative investor put at least 60 percent of the money in a large company U.S. stock fund (such as T. Rowe Price's Equity Income Fund). The rest, they say, could be divided between international stocks, small company stocks, and bonds. Your company should provide meetings about the various investment choices and how they pertain to you. If it doesn't, ask to have the service provided. You must understand your choices; your future depends on it.

Keep in mind that your 401(k) money is long-term money that you shouldn't plan to use until your retirement. This makes it conducive to equities—what most people consider the stock market—where you have to accept that your money is in for the long haul, and be willing to ride out the ups and downs of the market.

> **Pocket Change**
>
> If you want a more detailed explanation of 401(k)s, check out Mary Rowland's book, *A Commonsense Guide to Your 401(k)*. Rowland is a former personal finance columnist for *The New York Times* and the author of another book on mutual funds.

Tax Advantages of 401(k) Plans

Another great advantage of 401(k) plans is that the money you put into them is both pre-tax money and tax-deferred money. That means you win twice. Your 401(k) contributions are taken out of your salary before your salary is taxed for federal income taxes. The contributions are still subject to Social Security taxes, and some states subject the contributions to state and local income taxes. Still, not having to pay federal income tax on the money you contribute is a great benefit.

The money you contribute is also tax-deferred, which means you don't pay any tax on it or the money that it earns for you until you withdraw it, either prematurely or during retirement. An individual in the 25 percent tax bracket will pay 25 cents less tax on every $1 invested in a 401(k). (You'll learn about tax brackets in Chapter 14.) Here's another way of looking at it: If you are a person in the 25 percent tax bracket who invests $100 per month in your 401(k), your federal tax liability will be $300 less per year than if you didn't invest in the 401(k).

Getting Money Early from Your 401(k)

Many people in their 20s and 30s balk at the idea of putting away a significant portion of their income in a retirement fund. Retirement is still 35 or 40 years down the road, and they fear that their money will be locked away somewhere, never to be seen until they leave work for the last time.

Often, your employer will let you borrow against your plan and will deduct the repayment from your paycheck. The money you repay goes right back into your account, and you pay yourself, not a bank, with the principal and interest. If your employer doesn't have such a loan program, you'll be unable to withdraw funds from the 401(k) unless you leave your employer. You'd have to change jobs in order to gain access to your funds, which seems harsh, but helps to guarantee that the funds are there when you retire. There are certain situations in which you may withdraw from your 401(k) for hardship, but you must demonstrate real need or hardship to your employer in order to be able to do so. There may be a lapse of several months between the time you leave a company and when the money in your 401(k) becomes available. This is due to the administrative work to calculate your share, its growth, and so on, by your employer's 401(k) administrator.

If you withdraw your 401(k) money before you're 59.5 years old, expect to pay some stiff penalties. You'll pay a 10 percent penalty, and the money will be taxable, which can be a significant blow at tax time. The IRS directs that people who withdraw funds from their 401(k) plans have 20 percent withheld from the money to be used for tax payment. The problem is, that amount usually isn't enough money to pay for both the penalty and the taxes owed on the withdrawal.

> **Dollars and Sense** _____
>
> A **403(b) plan** is similar to a 401(k), except that it's offered only by hospitals, schools, and nonprofit employers. Assets from 403(b) plans normally are held with an insurance company in an annuity format. Participants can contribute up to 15 percent of their salary to an annual maximum of $13,000 in 2004. After that, the amount that participants can contribute will increase by $1,000 every year, up to a maximum contribution of $15,000 in 2008.

For example, if you withdrew $5,000 from your 401(k) plan and had the standard 20 percent withheld ($1,000), then you would receive $4,000. But if you were a taxpayer in the 27 percent bracket, you'd owe $1,350 in taxes, plus $500 for the penalty, for a total of $1,850. The 20 percent taken out wouldn't cover those costs, and you'd be

$850 short on April 15. Not a nice surprise! Still, the 401(k) is your money, and you can get it if there is a real need, and if you're willing to pay the penalties. The 401(k) plans continue to gain popularity and are giving many people an incentive to start saving for retirement. One thing to watch for is this: Some employers make you wait a year until you can start contributing to a 401(k), so check with the company's benefits department if you have questions.

Vesting

You may hear about *vesting* of funds when your employer discusses your 401(k). Vesting is the amount of time you are required to work for a company before you are entitled to the funds your employer has put into your retirement account on your behalf.

Cliff vesting (usually three years) means you must work for your employer for three years before you are entitled to the matching funds placed in your 401(k). If you change jobs after only two years and your company has three-year cliff vesting, then you will only have your own contributions available to move elsewhere. This portability is what makes 401(k)s so popular. If you leave this employer after three years, then you receive the employer's match as well as your own contributions.

When you are thinking of changing jobs, consider whether to change immediately or to wait a bit until you are vested. Always know how much of your retirement plan is employer-matched, and how much you have to lose if you leave.

The second way for an employer to vest is via *graduated vesting*. You are partially vested after two years, but you must stay with your employer for six years before you are 100 percent vested. The schedule goes as follows:

> **Show Me the Money**
>
> **Vesting** is the amount of time required for an employee to work for a company before he or she is entitled to the employer's contributions to the plan. There are two types of vesting: cliff and graduated.

Years Employed	Percent Vested
2	20%
3	40%
4	60%
5	80%
6	100%

When you change jobs, whether you are vested or not, you have your contribution to your 401(k). These funds can be withdrawn (but let's remember income tax liability and penalty), rolled over into an IRA, or even possibly rolled over into your new employer's 401(k) plan.

If your new employer has a 401(k) plan, then see if you can transfer directly from a former employer's 401(k) plan to your current employer. If you can't, roll the funds into a separate IRA, and then roll it into your new 401(k) later, if permitted.

Money Purchase and Cash Balance Plans

While not as popular as 401(k)s, you might encounter two other types of retirement plans offered by your employer—money purchase plans and profit sharing plans. They both work much the same as a defined contribution pension plan.

A target benefit plan is an age-weighted retirement plan that would normally be put into place when a company wishes to have a specified sum available for an older employee (usually an owner) at the time of retirement.

Money purchase plans are usually used by small employers who want to get a great deal of money into a retirement plan. Money purchase plans are really profit sharing plans, but they require the company to contribute a set amount of money into a retirement account, regardless of whether or not the company generated profits.

This chapter is only a crash course on places to invest your hard-earned money. Before you start seriously investing, you should check out some other resources for more detailed information. See Appendix A for some suggestions.

The Least You Need to Know

◆ People think that you need to have thousands of dollars to invest, but it's not true. You can begin investing with $50 or less.

◆ Investing your money will be a less daunting task if you start small and learn what investment opportunities are available before you start putting out money.

◆ Mutual funds offer diversification and are a great place to start investing.

◆ Money-market funds are generally safe places in which to place funds, although not too exciting as investment vehicles.

◆ CDs can be good investments, but they require a little homework.

◆ The very popular 401(k) plans offered by employers these days are a great incentive to begin retirement savings.

A Taxing Topic

In This Chapter

- ◆ Understanding what taxable income is
- ◆ Reducing your taxable income
- ◆ Checking out your tax bracket
- ◆ Preparing your tax returns
- ◆ Using a computer to help you prepare your tax returns

For most people, taxes are an annoyance to be dealt with at various times throughout the year. They get the most attention in April, when people line up at the post office, minutes before the mid-month deadline, to get their federal income tax returns in the mail on time. But taxes aren't restricted to the springtime. They bug you in the form of the pesky tax bills that show up in the mail, and they annoy you every time you see them deducted from your paycheck.

The trouble with taxes is that you can complain about them all you want to, but you've still got to pay them. Not only that, but you've got to go to a lot of trouble (or pay somebody else to go to the trouble) to figure out how much you're supposed to pay, and exactly what it is you're paying on.

There are ways, though, of reducing the taxes you pay, and one of the goals of this chapter is to educate you on these methods. We tell you about ways that you can make less of your income taxable, which will reduce your overall tax rate. There's nothing magic (or illegal) about it; it's just a matter of getting a better understanding of how the tax system works and using it to your best advantage.

How Did Taxes Happen, Anyway?

The personal income tax as we know it today became permanent in 1913. The Sixteenth Amendment to the Constitution gave government the authority to tax the income of individuals and corporations. Back then, the tax was between 1 and 7 percent, a lot less than today. Taxes have traditionally risen during times of war and decreased in times of peace.

What's Your Taxable Income?

Before we begin the process of understanding taxes, take a look at the formula below to calculate our taxes:

> **To Calculate Taxes Payable:**
>
> Add all Taxable Income
> (Subtract Adjustments)
> Result is known as *Adjusted Gross Income* (*AGI*)
> (Subtract Standard Deduction or *Itemized Deductions*)
> (Subtract Number of Exemptions × $3,100)
>
> Result is your Total Taxable Income
> Calculate Tax
>
> (Subtract Tax Credits)
>
> Result is the actual tax to be paid

Taxable income is the amount of your income on which you pay taxes. Yeah, we know. You thought for sure you were paying taxes on every cent you make, or your taxes wouldn't consume such a large chunk of your income, right? Well, if it seems that way, you're right. We work for a good part of the year just to make the money that we pay in taxes, and it can be mighty discouraging if you dwell on it.

But you're not going to dwell on it. Instead, you're going to figure out how to make less of your income taxable. You're still going to pay taxes; don't get us wrong. But you might be able to whittle them down a little bit and give yourself a little more money for other things.

You have to pay taxes on the money you earn by working, but as you'll remember from Chapter 7, your income may come from sources other than your paycheck. For instance, the interest you earn on the money in your 401(k) plan is income, but it's not taxable income. This income is referred to as *nontaxable income.* You get to earn it for free (for now, anyway). Theoretically, you could make all your income nontaxable. Of course if you did that, then you wouldn't have a salary or any money to live on. But at least you wouldn't be paying any taxes!

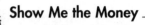

Show Me the Money

Your **taxable income** is the amount of your income on which you begin calculating your final tax liability. **Nontaxable income** is income that is excluded from tax liability.

Let's have a look at what's taxable income and what's not. Taxable income includes the following:

- Your salary, with the exception of money you may have deducted and put into a 401(k) plan

- Interest earned on savings and checking accounts

- Interest on all bonds except municipal (tax-free) bonds and dividends on investments

- Bonuses, severance pay, and sick pay from your employer

- Unemployment compensation

- Tips

- Capital gains on mutual funds and other investments. (Capital gains are the amount by which proceeds from the sale of a capital asset exceed the cost. They're the profit you make.) Although the tax rate on capital gains is different than regular taxable income, it's still considered taxable income.

- Bartering, royalties, and gambling winnings, including lottery winnings

- Most withdrawals from an IRA or annuity

Nontaxable income includes the following:

◆ Money you contribute to certain types of retirement accounts

◆ Disability income on benefits you paid for with after-tax dollars

◆ Funds contributed to a Flexible Spending Account used for childcare or medical expenses through work

◆ Return of invested capital—that is, your money invested that is returned to you

◆ 401(k) money that's rolled over into another 401(k) or IRA when you change jobs

◆ Child support payments

◆ Money you've lent that is repaid

Use this information about taxable and nontaxable income to help you to be smart when it comes time to figure out what to do with the money from your salary that you don't need to cover your expenses.

How to Make Less of Your Income Taxable

Once you have calculated your taxable income by totaling lines 1 through 21 of your federal income tax return (1040), you may be able to take off what are called *adjustments*. Adjustments from gross income are such things as IRA deductions (a tax-deductible contribution to an IRA account), moving expenses, and so on. Here are two kinds of adjustments in more detail:

◆ **Moving expenses**   If you move because you get a new job that's at least 50 miles away from your previous employer, you can deduct the cost of moving your things from your old home to your new home, plus the miles you drive at a rate of 12 cents a mile. You can't, however, deduct meals, house-hunting expenses, or costs of temporary living.

◆ **Student loan interest**   The Taxpayer Relief Act of 1997 allows taxpayers who pay interest on certain higher education loans for themselves or their spouses to deduct interest paid on the loan. The amount of deduction, which previously was $1,000, increased to $2,500 in 2001. The interest deduction is available to taxpayers regardless of whether they itemize their other deductions. Married couples must file a joint return to claim the deduction, and the deduction has certain income limitations.

When you have totaled your taxable income and subtracted your total adjustments, you have what is known as your *adjusted gross income (AGI)*. Once you have your AGI, you're ready to take your deductions.

Deductions

To make less of your income taxable, you can contribute to accounts where it won't be taxed, such as 401(k)s and childcare plans through your employer. Or you can increase your itemized deductions of income, which lowers the amount that's subject to taxes.

Deductions are perfectly legal, but it's up to you to find out which ones apply to you. There are tons of deductions, but you can't just help yourself to them as you would at a smorgasbord. For instance, you can't take a deduction on mortgage interest if you don't own a home. The IRS frowns on that sort of thing, and we don't want to see our readers paying large fines, or worse. The idea is to lower your taxable income by putting as much as you can into legitimate tax-sheltered accounts and by taking all the deductions that apply to you.

There are two methods for figuring out your total deductions:

- ◆ Standard deductions
- ◆ Itemized deductions

The good news is, each year you can figure out which method gives you a better deal, and go with it.

Standard Deductions

Most young people take the *standard deduction*, which is the amount allowed by the IRS, because their financial situations are reasonably simple, and they're not eligible for a lot of deductions associated with owning property and

> **Pocket Change**
>
> The latest statistics from the Tax Foundation, a Washington, D.C.–based watchdog organization, show that the average American works until April 11 just to pay his or her taxes. That's the bad news. The good news is, due to the recent federal tax cuts, that's 21 days shorter than in 2000, when we worked until May 2 to pay off our taxes.

> **Show Me the Money**
>
> A **standard deduction** is the lump-sum amount of allowable deductions that you can subtract from your total taxable income. The IRS sets this amount. **Itemized deductions** are deductions that you list separately if you've incurred a large number of deductible expenses.

other investments. If your income is not exorbitant, and you rent rather than own where you live, you'll probably be better off taking a standard deduction. It's set right now at $4,850 for single people and $9,700 for married couples filing jointly.

If your financial life is a bit more complicated, you should figure out whether you'll do better by itemizing your deductions. You also might want to itemize your deductions if you've had an unusually large number of medical bills during the tax year, a high amount of charitable contributions, or significant loss because of theft, fire, or natural disaster. You need to get a copy of Schedule A of the IRS form 1040 on which to itemize. Check out Chapter 24 for a sample Schedule A.

Itemized Deductions

You have to know exactly what deductions you can take as *itemized deductions*, and that's where many people go wrong. They don't keep records of things they buy that could be counted as deductions, so they have no idea how much they can deduct.

These expenses can be itemized:

- **Taxes**   You can deduct state and local income taxes, real estate taxes, foreign taxes, and personal property taxes.

- **Interest expenses on home mortgages, home equity loans, and points charged when buying a home**   The catch with this one is that you've got to own a home. Points are those pesky fees that you have to pay to a mortgage lender to cover the loan-application fees. Chapter 24 explains how owning a home affects your taxes, so you'll read all about it then. For now, we'll just say that if you've bought a home, you're in for some tax advantages.

- **Charitable work and contributions (money or property) to tax-exempt organizations**   If you drive for Meals on Wheels or deliver baskets to shut-ins for the Salvation Army, you can deduct your mileage. The standard charitable mileage deduction is 14 cents per mile, plus tolls and parking fees. You'll need to use your odometer for each trip and keep a log of the miles you've driven. As with all itemized deductions, thorough documentation is essential. If you donate property like an old couch, loveseat, or end table to a charitable organization such as Goodwill, you can deduct the furniture at its current *fair market value*. Fair market value means what it's worth at the time you donate it, not what you paid for it. When you drop off the furniture, be sure you get a receipt showing the charity's name and a description of the property. You must keep a list of the property you gave, along with its fair market value. To access a guide suggesting the fair market value for items commonly donated to charitable agencies such as the Salvation Army and Goodwill Industries, go to www.goodwill.org and follow the links to "Claiming Tax Deductions."

Pocket Change

The charity to which you donate property usually will indicate the **fair market value** of your donation based on what it's worth when you drop it off (not what the original cost was). If not, you can estimate what the value is, unless it's valued at more than $5,000. If it is worth more than $5,000, the IRS requires a qualified appraisal. If you donate property valued at more than $5,000, you'll need to attach a special form to your tax return.

- **Home office expenses**   If you work from your home, you can deduct a portion of your utilities and home real estate taxes, and you can depreciate a portion of the costs of your home. You can only do this, however, if your home office is your only place of business. If your boss lets you work from home every now and then, you can't claim deductions on a home office. Your home office must also be an area of your house that is used only for business, and it must be used regularly. If your computer is on one end of your dining room table and you eat at the other end, you're going to have a hard time convincing the IRS that it's a home office. Still, if you do work exclusively out of your home, the home office deduction is worth looking into. You also can deduct business expenses, such as computers, fax machines, and the like. Just remember that many tax preparers feel that deducting home office expenses on your return can trigger an audit if the expenses are out of line with your income.

- **Gambling losses**   You can deduct these up to the amount of gambling winnings (are you surprised?).

- **Job-search expenses**   You can deduct these expenses if you're looking for work in the same trade or business in which you're currently employed, but not if you're looking for a different line of work (nobody ever said tax laws made a lot of sense). You also can deduct job-hunt–related travel expenses and costs such as having a resumé prepared, postage, and so on. You don't need to get the job in order to deduct the expenses.

Show Me the Money

Your **adjusted gross income** is all your taxable income, less certain permitted adjustments. Examples of adjustments are moving expenses and contributions to an IRA.

◆ **Nonbusiness casualty and theft losses**   Such losses would include storm damage to your home or the theft of your brand-new computer. The amount of the deduction can be no more than 10 percent of your adjusted gross income. You can figure out your *adjusted gross income* by subtracting all allowable adjustments from your taxable income.

◆ **Impairment-related work expenses for people with disabilities**   This would include, for example, the cost of a special handicapped-accessible desk or computer.

You can itemize the following expenses if they total more than 2 percent of your adjusted gross income:

◆ **Job-related car expenses**   Car deductions include the cost of gas, oil, maintenance, insurance, repairs, car registration, licensing, and so on. You also may be able to take a depreciation allowance if you own your car, but only if your car is used for business purposes and only on the percentage of use that is job-related.

◆ **Business expenses not covered by your employer**   These expenses can include travel and entertaining.

◆ **Educational expenses**   These expenses are deductible if you spent money to maintain or improve skills required by your job or by law. For instance, insurance agents are required to take continuing education courses in order to remain licensed. If you decide to go back to school in order to change careers, however, or because you think an advanced degree will help you along in your career, those expenses are not deductible. However, they may apply toward the tuition and fees adjustment or be eligible for an education tax credit.

◆ **Tax preparation fees**   If you wimp out and decide to have your taxes prepared for you, you can deduct the cost of the work. Most people with fairly simple financial lives, though, are able to prepare their own tax returns.

◆ **Safe deposit box fees**   These bank fees are deductible as long as you use the box to store taxable bonds or stock certificates.

You can also deduct medical and dental expenses that you paid for you, your spouse, or any dependents, if they total more than 7.5 percent of your adjusted gross income.

After you reach this 7.5 percent mark, you can start deducting expenses for things such as contact lenses, weight-loss and stop-smoking programs (if they're recommended by your doctor), childbirth classes, travel to Alcoholics Anonymous meetings (if the meetings are recommended by your doctor), and remedial reading classes for a dyslexic child.

If you qualify for these types of deductions, you can significantly reduce the amount of your taxable income. If you don't have a lot of itemized deductions, take the standard one and be glad for the $4,850 for singles or the $9,700 for married people filing jointly.

You can't deduct these things:

♦ Political contributions

♦ Trash collection fees

♦ Homeowners association charges, except the portion used to pay real estate taxes, and perhaps the portion used to pay interest

♦ Water bills (unless they're for a business)

♦ Estate, inheritance, legacy, or succession taxes

♦ Credit card interest (except for a business)

♦ Car loan interest

♦ Interest on loans where proceeds are used to purchase tax-exempt investments

♦ Points if you are the seller of the property

Money Pit

Remember, if you itemize your deductions, you must have documentation for each one. Don't deduct the cost of that computer you bought in September unless you can prove when, where, and why you bought it and how much you bought it for. If you would happen to be audited and had no documentation … let's just say it wouldn't be pretty!

After you've deferred all the money you can into nontaxable accounts, used as many adjustments as possible, and taken all the deductions you're eligible for, you're ready to compute your taxable income.

Pocket Change

Recent tax changes upped the standard deduction for married couples filing joint tax returns. Prior to changes enacted in May 2003, the standard deduction for married people filing a joint return was less than the total of two single deductions. The tax changes upped the amount to exactly the amount of two single deductions. However, the change is only in place for 2003 and 2004, which means the marriage penalty could be back in 2005. If you're married, or even if you're not, it's worth your time to call or write your area legislators, asking that the marriage penalty relief be made permanent.

Fitting In: Tax Brackets

If your salary isn't as much as you think it should be and you're having a hard time getting your boss to give you a big raise, then you can comfort yourself by knowing that you're paying less in taxes than Mr. Big Shot down the hall who makes $40,000 more a year than you do. You're paying less not only because you don't have as much taxable income, but also because you're also being taxed at a lower rate since your income is lower.

Of course, it's good to make more money. Nobody's going to argue with you on that point. However, if you nudge up just over the cut-off point, you will increase the rate of tax on the excess earnings. That situation doesn't happen very often, though, so it's not worth losing sleep over.

Something most people don't realize is that every taxpayer filing as a single person is taxed at 10 percent on the first $7,150 of taxable income (the income after adjustments, deductions, and exemptions). The tax rate is graduated, meaning that people who make the lowest income pay the lowest taxes, while those earning the most income pay the highest rate (35 percent).

Regardless of how much you earn, however, the first $7,150 of your taxable income if you're single, or $14,300 if you're married and filing a joint return, are taxed at 10 percent.

If you're single and you earn between $7,150 and $29,050 a year, your tax rate will jump to 15 percent on taxable income over $7,150, and then up to 25 percent once you earn more than $29,050. You'll be taxed at 25 percent until your earnings reach $70,350, at which time you'll have the privilege of turning over 28 percent. When your earnings hit $146,750, your tax rate will jump to 33 percent, and when you reach $319,100, you can plan to kiss 35 percent of it good-bye.

If you're married and filing jointly, you'll pay 15 percent of anything between $14,300 and $58,100. Your tax rate will jump to 25 percent once your combined income hits $58,100, and to 28 percent once your earnings reach $117,250. When you pull in $178,650 in combined income, you'll reach the 33 percent tax bracket, and, if your combined earnings are $319,100 or higher (same as a single earner), you'll pay the top rate of 35 percent.

Notice that the biggest jump, by far, is that from 15 percent to 25 percent. Just when you're starting to get somewhere, wham! You're socked with a much higher tax rate. All other bracket increases are at a 5 percent tax increase.

Such is the way of the American tax system. The tax rate that you end up paying, based on your income dollars beyond $29,050 (if single, and $58,100 if married, filing jointly), is called your *marginal tax rate*. If you're a single taxpayer with a

taxable income of $37,350 a year, your marginal tax rate is 25 percent, on the last $8,300 of your income. By knowing the amount of your marginal tax rate, you can figure out any additional taxes you'd have to pay if your taxable income were to increase. Reviewing the total amount of taxes you pay per year and dividing this amount by your adjusted gross income, will give you your average tax rate.

Show Me the Money

Your **marginal tax rate** is the tax rate that you pay on your next dollar of income. It is your highest income tax bracket.

Marginal tax rate is tricky to grasp because of how taxes are deducted from paychecks. If you have the same salary throughout the year, the amount of state and federal income tax taken from your check each pay period will be the same. So it appears that all your income is being taxed at the same rate, even though it's really not.

Preparing Your Tax Returns

April 15 is fast approaching, and you have taxes on the brain. You know you have to get a return prepared and in the mail, but you've been putting it off. Preparing a tax return is one of those things we tend to build up in our minds as a big deal, when it doesn't have to be. It's like painting the living room. You know it's a one-day job, but the longer you think about it, the bigger a task it seems to be. Eventually, it's like a monster looming over you. When you finally get around to painting the room, you wonder why you turned it into such a project in the first place.

I Can Do That!

If your financial situation is not very complicated, then you probably can prepare your tax return yourself. In fact, it's probably a good idea to do it yourself, because it forces you to learn a little about the tax codes and to become more familiar with your personal finances. Seeing in black and white what you earned, what you invested where, and what deductions you're eligible for can give you a better understanding of where you stand financially.

> **Pocket Change**
>
> For an IRS booklet on preparing an individual tax return, call 1-800-TAX-FORM and request Publication 17, *Your Federal Income Tax.* Find the IRS online at www.irs.gov.

The IRS tax return instructions contain an introduction that gives you basic directions on how to fill out the return. If your return is not at all complicated, you should be okay using just those instructions. If you want more information, you can get it for free from the IRS.

If you want more than IRS information, plenty of books are available to help you with your taxes. We've listed a few here, but you can find many more in your library or local bookstore. Be sure you get the most recent books you can find, because tax laws change constantly:

- ◆ *The Complete Idiot's Guide to Doing Your Income Taxes,* by Gail Perry and Paul Craig Roberts

- ◆ *The Motley Fool Investment Tax Guide 2002,* by Roy A. Lewis and Selena Maranjian

- ◆ *J. K. Lasser's Your Income Tax 2004,* by the J. K. Lasser Institute

- ◆ *Kiplinger Cut Your Taxes,* by Kevin McCormally

- ◆ *Taxes for Busy People: The Book to Use When There's No Time to Lose,* by Robert A. Cooke

If you're going to do your own taxes, just be sure that you don't wait until the last minute. It's much more likely that you'll end up frustrated and making mistakes if you do.

Help! I Need Somebody (Not Just Anybody)

If you decide not to do your taxes yourself, there are plenty of people around who will do it for you. If you look in the Yellow Pages, you'll see the names of a bunch of people who will prepare your tax return. But they call themselves different things. There are tax preparers, enrolled agents, certified public accounts, and tax attorneys. How do you know whom to pick?

Different people who work with taxes have different levels of expertise, beginning with a tax preparer and ending with a tax attorney. The more expertise someone has, the higher his or her rate generally will be. If you're filing a simple tax return, there's no reason you need to hire a tax attorney to do it for you.

CAUTION

Money Pit _____

Nearly everyone has a friend or relative who prepares taxes. Maybe you know a CPA or someone who works part-time during tax season for H&R Block. Don't assume, however, that just because you know somebody who works with taxes, that he or she is qualified to prepare *your* taxes. Good friends do not necessarily make good tax preparers. And do you really want your friend or relative to know all the personal financial information that your tax return includes?

Let's have a quick look at the different categories of tax help, so that you can decide which one is right for you:

♦ **Tax preparers**   As a group, tax preparers have the least amount of training. They don't need to be licensed, and many of them work part-time. H&R Block is a well-known company that prepares taxes. The people who work for Block are tax preparers. Preparers are normally reliable if your tax return is fairly straightforward, and they won't break your budget. They usually charge about $125 for a basic tax return.

♦ **Enrolled agents**   Enrolled agents are licensed and can represent clients in front of the IRS in the event of an audit. Enrolled agents generally have more training than tax preparers, and they're required to participate in continuing education. As a group, they charge more than tax preparers.

♦ **Certified public accounts (CPAs)**   CPAs undergo a lot of training and must pass an exam to receive their credentials. They have to complete continuing education courses each year in order to remain certified. If your taxes are complicated, because you have your own business or for other reasons, you might need a CPA. CPAs usually charge about $150 an hour, so you could be looking at a hefty bill.

> **Dollars and Sense**
>
> If you hire someone to do your taxes and you feel that they're not doing a good job for you, get someone else to look at their work. Anyone, even a hotshot CPA, can make a mistake—and unfortunately, his or her mistake could become your problem. If that does occur, a reputable CPA should be willing to pay any penalties.

♦ **Tax attorneys** You probably will never need a tax attorney to complete your tax return, unless your financial life gets incredibly complicated, with all kinds of legal ramifications. If you do need one some day, be prepared to pay, big time! Many tax attorneys charge up to $350 an hour.

If you find someone whom you like and trust to prepare your taxes, consider yourself lucky. There are many excellent people around, and finding one makes your life a little easier. Once you find someone, try to stick with him or her, if you can. They'll have your files in case you ever get audited, and there's a lot to be said for continuity.

Websites and Software To Help You Prepare Your Taxes

An increasing number of Americans are relying on their personal computers to help complete their tax returns. There's more and more tax-preparation software coming out all the time, and it can provide some real advantages. The programs provide great information and guide you through your return preparation, clearly answering your questions. We recommend at least doing your return on your own with a tax prep software package, and then having it checked by a professional. See how close you get to being correct!

The tax forms you need are contained in the software, so you don't have to zip down to the post office to get them, only to find out the post office has been out of them for a week. The software enables you to file your return electronically, and the IRS sends you a confirmation when the return is received.

Tax-preparation software programs generally aren't very difficult to work with. They merely require you to enter or even directly download the information requested, and the programs zap your info into the appropriate tax form. Two popular tax software programs are Intuit's Turbo Tax (or Turbo Tax for Macs for Macintosh) and Block Financial's Kiplinger Tax Cut. You can file your tax return online using Turbo Tax for the web. It's on the Internet at www.turbotax.com.

Here are some websites to check out for information and tax advice:

◆ Quicken.com Taxes at www.quicken.com/taxes

◆ Smartmoney.com Tax Guide at www.smartmoney.com/tax

For another online tax preparation program, go to this site:

◆ Secure Tax, located at www.securetax.com

Tax forms (and accompanying instructions) are also available on the IRS website at www.irs.gov. These forms are a convenient means of filing your tax return.

Regardless of how you decide to prepare your tax returns, make sure that you check everything before you send them in. Prepare the returns and then put them aside for a few days. Bet you'll find some mistakes when you come back refreshed and look them over again. According to the IRS, a high percentage of completed forms contain mistakes. Also, make sure that you start far enough in advance, so you don't end up in a panic on April 1.

Dollars and Sense

Don't overlook your state income taxes when working online. There are software programs for state taxes, too.

Paying Your Taxes Online

The Internal Revenue Service reported that 59,745,000 individuals filed their tax returns electronically in 2004, a 15 percent increase from the previous year. E-filing is apparently becoming the preferred method of filing taxes. In fact, the IRS is hoping to have 80 percent of all returns filed electronically by 2007.

The IRS, in partnership with a consortium of companies, offers free filing online for qualified taxpayers. To find out if you're eligible for free filing, go to www.irs/gov/efile.

The Least You Need to Know

◆ Not all of your income is taxable income.

◆ You can reduce your taxable income by taking advantage of certain adjustments and deductions.

◆ Not all of your income is taxed at the same rate.

◆ You can prepare your own tax returns or hire someone to do them for you.

◆ More and more software programs are available to help you prepare your tax returns, and many tax returns can be filed electronically.

Looking Out for What You Have

In This Chapter

◆ Understanding how insurance works

◆ Thinking big is the way to go

◆ Knowing what kinds of insurance you need and don't need

◆ Shopping around to get the best rates

◆ Fighting back for fair treatment

Insurance is one of those things most people don't like to think about, much less sit around and discuss with friends. It's sort of an unsavory area of life. First of all, you have to buy the darn stuff, and it's expensive. Even as you're shelling out the bucks to pay for it, you're hoping you never need it. If you do need it, something bad has happened. Let's face it— insurance can be a drag.

Still, it's better to have insurance than not to. Because we can't see ahead to what losses will befall us (and who would want to?), we need to protect ourselves against possible catastrophic losses. Insurance is a method of sharing risk among a large group of people.

If you learn one thing about insurance from this chapter, let it be this: Insurance is meant to protect the important things in your life, such as life itself, your health, the health of your family, and your home, against big losses. If you get sick and can't work, though, you'd better have insurance to cover your lost income, even if you're supporting only yourself. If you have a house and it burns down, you'd better have insurance to rebuild and replace the stuff you lost. Whenever you walk outside and get into your car, there's the potential for an accident, and you need to be insured just in case.

Pocket Change
It's been estimated by the National Insurance Consumers Organization that 90 percent of Americans have the wrong kind of insurance, in the wrong amounts, from the wrong companies. Sounds like we all could use some insurance education! Read on to find out what's right for you.

Dollars and Sense

Try to think of insurance as a tool that helps you deal with trouble, should trouble arise. That way it seems less like a necessary evil, and more like, well … insurance.

Welcome to the Insurance Jungle

There are more kinds of insurance policies available to Americans than you probably can imagine, and we buy tons of it. Most people, though, don't understand the insurance industry, or even what kinds of insurance they should have.

The insurance industry is huge, and it commands a large chunk of our nation's economy, as well as its attention. Not a day goes by when you don't read or hear some news related to the insurance industry. There are tens of thousands of insurance companies in this country, and more than 2 million people are employed in the industry, making it one of the country's largest employers. Insurance is a powerful industry, as well. It has an extremely strong lobby that exerts tremendous pressure on the government agencies that are supposed to oversee it. As a result, it has become a formidable force in our society.

Insurance is an issue we all need to think about, because we need to have it.

Insurance 101

Most insurance is sold through agents or brokers who work for insurance companies such as Allstate, State Farm, Nationwide, Liberty Mutual, and thousands of others. The agents earn commissions from the insurance companies, based on how much and what type of insurance they sell. Certainly, insurance agents aren't the only people out there who work on commission. Real estate agents do, and many other types of sales-people do, as well. There's nothing wrong with a commission system, but you should be aware that that's how the insurance industry works.

If an agent is going to get a big commission for selling a certain type of policy, you can be sure he's going to knock himself out trying to sell it. That's how he makes his living, and some agents are really good at convincing you that you need something that's completely unnecessary.

After you read this chapter, you'll have a better understanding of what you need and don't need. Don't let an agent talk you into buying something you don't need, for which you'll end up paying a large premium. The *premium*, by the way, is the amount of money you pay for a particular insurance policy. Be sure that he or she understands your situation so that you get the kind of coverage you should have.

> **CAUTION**
>
> **Money Pit**
>
> Some analysts say that nearly 50 percent of insurance agents and brokers try to sell you policies that generate the highest commissions for them. If you don't know what you want or need, you could be suckered into buying unnecessary coverage while lining the pockets of the agent.

> **Show Me the Money**
>
> A **premium** is the amount of money you pay, at regular predetermined intervals, for a certain insurance policy.

If you don't know anyone who sells insurance, you'll have to take your chances with a referral or someone you find on your own. Choose someone with a CLU (Chartered Life Underwriter) or ChFC (Chartered Financial Consultant) designation, which demonstrates that the agent has taken courses to further educate him- or herself about the industry. It also implies that the agent has affirmed to practice ethically.

Sometimes You Need It, Sometimes You Don't

You've already learned to think big when it concerns insurance. Forget the little stuff, even if it's tempting because it doesn't seem to cost very much. In many cases, the same coverage offered with "specialty" policies, such as mortgage life insurance or flight insurance, is already provided for in your regular life insurance policy.

If you buy a lot of little insurance policies hoping to cover every possibility for loss, you'll end up spending a lot more on the policies than you would fixing the things that go wrong. If your computer does break down, by the time you pay the deductible, spend an hour or two filling out the claim, and try to cut through the inevitable red tape, you're probably better off having it fixed on your own. Make no mistake about it. You can buy as much insurance as your heart desires. You can insure

> ### Pocket Change
>
> Insurance companies pay out an average of 60 cents in benefits on every dollar they pull in for premiums. Some policies, though, such as repair plans, average less than half of that amount. Skip the little stuff and worry about the big stuff.

your stereo equipment, your mountain bike, your drum set, your cell phone, and your snowboard if you want to. You can pay anywhere from $12 to $40 a month to buy health insurance on your five-year-old golden retriever. Before you start buying insurance on everything you own, however, consider what you really need.

The types of insurance you need depend on where you are in your life. A thumbnail sketch of the types of policies you may need follows:

- **Single with no dependents**   At this point in your life, you need health insurance, auto insurance, homeowners insurance, and enough life insurance to cover your burial, final expenses, and any outstanding loans. If you rent, consider getting renters insurance (see Chapter 5 for more details). Disability insurance also makes sense for you now.

- **Married with no kids**   Now you'll need some life insurance, especially if your spouse doesn't work or if you own a home. Auto and homeowners or renters insurance is necessary, as are health and disability insurance.

- **Married with kids**   Kids bump up the amount and types of insurance you need. If you don't have life insurance yet, you'll definitely need it now. Term life insurance, where you pay a certain amount per year and your survivors receive a certain amount if you die (more about this later in the chapter), is probably your best bet. You'll still need health and disability insurance, too, along with auto (pay special attention to that one once the babies get to be teenagers and start driving!) and homeowners insurance. It's a good idea at this point to re-examine all your policies to make sure you're adequately covered. Having kids makes you responsible for them, and you want to make sure they'd have sufficient resources if you were to die or become disabled.

We're going to concentrate on the types of insurance necessary for people in the first two categories: single with no dependents and married with no kids. We'll also touch briefly on what you need if you're in the third category: married with kids.

Health Insurance

In the past few years, health-care insurance has become a hot political issue, a topic of discussion at dinnertime and parties, front-page news, and a growing headache for

many Americans. The United States spends more of its gross domestic product on health-care than any other major industrialized nation, according to the Washington, D.C.–based National Coalition on health-care (NCHC), and patients are being asked to pay more and more out of their pockets while an increasing number of people are uninsured.

If you get health insurance through your employer, breathe a big sigh of relief. Even though many companies have started requiring that employees *co-pay* (that means you contribute a portion of your salary to offset the employer's cost for your insurance plan) and pay higher deductibles, you're still better off than having to buy insurance on your own. If you do need to buy your own health insurance, be sure you get a plan that covers the big stuff. You need to be covered for hospitalization, physician costs, and charges for things such as X-rays, lab tests, and diagnostic tests. If you're a woman who plans to have a baby in the not-too-distant future, look for maternity benefits, too.

> **Pocket Change**
>
> If you think health insurance is expensive now, just wait. The National Coalition on Health Care predicts that the average cost of health insurance for a family in America will cost more than $14,500 a year by 2006, jumping more than $5,000 between 2003 and 2006.

> **Show Me the Money**
>
> A **co-pay** is the amount an insured person is expected to pay for a medical expense at the time of the visit. It can also refer to the difference between what your doctor charges and what your insurance company will cover for a particular service.

If you're leaving a job where you have an insurance plan, look into the possibility of extending your coverage when you leave. COBRA (Consolidated Omnibus Budget Reconciliation Act of 1985) requires your employer to continue your health coverage after a job loss, death of an employee, divorce, or attaining a certain age (as when a child reaches an age when he or she is no longer covered under the plan). Your employer is required to offer COBRA coverage for 18 months after you quit your job, or 36 months for other situations (such as divorce). You have to pay for the insurance, but at least you'll be covered and your insurance won't lapse.

It used to be the general rule of thumb—and still is, in some states—that you could probably get a better rate with a *health maintenance organization* (*HMO*) or *preferred provider organization* (*PPO*) plan, both of which limit your choice of health-care providers, than on a plan that lets you see whomever you want. The health insurance arena is changing, however, and HMOs and PPOs aren't always available in all areas, or always the most economical types of plans.

> **Dollars and Sense** _____
>
> If you're buying your own health insurance, take the largest deductible you can afford, which is an amount you'll be required to pay before the insurance company will pay a claim, to keep the cost down. Also, consider a co-payment option, in which you'd pay a percentage of your health costs. Make sure the co-payment option includes a maximum out-of-pocket limit though.

If you can get an HMO or PPO plan in your area, go ahead and check them out. They may still be your best deal. Don't reject HMOs and PPOs because you think they limit your choice of doctors. Many HMOs and PPOs probably include your current doctors, so ask to see a list of which doctors are included as providers before you make your decision.

Check out a big health-care insurer such as Blue Cross Blue Shield if you're shopping for a policy. They normally can get better rates from health-care providers and are more stable than many smaller companies. Look for a plan that has the highest lifetime maximum benefits you can find and is guaranteed to be renewable.

> **Show Me the Money** ___
>
> Health maintenance organizations (HMOs) and preferred provider organizations (PPOs) are health plans that restrict your choice of health-care providers. As a result, these plans often—but not always—cost less than those that don't restrict providers.

Because health-care insurance changes so often and so quickly, and the regulations vary greatly from state to state, shopping for a policy can be extremely challenging. If you need to find your own insurance, consider the suggestions that follow:

♦ Go online. If your state enables you to choose whatever health-care plan you want, you can get immediate quotes online from sites such as eHealthInsurance.com and DigitalInsurance.com. These sites can at least give you an idea of what's available and how much it will cost.

◆ Find a health insurance broker. Using a broker can be helpful because he or she should be able to guide you not only on price, but also on the ins and outs of whatever company you're looking to insure with. The National Association of Health Underwriters, located on the web at www.nahu.org, can lead you to a broker in your area.

◆ Check out your state insurance department's website. Most of these sites include the names of companies that offer policies within your state and some information about them. State sites may also include a record of complaints against various companies.

Dollars and Sense

If you're having a difficult time finding insurance because of a medical condition, check to see if your state has a high-risk insurance pool.

Some innovative folks have joined together and obtained small group insurance on their own. In some states, members of these small groups may be eligible for group policy rates, which can cost 20 to 50 percent less than individual rates. You might also check in your area to see if you can join an organization that offers group health-care benefits, such as a chamber of commerce.

Another option for certain people is a medical savings account. As the name implies, this is a savings account created for the purpose of paying for medical expenses. It works in conjunction with qualified major medical insurance and can be used to help pay deductibles and expenses that insurance doesn't cover. Generally, these plans are options for people who are self-employed, who work for a company with 50 or fewer employees, or who employ 50 or fewer workers. The Internal Revenue Service offers a form on medical savings accounts. You can access it by going to the IRS website at www.irs.gov and clicking on "Forms and Publications"; the form number is 969.

Auto Insurance

You must have car insurance, because the liability risk if you're in an accident is too great to ignore. Auto insurance is expensive, but it's required by law in nearly every state. Even if it weren't, you couldn't afford to be without it.

Different types of coverage are associated with car insurance, but the one that's required by almost all states is liability. Liability coverage is twofold: bodily injury and property damage. The bodily injury liability coverage protects you against lawsuits in the event that someone is injured in an accident in which you're involved. Although it varies from state to state, most states impose a minimum amount of bodily injury coverage, between $10,000 and $30,000 per person, and up to $100,000 per accident. If you lend your car to someone else to drive, remember that the insurance follows the car. Thus, your coverage is the primary insurance in the event of an accident.

The property damage liability covers damage to other cars and property that's caused by your car. It would not only cover the cost of fixing a car that you hit, but it would pay to repair or replace the fence you ran over, too. Most states require a minimum of $10,000 in property coverage.

> **Pocket Change**
>
> Although $100,000 sounds like a lot of bodily injury coverage, experts say that to protect your assets in case you're sued, you should have up to $300,000 in coverage. If you buy only the minimum amount, it might not cover all your liability in the event of a lawsuit.

> **Pocket Change**
>
> Certain vehicles are more likely to be stolen than others, according to police statistics. Honda Accords and Toyota Camrys are two vehicles frequently targeted by thieves.

If you have a loan on your car, you'll need collision and comprehensive coverage, as well. Collision coverage pays for damage to your car if you're in an accident or pays to replace a car that's totaled. Comprehensive coverage protects you from car theft or weird things that could happen to your car, such as a tree falling on it or it being damaged during a riot, fire, or flood.

If you get hit by someone who doesn't have insurance (this isn't as unusual as you might think), you'll need uninsured motorist coverage. This insurance covers your medical expenses and lost wages in the event that you're injured by an uninsured motorist.

When you rent a car, your policy provides coverage unless it states otherwise. Read your policy, and always call before you go on a trip. If your deductibles are high, you should purchase coverage from the rental company.

There's a big difference in auto insurance rates, so be sure you look around. Be aware that a poor driving record will dramatically increase your insurance rates. Look for cars with good safety records (a Volvo anyone?), and stay away from hot sports cars or convertibles if you're interested in keeping your rates down.

If you're over 25, you'll generally get a better rate than someone who is younger. Also, being married, living in what is considered a safe neighborhood, and having a relatively short work commute (driving less than 7,500 miles/year or not using your car for work) will lower your insurance rates.

Property Insurance

You're required to buy property insurance before you can get a mortgage, so if you own a home, you already have homeowners insurance. You'll read all about that type of insurance in Chapter 26.

If you're renting an apartment, you'll need renters insurance if you have a lot of stuff you want to protect. Damage to the building is not your responsibility, but if your TV or VCR is stolen or damaged, you'll need insurance if you want to replace it without paying out-of-pocket. If you have a bunch of good computer equipment or a rare coin collection, you definitely should look into renters insurance.

Disability Insurance

What would happen if you had a serious accident while skiing that resulted in a head injury? Pretty gruesome to think about, huh? Still, nobody is immune to accidents or injury. You have a greater chance of being disabled by age 65 than dying, and if you were hurt and unable to work for a long period of time, you'd be out of luck. You'd be a little less out of luck, though, if you had *disability* insurance, which would provide you with an income to live on until you could work again.

Most large companies provide disability insurance to employees who are unable to work because of a physical or mental disability. But if you work for a small company or are self-employed, you might have to buy it on your own. If you can't afford to be without a paycheck for an extended period of time, you'd better have disability insurance. By the way, if you don't work, you can't get disability insurance.

How much disability insurance you need depends on how much money you have. If you've been living paycheck to paycheck and have no money saved, you'd better have enough insurance to cover the full amount of your paycheck. If you have enough money in the bank to live off of for six months or a year, you can skimp a little.

Show Me the Money

Disability is not an old person's condition; it's the inability to work because of a physical or mental condition. More than one third of all disabilities are reported among people who are under 45 years old.

Disability insurance becomes increasingly important as you gain dependents. If you're married and your spouse doesn't work or doesn't earn enough to support both of you, then you can't be without it. If your spouse is making enough to support both of you, then it's not as important. Once you have kids, however, you've got to have disability insurance, unless your spouse makes enough money to support the entire family for an extended period of time.

> ### Dollars and Sense
>
> If you don't have disability insurance through your employer, you might be able to purchase it through a professional organization in which you're eligible for membership. Groups are often able to buy insurance for less than individuals, so you should be able to get a better rate. The American Medical Association, National Education Association, Writers Guild, CLU, and ChFC Society are all professional organizations. If you need coverage, find out if you can qualify under such a group.

Make sure you know what is included in your disability coverage if you get it through work. Many people don't take the time to find out, and you can't depend on the benefits department to seek you out and tell you that you're eligible for coverage. Most companies have short-term and long-term provisions, so if you find out you need an operation and will be out of work for a couple of weeks, you'll want to know whether you're eligible for benefits.

If you need to buy your own disability insurance, go for the longest elimination period (the number of days you must be disabled before the insurance kicks in) you think you could handle. This will result in a significantly lower rate. A 90-day elimination period often is recommended, but you'd need to be able to support yourself (and your family, if applicable) for that period of time.

Also, be sure you understand how the policy defines "disabled." Some policies require that you be hospitalized in order to receive benefits. You should look for a policy that will keep paying you as long as you're unable to perform the duties of your job.

Don't depend on government programs such as Social Security or Worker's Compensation to provide you with benefits in the event of a disability. If you are eligible for coverage, your benefits won't be as much as you need. Also, your chances of being injured off the job are probably as good, or better, as those of being injured at work. You need coverage in the event of any disability.

Life Insurance

You need life insurance so that your family will have financial support if you die and thus can no longer provide for them. If you're single and without children, then you probably don't need life insurance. If you do, the amount should be only enough to cover your funeral, final expenses, and any outstanding loans. If you're married but have no kids, then you should think about life insurance if your spouse would have to drastically change his or her lifestyle if you died. If you have kids, you need life insurance.

How much life insurance you need varies depending on your situation, but experts say it should be for five to eight times the amount of your current salary. After you figure out about how much coverage you need, it's time to decide what kind of coverage you want. As mentioned briefly earlier in this chapter, there are two basic types of life insurance: term insurance and cash-value (sometimes called whole-life) insurance. Nearly everyone (except for those who are rolling in wealth) benefits more from term insurance than cash-value insurance when they are young. Cash-value insurance makes sense for older people, but for people in their 20s and 30s, term is probably better.

Term life insurance is the least-expensive kind of life insurance. In exchange for your annual premium, term life will give a predetermined amount of money to your beneficiaries if you die during the term in which you're insured. All you need to do is keep paying the premium. The premium, however, will keep increasing as you get older and someday might be prohibitive. It's a good idea to review your policies periodically to be sure they make sense for you.

Show Me the Money

Term life insurance is a policy in which you pay an annual premium, in exchange for a predetermined amount of money that will be paid to your beneficiaries if you die during the term that you're insured. **Cash-value insurance** combines a life insurance policy with a type of savings account, where you actually earn interest on part of the money you pay into the plan.

Dollars and Sense

Cash-value insurance can cost up to eight times as much as term life insurance for the same amount of coverage. Unless there are special circumstances, like if you're very wealthy and anticipate an estate-tax problem if you should die, term insurance is a better deal for young people.

The other kind of life insurance, cash-value insurance, combines life insurance with a sort of savings account. Your premiums not only insure that your survivors will receive money if you die, but some of the money from the premiums is also credited to an account that will increase in value as long as you keep paying premiums.

Cash-value insurance might sound like a better deal because you think you'll be getting something back from it. An agent hawking cash-value life insurance will tell you that after you pay on the policy for so many years (usually 10 or 20), your policy will be all paid up, and you won't have to make more payments. The problem is, that cash-value insurance is much more expensive to buy than term when you are young, and the only reason you might be able to stop paying premiums at a certain time is that you've already paid in a great amount of premiums. Agents love cash-value life because they get a much higher commission from selling it than they do on term policies. Don't let an agent or broker talk you into buying cash-value insurance. At this point of your life, it's not likely that you'll need it.

> ### Pocket Change
> There is an argument for buying a cash-value policy at a young age. When you buy term life insurance, you need to provide proof of insurability to get a new policy when the current term expires. If it turns out you're uninsurable due to an emerging disease or other medical problem, you could end up without life insurance. Once you have a cash-value policy, as long as you make the premium payments, it can't be cancelled.

You Just Don't Need It

In addition to extended warranties for your computer, washer, and hairdryer, there are some other insurance goodies you can live without. If an agent tries to get you to buy these sorts of policies, just say no:

- **Dental insurance** If your employer offers dental insurance, by all means, go ahead and use it. If not, though, don't bother getting it on your own. It usually doesn't pay for extensive work, and it's not worth buying to cover having your teeth cleaned a few times a year.

- **Flight insurance** This novelty insurance plays on the fears of people who don't like to fly, especially after the awful airline crashes of 9/11. If your life is worth a lot of money, you'll have your life insurance up-to-date anyway.

- **Credit life and disability insurance** Sold by credit card companies, these policies will pay a small amount to your beneficiaries if you die with a credit card balance. The policy only covers the debt on that one card. Don't bother.

- **Life insurance for your kids** Life insurance is to protect income, and children generally don't have income. If your child dies, a small amount of insurance money isn't going to make things better for you. You may purchase a child rider on your life insurance policy to cover a funeral and final expenses, if you wouldn't be able to afford these if your child were to die.

My Mama Told Me: You Better Shop Around

To keep the costs of your insurance policies down, you must comparison shop. Costs can vary greatly.

We mentioned earlier that you should take the highest deductibles you can afford on your insurance. Of course, you'll pay more in the event that something happens, but you'll pay less on your premiums. Chances are, you'll end up paying more in premiums than you will on a higher deductible for an occasional claim. If you have a very low *deductible*, you'll end up filing claims a lot more often than if your deductible is higher.

Say that your roof leaked during that last nasty thunderstorm. It's nothing too bad, but the estimate to repair the drywall and repaint the wall was for $175. If your deductible is $100, you're going to spend a lot of time filling out claim forms and hassling with the insurance company for the sake of $75. Also, if you report every minor claim, you can bet that the insurance company will soon be hiking up your rates. If you have a $300 deductible, though, you'll save significant money on your premiums, a savings you can use to make minor repairs. Comparison-shop the premium savings and the deductible limits, and then determine what you can afford to pay out if you have a claim.

Show Me the Money

A **deductible** is the amount of money that you have to pay before your insurance coverage picks up the cost.

Pocket Change

Call Marketing Direct Insurance Services at 1-800-924-LESS for some proposals from insurance companies that have high ratings but low costs. You'll get an idea of what's available, but you won't be under any obligation to buy. Or check it out online at www.marketing-direct.com.

Also mentioned earlier was the advantage of getting a group rate on an insurance policy, rather than buying it on your own. Whenever possible, check out group rates through your employer or an organization you belong to for the insurance you need. You can often save significant money by doing so.

Finally, when you're shopping around, check out the rating of the insurance company you're thinking of doing business with. Various organizations evaluate and rate insurance companies, judging them on their financial stability and health. Look to A. M. Best, Standard and Poor's, Weis Research, or Moody's rating services. Directories published by these services are available in most libraries.

What Do You Mean, I'm Not Covered?

Coming from your insurance agent, the words "you're not covered" can strike fear in even the staunchest hearts. If you've filed a claim and your insurer doesn't want to pay it or wants to pay you only part of what you believe it should, don't roll over. There are things you can do to assure your best shot at getting what you deserve:

- **Document your losses.** If you're in a car accident, get the names and addresses of all possible witnesses. If your property was damaged, take photos or videotapes of the damage. File police reports when necessary, and get several estimates for what it will cost to repair or replace whatever was damaged.

- **Don't give up.** If you file a claim for $2,286 for repairs to your car after a wreck, and the insurance company says it will give you $1,500, find out why. If you don't get any satisfaction from the *adjuster*, the person who surveyed the damage and determined what you should be paid, find out who the supervisors and managers are and ask to talk to them. Ask your agent to help you.

Show Me the Money

An **insurance adjuster** is a person who inspects damage and determines the amount that the insurance company should pay for repairs or replacement.

- **Prepare your claim carefully.** Make sure that your policy covers the claim you're about to make and write out your claim report carefully and clearly. By all means, keep a copy of the report, and document all conversations you have with anyone concerning your claim.

- **Get legal help.** If you've been denied coverage for a major claim that you feel you're entitled to, you might want to hire a lawyer who specializes in insurance concerns. It will be expensive, but if there's a significant amount of money at stake, it might be worth it.

Insurance is a big, powerful industry, and it's in the business of making money. Don't expect that your insurer will go out of its way to please you and make you happy. Although you shouldn't assume an adversarial position with your insurance company, you should remain alert to the possibility that you'll have to do a little haggling to get what you deserve. Good companies do, and all companies are expected to, honor their commitments and promises to their customers.

If you aren't satisfied with the service or coverage you've received, you can contact your state insurance department. Just make sure that you're entitled under your policy to whatever compensation you're seeking.

The Least You Need to Know

- ◆ Hardly anyone likes insurance, but we all need to have it.
- ◆ The insurance industry is large and powerful, and we're pretty much at its mercy.
- ◆ Purchase insurance to cover major losses, not to protect you against every little thing that could go wrong.
- ◆ There are some types of policies that almost everyone needs, and some that hardly anyone should buy.
- ◆ There are ways to save money when buying insurance, so it pays to know what you need and to look around before you buy.
- ◆ If your insurer hassles you about paying a claim, be prepared to fight.

Part 4

To Everything There Is a Season

Things change. Your old pals and roommates are getting married. People are getting new jobs and moving away. A couple of your friends even have babies. It seems the only thing you can count on anymore is the fact that nothing stays the same.

You find that you're taking life a bit more seriously yourself these days. You're not all business, though; you still love to have a great time, but you're finding you've got more responsibility. Your finances reflect these changes in attitude, too. You're looking past your 401(k) plan and even thinking about getting into the stock market. Maybe your work situation has changed and you're working from home. What does that mean to your life and your finances? Maybe you've started asking around for a good financial advisor. You're looking down the road, that's for sure.

There's an awful lot involved in these kinds of decisions, and we cover a lot of material in this part, everything from weddings to home offices to market risk. By the time you're finished reading this part, you should feel a little more comfortable and ready to move ahead.

Working from Home

In This Chapter

- ◆ The growing trend toward working at home
- ◆ Assessing your aptitude to work at home
- ◆ Being accountable to an employer—and to yourself
- ◆ Setting up a home office that's right for you
- ◆ Paying taxes and taking deductions
- ◆ Protecting yourself and your business

There are many reasons why more and more Americans are staying home to work, or at least completing some of their work from home. Technological advances have made it possible for many people to work from almost any-where, without the confines of an office cubicle. Attitudes about working from home have also changed dramatically during the past decade or two.

People who worked at home used to be looked at as somehow suspect—they didn't fit into the norm of commuting office workers. That, however, was before the days of laptops, e-mails, and home fax machines, which made being in the office unnecessary in many cases. As employers became more receptive toward employees working from home, attitudes toward home workers began to change and the work-from-home revolution got underway.

Can 20 Million Americans Be Wrong?

According to the U.S. Bureau of Labor Statistics, about 20 million Americans do at least some of their work from home. The National Association of Homebuilders surveyed Americans and found that more and more are looking for home offices when they buy new homes. Millions of others have carved out space in their existing homes to create home offices.

People who work from home value the independence and flexibility it affords. Parents enjoy the ability to blend work and family, and, let's face it, wouldn't most people rather go to work in comfy jeans and a sweater rather than a business suit or high heels?

Not everyone, however, is suited for working from home. Some people miss the camaraderie and social aspects of a workplace and end up feeling isolated and resentful. For others, it becomes too difficult to separate work time from family time, or children become resentful at having Mom or Dad at home but unavailable to them because she or he is working.

If you're thinking about going the work-from-home route and have the opportunity to do so, consider whether or not your situation meets the criteria for successfully working at home, as listed below.

- I have good organizational skills and am disciplined enough to avoid distractions.

- I have a family (if applicable) who will support my decision to work at home and respect my work time.

- I have the necessary private space and equipment to work from home.

- I am comfortable working by myself without social interaction.

- I am motivated enough to finish work without prompting.

- I believe I can achieve a good balance of work and family while working in my home.

- I know where to look for resources that would aid me in working successfully from home.

If many of these attributes don't apply to you, you'd be wise to think carefully about whether or not you're suited to be a stay-at-home worker.

Working at Home for Somebody Else

As attitudes toward working from home change and technology makes it easier and easier to do so, an increasing number of employers are finding that granting employees flexibility as to where they work actually benefits their company. According to Gil Gordon, a telecommuting consultant, studies have shown that people who work at home achieve 15 to 25 percent greater productivity than those who work in traditional offices.

Employers are also learning that allowing employees to work from home attracts good people who might otherwise not apply with their firms. There's also a high level of job satisfaction among employees who can work from home, cutting down on turnover, training costs, and lost time.

If your employer allows you to work from home, be sure that you both have the same expectations concerning what you'll do and how you'll be held accountable. Perhaps you'll be required to spend half a day each week in the office to meet with supervisors or co-workers. Or you might be required to file daily reports that account for your productivity.

Whatever arrangements you make with your employer, be sure to report frequently as to what you're doing and be accessible at the times you say you will.

Another route is to work at home as an independent contractor, which means you're doing work for someone, but not as an employee. You're a self-employed person performing a particular job for a particular person or company. Employers must withhold taxes and pay unemployment taxes on employees' wages. That is not the case with independent contractors, who are simply paid a fee for work completed. The advantage of working as an independent contractor is that you truly are independent—you set your own schedule and working conditions. Don't forget, however, that you won't have benefits provided by an employer, and you'll be responsible for paying your own taxes.

> **Pocket Change**
>
> Gil Gordon is a recognized expert in the areas of telecommuting and working from home. You can check out his website at www.gilgordon.com.

> **Pocket Change**
>
> According to the U.S. Census, 76 percent of U.S. workers drive to work, with an average commute time of 25.5 minutes each way. Other benefits of employees working at home are less crowded highways, a decrease in gas consumption, and cleaner air.

Going It Alone From Home

The Bureau of Labor Statistics reports that 10.3 million Americans were self-employed in 2003. If you are among that number, you already have an idea of the challenges and rewards of being your own boss.

Everyone has strengths and weaknesses. When you're in charge of yourself, these can become more obvious, both to your delight and dismay. Perhaps you never noticed how many coffee breaks you took when you worked in an office because everyone else was taking them, too. Now that you're working from home, however, those trips to the kitchen seem way too frequent. Or perhaps you're pleasantly surprised at how much you're able to accomplish in a short amount of time, undistracted by the office chatter, politics, and gossip.

> **Dollars and Sense**
>
> If you work at home, you'll need to establish a routine and boundaries, even if you're the only one in the house. While there's no single formula that works, most people find they need to limit distractions in order to be able to concentrate and be effective in their work.

Most people who are working for themselves, or themselves and their families, are highly motivated. And with good reason—if you don't complete your work as a self-employed person, it's a good bet that you won't get paid. Working for yourself is way different than being on a company payroll, where, if you're a bit less productive during a pay period than you are normally, there generally are not grievous consequences.

As a self-employed person, it is imperative that you are disciplined enough to finish your work on time, contact clients as arranged, and keep to your necessary schedule. Your credibility will erode quickly if you don't deliver what you say you will—and on time.

Setting Up a Home Office

While we can't begin to cover every aspect of creating a home office in this short section, we can offer some suggestions to get you started. You'll need to find the right space for an office, outfit it with a phone, computer, and other equipment; consider zoning and legal issues; and, of course, figure out how you'll pay for what you'll need. The first thing to consider is whether you can legally work from your home.

Zoning and Other Legal Issues

Before you go ahead and set up a fancy home office, you need to make sure there are no zoning restrictions in your area that prohibit you from working at home. While many communities limit the types of businesses that can be run out of a home, it's unlikely that you'll run into trouble for simply working at home, but it's best to check.

If you're setting up a business that will be run out of your home, the extent and type of business might be restricted by zoning. Check with your municipality about any existing zoning ordinances. If there's an ordinance that restricts or prohibits at-home businesses, you may have to file for a variance or consult with a lawyer. The majority of communities, however, do not restrict work you do within your home as long as it doesn't affect your neighbors or present a hazard. As long as your work is conducted quietly and you don't bother anyone, you're not likely to run into zoning problems.

However, many municipalities do restrict the use of signs in residential areas, and there may be parking restrictions and limits on the number of employees you can have. An increase in traffic often is restricted, and there might be noise restrictions as well.

Even if the zoning allows working from a residence, the need for permits, business licenses, and registrations varies greatly according to your location. You should check with your municipality to see if you need any of these in order to work from home.

Finding the Right Space

Whether you live in a three-room apartment or a ten-room house, you'll need to designate a space for your office. Some people find it works just fine to have their desk in the living room, while others need to be in private spaces, behind closed doors.

> **Pocket Change**
>
> To learn everything you'll need to know about starting a business and running it successfully, check out *The Complete Idiot's Guide to Being a Successful Entrepreneur*, by John Sortino.

> **CAUTION**   **Money Pit**
>
> A common problem of people who work from home is the temptation of the refrigerator. Many people find themselves taking too many fridge breaks, which results in decreased production—not to mention added pounds. If you find yourself having this trouble, establish your office as a no-food area, and put the refrigerator off-limits except for during established break times.

A spare bedroom, basement, attic, side porch, garage—even a large closet or breakfast nook—can all be candidates for a home office, depending on what you're able and willing to do to convert the space. Following are some tips to remember when choosing a space:

♦ Find a space you can call your own. You'll need a space where you can have some privacy and quiet when you need it. Be creative and claim a space for yourself. This is especially important if you plan to claim a home office deduction on your income tax return.

♦ Make sure your office has enough space to keep you organized. You might think a tiny office would be easier to organize than a larger one, but attempting to work in too small a space will prove difficult. Remember that you'll need room for filing cabinets, shelves, a desk or computer table, and other equipment.

♦ Choose a space that makes it easy to set limits on other people "visiting" you in your office. If you locate your office in a spot where everybody has to walk by as they come in the door, the temptation to stop and chat will be great. If you're in a corner of the basement, however, chances are they'll almost forget you're there.

Setting up a home office can be as simple as moving some stuff around, or as complex as hiring a contractor to convert or add a room to your house. The important thing is to find a space that works for you. Be realistic about your needs and expectations. If you'll be receiving clients at your home, you need to also consider the needs of your clients and the impression your office will make.

Dollars and Sense

A separate phone line for business is highly desirable, but if you're the only one in the house during business hours, you might be able to get away with one line for business and personal use. Do not let a child answer the phone if there's a possibility that the call is business related.

Getting the Equipment You Need

Many people, when just starting out in their own business or converting to a work-at-home situation for an employer, can't afford to spend thousands of dollars on fancy office equipment. There are, however, some things you're probably going to need.

One of the most important things you'll need is a comfortable workstation and a good chair. Using a dining room chair at a desk that wasn't designed for a computer might work all right for a short time, but you're sure to feel the effects before long. Pay attention to ergonomics when you're selecting office furniture and make sure to get a good chair.

These days, with the proper equipment and planning, it's easy to communicate easily with practically anyone. When you begin to equip your office, think about your communication needs and the equipment you'll need to satisfy those needs. Consider the phone system you'll need. If you still have dial-up computer access, you'll need a second phone line so you're not tying up the only line when using the Internet. A fax machine might also require a separate line. Other equipment to consider includes:

◆ Appropriate computer system with Internet connection and all necessary software (don't forget financial software)

◆ Laser printer

◆ Answering machine with a business message

◆ Fax machine

◆ Copy machine (some printers can double as copiers, but might not be practical if you need to make multiple copies on a regular basis)

◆ Filing cabinets with appropriate files and labels

◆ Adequate lighting

◆ Telephone with a headset to allow you hands-free use

◆ Adequate shelves for storage

Many home offices have started with little more than a desk, chair, and computer, so if you can't buy all the desirable equipment right away, don't worry. Add what you need as you can, and remember that the most important attributes of a home office are those you offer: enthusiasm, determination, and perseverance.

Financing the Stuff You'll Need

After you've compiled your wish list of supplies and equipment for your home office, you'll need to figure out how you'll pay for them.

Experts highly recommend that if you're going to be working for yourself, you set up separate business accounts for credit cards, bank accounts, and so forth. This will make your accounting much easier. A new business owner can have a difficult time

Pocket Change

The Small Business Administration, an independent agency of the federal government, is a gold mine for anyone starting a business. In addition to business loans, the SBA provides models for business plans and a wealth of advice and information. If you're even thinking about working for yourself, check out the SBA web site at www.sba.gov.

getting a business credit card when first starting out. If so, get a new personal card and use it only for business. Having a credit card used strictly for business will help you to establish business credit.

If you need to get a loan, there are several routes you can take. The Small Business Administration (SBA) provides loans under certain conditions to those starting their own businesses. Many new business people start out by getting an equity loan, often using the equity in their homes. Or they may have a family member co-sign a starting loan. There also are government loans and grants available for small business startups.

Challenges and Opportunities for the Self-Employed

When starting your own business, you can expect some challenges along with the rewards. Working for someone as an employee generally includes benefits, and your employer is responsible for the taxes on your salary. When you're working for yourself, however, you must plan for your own benefits, such as health care and retirement, and take care of paying the applicable taxes. These can be quite a drain on your income. The good news is that there are deductions you can take on your income tax to help offset the expense.

Taxes

If you are self-employed, there are some tax considerations you'll need to understand. Generally, a person who is self-employed is categorized as one of the following legal entities:

- ◆ Sole proprietor
- ◆ General partnership
- ◆ Limited liability corporation (LLC)
- ◆ S Corporation or C Corporation

The simplest and most common form of ownership for people just starting a small business is a sole proprietorship. That means that you are the sole owner of the business. In a sole proprietorship, you are required to file a Schedule C, Profit or Loss From Business, with your tax return. All you need to do is keep track of your income and your expenses, then place the information on the Schedule C.

There are legal and accounting expenses associated with starting up a partnership or corporation and different considerations concerning taxes. Business owners usually set up a LLC or a corporation so that their liability is limited to the assets of the business. This protects personal assets from being lost due to a lawsuit.

The economic concept that seems to confuse the self-employed the most is double-paying Social Security and Medicare taxes. When you are an employee, you pay 6.2 percent Social Security tax and 1.45 percent Medicare tax. Your employer pays the same amount, meaning that a total of 15.3 percent of every employee's salary (up to a certain amount) goes into the U.S. Treasury.

When you are self-employed, you must pay the entire 15.3 percent yourself. That, along with local, state, and federal income taxes, can take a big bite out of your income. If you make $100, for instance, and are in the 15 percent tax bracket, you'll lose $30.30 off the top to the IRS and Social Security.

Also, when you're self-employed, you are required to pay quarterly estimated tax payments to the IRS. Payment due dates fall on April 15 (this payment is always tough because you owe the balance due from the prior year, plus a payment on the first three months of the current year), June 15, September 15, and January 15. These payments are made on a Form 1040-ES.

Schedule SE (Self-Employment Tax) is the form to use to figure out how much Social Security and Medicare tax you'll owe. It's a good idea to get this form early and calculate how much money you'll owe so you can plan to pay the

> **Dollars and Sense**
>
> A sole proprietorship is easy to start and easy to end. If you're thinking of starting a business, it's probably the best way to begin, unless you have special circumstances. A Schedule C can be filed for a partial year.

> **Dollars and Sense**
>
> If you're self-employed, it's a really, really good idea to establish a bank account into which you pay taxes on all your income. That way, when taxes come due, you aren't left scrambling for cash to pay them.

> **Pocket Change**
>
> While paying quarterly taxes can seem cumbersome, it actually is a safer practice than trying to pay just once a year, because it forces you to keep money in reserve and be accountable at regular intervals.

taxes each quarter and not be hit with a big tax bill (and possible penalties) when April 15 rolls around.

Dollars and Sense

If you're self-employed, be sure to look into Individual Retirement Accounts designed especially for you. Called SEP-IRAs, these allow you to contribute up to 25 percent of your income, up to $41,000 a year. You'll learn more about SEP-IRAs in Chapter 18.

These same taxes are due if your business is a corporation or a partnership, but they are reported differently on your tax return. Partners and corporate owners receive a Schedule K-1 on which income is reported for their tax return.

Paying taxes can be daunting for the self-employed, there's no question about it. You might need to consult with an accountant or tax advisor if you have special concerns. Software programs such as Quicken, QuickBooks, Microsoft Money, Turbo Tax, and TaxCut can help you through the tax maze.

Deductions

If you work from home for an employer, you may be able to deduct nonreimbursed expenses from your federal income tax. You would use Form 2106 to take deductions for parking fees, tolls, travel expenses, car rentals, and so forth. You're even permitted to deduct 50 percent of the costs of meals and entertaining. You can also deduct office expenses that exceed 2 percent of your income, which may be advantageous if you need to buy a lot of equipment when you're first starting to work from home. If your employer reimburses all your expenses, however, you cannot claim them as deductions.

If you use your own car for business and are not reimbursed for mileage, you can also deduct that. You are required, however, to keep track of how many miles you rack up for business. The standard mileage rate, set by the IRS, is set at 37.5 cents per mile in 2004.

If you are an independent contractor with your own business, the vehicle deductions are calculated the same as for an employee. Instead of using Form 2106, however, you'd list your vehicle expenses on Schedule C.

Independent contractors and some employees are able to take the "Expense for the Business Use of their Home" deduction, as listed on Form 8829. The rules regarding that deduction are as follows:

◆ Business space must be used exclusively for business. Having a computer on the dining room table doesn't count as business space. A workspace in an area of the family room used only for your work does count as business space.

◆ Know what percentage of the overall living area of your home or apartment your workspace occupies. That number will be important.

Money Pit _____

If you're planning on deducting expenses incurred while working at home, especially for business space, be careful. Although it's more common for taxpayers to claim these deductions than it used to be, they still can be a red flag to the IRS.

◆ Total all expenses related to your living area, including the cost of heat, electricity, rent or mortgage, and so forth. If your work space occupies 15 percent of your living space, you may deduct 15 percent of your heating bill (and so forth) as a business expense.

◆ Know if an expense is direct or indirect. Indirect expenses, such as electricity, are a percentage of your total expenses. Direct expenses are completely attributed to the business, such as the installation of an entrance door for your office space.

◆ If you own your home and use it for business purposes, you may be able to depreciate a portion of the cost of the property each year. This means the cost of the building only—not the land. There's a formula for this based on 27.5 year increments, along with the percentage of space used for business.

Pocket Change

Starting in 2003, self-employed folks can deduct up to 100 percent of their premiums if they buy their own health insurance. To make it even better, they get to subtract the deduction from their total income, which lowers the amount of taxable income. And even those who don't itemize their deductions or qualify for the itemized medical deduction can take this insurance deduction. To find out more about it, check out www.turbotax.com/articles/DeductingSelfEmployedHealthInsuranceCosts.

While claiming deductions can be a little tricky, it's still important to know what you are entitled to so you can maximize your deductions. Save receipts for everything— and that means everything—you think you might deduct.

Insurance Is Especially Important

As you read in the last chapter, insurance is crucial. Unfortunately, many self-employed people don't have all the insurance they need, especially in the area of health insurance.

Health-insurance is expensive, and the rates continue to rise. According to a March 16, 2004 piece in *USA Today*, the average health insurance premium for a family in America is $9,086 a year. That's 21 percent of the average family's income of $42,409. If you have a job where your employer pays all or most of your health insurance, you don't think much about the cost, although many employees are facing increasingly higher co-pays and deductibles. If you're self-employed and need to pay for your own insurance, however, it's a different story. There's no question, however, that you need health insurance.

> **Pocket Change**
>
> To learn more about buying your own health insurance and where to find an affordable policy, check out www. healthinsuranceindepth.com. For insurance information relating specifically to those who are self-employed, see the National Association for the Self-Employed at www.nase.org.

In addition to the types of insurance covered in Chapter 15, self-employed individuals may need to obtain special business coverage. If you have a lot of computers and other equipment, you might want to look at special computer insurance or business property insurance. You might also need to consider malpractice, errors and omissions, or product liability insurance, depending on the type of business you have.

Insurance is always important, but, the more you have to lose, the more important it becomes. As your business expands, so should your insurance.

The Least You Need to Know

♦ More and more people are working from home, but it's not the best option for everyone.

♦ If you work at home for an employer, be sure to be accountable for your time and the work you're expected to complete.

♦ You can design a home office that will work for you if you consider your space, your needs, and your budget.

♦ Among the challenges and opportunities for self-employed people are both paying additional taxes and being able to claim tax deductions.

♦ Insurance can be expensive, but the more you have to protect, the more of it you'll need.

Chapter 17

The Game of Life

In This Chapter

- ◆ Understanding that your life situation affects your finances
- ◆ Being single and earning a paycheck
- ◆ How living together affects your personal finances
- ◆ How marriage affects your checkbook, your insurance, and your taxes

Life, in many ways, is not a game of chance. It moves along at its own pace. Days pass, seasons change, and all of a sudden, you're another year older. Your life is changing, too. You're probably better established in your career than you were a year or two ago, and it might seem like a lifetime ago that you left college and started working. Hopefully, your personal finances are on track, and you're enjoying having a little extra money—not only for things you want to buy, but for investing in your future, as well.

We spent a good deal of time in Chapter 8 evaluating your financial life-style and determining your expectations as they relate to your personal finances. Now, we're going to have a look at how different stages of life can affect your personal finances and how you can make the most of each of those stages.

Footloose and Fancy-Free

The single years can be some of the best ones of your life. You're getting your career off the ground and starting to be recognized for your accomplishments. You're meeting lots of new people and enjoying an active social life. You're not broke like you were in college and the first couple of years when you started working, so you can afford to do some things now that you couldn't do before. You're learning a little about investments, putting some money away in your 401(k) plan, and maybe even thinking about buying a place of your own.

If you're still living with your parents, you're by no means alone. Many Gen Xers are staying at home longer, and they say it's to be able to save money. Not all single people, however, are financially responsible. Some not-so-young-anymore singles haven't saved a dime, and they aren't looking into the future past their next paycheck.

> **Pocket Change**
>
> The median age for first marriages in America is 25 for women and 27 for men. That compares with 22 for women and 25 for men in 1980. Pass that little tidbit of information along to Mom the next time she starts making comments about your unmarried status.

> **Pocket Change**
>
> More young adults currently live with their parents than at any other time since the Great Depression of the 1930s.

We've covered some information in earlier chapters about investments, taxes, and other topics that can affect your finances and your future. Hopefully, you've learned something and are doing what you need to in order to both enjoy your single years and ensure your future. At the very least, you should by now be doing the following:

- Paying back college loans

- Working to reduce (hopefully to eliminate) credit card debt

- Saving money in an emergency fund

- Putting some money into your employer's 401(k) plan or another type of tax-deferred retirement plan

We'd never suggest that you miss out on the opportunity to enjoy those great single years because you're saving every penny you make and never have any money with which to do anything. Just don't lose sight of the fact that you have a lot of life ahead of you, and all the fun you have when you're footloose and fancy-free won't finance your retirement.

She (Gulp!) Wants Me to Move In with Her!

So you've met somebody you really, really like. Okay, you're in love. You're spending a lot of time together. Actually, you're together almost all the time. You talk about a future together, but neither of you feels like you're quite ready to start shopping for engagement rings. You're just hanging out one day, when it happens. She tells you she'd like you to move in with her.

There are many reasons why so many couples are living together these days. Some do it because it's convenient. It eliminates running back and forth between two apartments and shuffling your belongings all over town. Some couples use living together as a sort of "trial run" for marriage. They reason that it makes more sense to see whether it will work out before you get married than risk a divorce a year or two after the nuptials.

> **Pocket Change**
>
> If you decide that living together makes financial sense, you're in good company. More than 5 million unmarried couples are living together in the United States, according to U.S. census figures.

Financial considerations can also factor into a couple's decision to live together rather than get married. Many couples set a goal of saving a specific amount of money, or paying off their student loans, or getting enough for a down payment on a house before taking the plunge. Some wait to establish their careers before getting married and live together while they do.

Whatever the reasons, plenty of couples choose to live together. Although cohabitation doesn't raise eyebrows the way it did 30 years ago, it can still be a sticky arrangement. There are financial and legal ramifications, as well as the less tangible emotional aspects to consider. You're on your own to figure out the emotional particulars of living together, but we can tell you some things you should know about the legal and financial aspects.

Financial Advantages

There are definitely financial advantages to living together. If you each had an apartment before you moved in together, you've cut your housing costs by about 50 percent by sharing your space. That makes more sense than paying rent on an apartment that was empty most of the time, anyway. You'll also be sharing costs for utilities, so you'll see some savings there. If you were living a considerable distance apart, you'll save money on transportation and phone bills, too.

You'll also realize some tax advantages by living together instead of opting for marriage. Although you're living together, you'll continue filing your tax returns as singles. That can save you some money, especially if you and your significant other earn above-average salaries. Consider that if you each earn $45,000 a year, you'll pay about $1,500 more in taxes after marriage than if you were still single.

Financial Disadvantages

Although there are financial advantages to living together, it's not all a bed of roses. There are instances in which you'd be better off financially if you were married. Consider the following:

◆ **Health benefits** Many employers offer health and dental benefits to spouses of employees, but not to a person with whom the employee lives.

◆ **Life insurance** If an employer offers life insurance and the employee dies, benefits automatically go to the spouse of the deceased. An unmarried partner must be named beneficiary to get the benefits.

◆ **Pension** Many companies will pay some pension benefits to the spouse of an employee who dies before retirement. These benefits usually don't apply to unmarried couples.

◆ **Social Security** If a person dies while employed, the spouse might be eligible for some Social Security benefits upon reaching age 60. An unmarried partner isn't eligible for these benefits.

◆ **Memberships** Unmarried couples usually aren't eligible for money-saving "family" memberships in clubs and organizations. You'll sometimes end up paying almost twice as much as singles.

We're not trying to turn marriage into a business transaction, but as you can see, there are financial advantages and disadvantages to living together instead of getting married. One thing to remember, though, is that marriage implies love and commitment that extends far past the savings account. If you're putting off marriage because you'll be taxed at a higher rate, you might have to ask yourself whether you're looking for an excuse to stay single.

> **Pocket Change**
>
> *Living Together: A Legal Guide for Unmarried Couples* is a book/CD-ROM package that includes legal forms, explanations of legal issues as they relate to unmarried couples, and more. Currently in its eleventh edition, it's written by three lawyers: Frederick Hertz, Ralph Warner, and Toni Ihara, and is available in bookstores or from Amazon. com.

Breaking Up Is Hard to Do

As much as you both might want the relationship to work, sometimes things go wrong. Relationships end, and sometimes it's not under the best circumstances. When that occurs, couples who lived together, but weren't married, might have a hard time figuring out where they stand legally. Divorce laws are pretty clear-cut in most states, but there are few laws that deal with breakups of couples who have lived together.

What happens, for instance, if a man works two jobs to put his girlfriend through law school, and then the couple breaks up and the girlfriend moves out? Should he be entitled to reimbursement for her law school tuition? Or what happens to property when an unmarried couple breaks up? Even if there's not a house involved, there's likely to be furniture, maybe some art, computers, CD players, and TVs. Unmarried couples who split should try for congenial and equitable property division, because there's a lot of legal gray area out there.

If you're planning to live together, we wish you all the best. But if you have a significant amount of property between the two of you, you might do well to consult a lawyer before you move in. Some legal experts advise couples moving in together to set up an agreement, similar to a prenuptial agreement, of how property will be divided if the relationship ends.

Will You Marry Me?

You've finally decided to take the plunge and make it official by getting married. Hearty congratulations and best wishes to you both! Before you blissfully embark on your honeymoon, though, you need to think about some financial considerations.

A large number of divorces are caused by financial problems. Sometimes these problems are a result of a gambling or other type of addiction. Often, though, financial problems occur because the couple doesn't work together on their financial health.

Maybe they don't share common attitudes about money, but they never bother to work out those differences. Maybe they don't even know each other's attitudes toward money because they've never discussed it.

If you're planning to marry, it's absolutely necessary that you and your intended sit down and carefully and thoroughly discuss how you'll handle your finances after the wedding. You should establish some goals to work toward together and make sure you know about each other's debts, spending patterns, and investments.

You'll need to decide how you'll set up your bank accounts as a married couple. It's not necessary to have joint accounts, although most married couples have at least some of their money pooled. Some couples, especially when both people are earning, keep separate accounts, while also establishing joint accounts. Separate accounts give individuals freedom and independence, while joint accounts offer the convenience of allowing either spouse to sign a check. This is a decision that you and your partner need to discuss and figure out. Do whatever you agree will work best for the two of you.

> **CAUTION**
>
> ### Money Pit _____
>
> Love might be blind, but your understanding of your partner's financial situation shouldn't be. You'll be in for an unpleasant surprise if you find out your new husband owes $10,000 for something you know nothing about. If one of you does have a lot of debt or other financial problems, discuss those problems and reach an agreement before the wedding as to how you're going to handle them.

Earlier in this book we discussed financial personalities and attitudes toward saving and spending money. While contemplating marriage, be sure to consider the financial personality of your spouse-to-be. If you scrimp to be able to save 20 percent of every paycheck and your partner hasn't saved a dime during the eight years he or she has been working, you clearly have different attitudes about money. Learn your partner's attitudes concerning savings and the best means for savings. Do you have 401(k) plans? Any stocks? What about savings bonds you got as gifts when you were a kid? Talk about saving to buy a house. What about saving for kids?

Talk about whether you'll operate within a budget and together plan the budget you'll use. You don't want the stresses of adjusting to married life to be aggravated by a misunderstanding of how you'll be handling your finances. Get as many financial considerations as possible ironed out before the wedding to avoid conflicts afterward.

You should also discuss the following financial issues:

◆ How will your marriage affect your employer benefits? If one of you has a much better package than the other, make sure you both are covered by the better deal. Consider health benefits, retirement savings plans, and anything else that might affect your financial situation. Check to see whether either employer offers compensation to an employee who gives up benefits to be covered by the partner's plan.

◆ Figure out how much life and disability insurance you need. It costs more for two people to live than for one person. If your partner dies, can you continue your lifestyle on your own earnings? Or if your partner becomes disabled and can't work, can you both live on one income? If not, make sure you have sufficient life and disability insurance. If you already have life and disability insurance, rename the beneficiary if it's not already your spouse.

◆ Start an emergency fund if you don't already have one. When you're footloose and fancy-free, you're the only one you have to worry about. Now you have the additional responsibility of another person. You should start saving whatever you can to get three to six months' worth of living expenses in case of an emergency.

◆ Make or update your wills. If you don't already have wills, now is a great time to get them. If you do have them, they'll need to be updated. Contact your local Bar Association and ask for the name of a lawyer who will be able to prepare a will. Will kits are a nice way to obtain information, but any will completed through a will kit should be reviewed by an attorney. Note that in many states, a will is considered invalid if a marriage has taken place after the will was signed. You want to have your assets distributed per your wishes, not by the state.

Uh, Could You Sign Here, Please?

Prenuptial agreements—those handy little plans that spell out how assets will be divided in the event that the marriage fails—used to be primarily for Hollywood types who had tons of money but little staying power when it came to marriage. It's pretty clear that with about 1.2 million couples getting divorced each year that many of us average Joes have lost our staying power as well.

Show Me the Money

A **prenuptial agreement** is a legal document that protects your financial interests. The average estimated cost of a prenuptial agreement ranges from $1,500 to $3,000, depending on the complexity and the amount of assets to be considered.

Even if you don't have tons of money, some matrimonial lawyers and financial advisors strongly recommend prenuptial agreements, especially if one person has a child or children from a previous marriage or relationship. A prenuptial agreement also might make sense if one partner owns a business or makes a lot more money than the other. Such an agreement could also be important if one partner has major assets independently and doesn't want to risk losing them.

> **Pocket Change**
>
> It's not surprising that you now can get a prenuptial agreement on the Internet. One such site is LegalZoom, an online legal document provider. For $119, you can fill out a standard prenuptial agreement, have it checked over by a LegalZoom document reviewer, and have it sent to you via e-mail or regular mail.

Whether or not to have a prenuptial agreement is something you and your intended will have to decide together. If you can't agree on the need for one, or if you feel your partner is pressuring you to have one and you don't want it, it might be a good idea to get some financial or relationship counseling before the wedding. It might just be a matter of not fully understanding the other's concerns or wishes.

Goin' to the Chapel and We're Gonna Get Married

Once you decide to get married, you can kiss your free time good-bye. There's just so much to do. You need to make the official announcement, pick a date, and start making wedding plans. You've got to arrange for time off from work for your honeymoon, think about where you'll live, and pick out your wedding dress and tux.

As busy as you'll be, however, you've got to spend some time doing some serious thinking about your personal finances and how the wedding and marriage will affect them. A wedding can be unbelievably expensive (almost enough to make you want to elope!), and you'll be spending money on a lot of other things such as an engagement ring and honeymoon. Let's take a look at some of the expenses you might be faced with.

With This Ring

One of the very first expenses involved with getting married is buying an engagement ring. Of course, a ring is not required, but it's traditional and quite important to many couples. Just remember that it's not a smart move to buy a ring that you simply can't afford. An engagement ring should be a symbol of your love and commitment, not a statement of your financial situation. You'll have plenty of occasions to upgrade your ring after you're married.

If your girlfriend doesn't already know that you think she's the greatest, she probably won't want to marry you anyway. Don't let a jeweler talk you into buying a ring you can't afford.

> **Pocket Change**
>
> A recent survey by *Bride's Magazine* showed the average amount spent on an engagement ring is $3,044.

Ouch! Here Comes the Bill

Traditionally, most wedding expenses were paid for by the bride's parents. But times have changed, and the way we pay for weddings has changed as well. Nowadays, the bride and groom might pay for the entire wedding, the two families might split expenses, or each family may pay for the number of guests it invites.

Regardless of who is footing the bill, the first important thing to do when planning your wedding is to establish how much you can spend. This will require talking to everyone who might be contributing and finding out how much you'll have. If you learn that you'll have $25,000—great! Go ahead and throw yourself a bash. If you find out you have $7,500, then you'll need to scale down and work within those parameters. You can find some good tips on saving on wedding costs at About.com. It's on the web at htt://weddings.about.com.

> **Pocket Change**
>
> *Bride's Magazine* reports that the average cost of a wedding for 200 guests and five attendants is $19,104.

The budget for every wedding is different, because every wedding is different. This worksheet, however, gives you an idea of the way the average wedding budget breaks down, by listing the percentage for the total budget as it normally is allocated. Use these percentages as a guide to plan your wedding, so that you can stay within your budget.

Grab your calculator and you'll get an idea of how much money you'll have to spend for each cost area.

Total wedding budget $_____

Area	Estimated Cost	Actual Cost
Stationery items (3%)	$ _____	$ _____
Bridal attire (10%)	$ _____	$ _____
Reception (40%)	$ _____	$ _____
Flowers (8%)	$ _____	$ _____
Music (3%)	$ _____	$ _____
Photography (7%)	$ _____	$ _____
Gifts—attendants (2%)	$ _____	$ _____
Honeymoon (20%)	$ _____	$ _____
Misc. (e.g., special parties) (7%)	$ _____	$ _____
Total	$ _____	$ _____

Obviously, these percentages will vary, as you customize your own wedding. Be sure you keep track of all your wedding expenses by saving all receipts and filing them in a safe place.

Filing Jointly or Separately?

Have you ever heard of the marriage penalty? That term is used to refer to the traditional inequity for married couples who file joint income tax returns. It used to be that the deduction a married couple took didn't even come close to adding up to the total of the deductions of two people filing separately. However, the income tax revisions of 2003 lowered this burden somewhat.

As single people filing income tax returns, each of you was eligible for a $4,850 personal deduction. If you decide to file a joint return after you're married, your deduction will now be double that amount—$9,700. That's a lot better than it used to be, when the married deduction fell about $2,000 less than the total of two single deductions. As mentioned in Chapter 14, however, the break for married couples filing jointly is only a temporary measure.

And Then There Were Three

Life happens, and kids very often are a part of life. And, while they can be the best thing to ever happen to you, the little darlings are expensive. Very expensive. If you have a child or two, are thinking of having a child, or are expecting a child soon, there are some financial implications you need to consider.

How a Baby Affects Your Life

No one can tell you exactly how having a baby will affect your life. Suffice it to say, however, that your life will never be the same. Your sleeping schedule will change. Your relationship with your spouse will change. Your financial situation will change. Your expectations, hopes, and dreams will change. And, if you're lucky, you'll experience a profound, life-changing love for your baby.

How a Baby Affects Your Pocketbook

The first financial factor to consider when thinking about having a baby is the income you may lose due to time off during pregnancy and after the baby is born. If your employer doesn't offer paid maternity (or paternity) leave, check at work to see if you're covered by short-term disability insurance, which might cover you for time off due to pregnancy and childbirth. If short-term disability won't kick in, you could take time off under the Family Medical Leave Act, but your employer doesn't have to pay you when you're gone.

The next financial hurdles to clear are the medical bills for the pregnancy and birth. Check the provisions of your health insurance policy to find out exactly what pregnancy and childbirth expenses will be covered, and which you might have to pay for yourself. Don't forget to consider any deductibles or co-pays you might be responsible for. If you have to pick up some, or even all of the cost, most hospitals and birthing centers will work with you on setting up a payment plan.

Not only are babies expensive to birth, they're expensive after they arrive in the world. A crib, stroller, high chair, baby swing, car seats, mobiles, sheets, diapers, lotions ... the list goes on and on, and there's more baby gear being invented by the minute.

> **Dollars and Sense**
>
> If you've decided to go the adoption route, expect to encounter a variety of expenses. Statistics show it can cost between $8,000 and $30,000 or even more to adopt an infant. For more information on the cost of adoption, check out www.adopting.org/cost.

While you definitely need furniture and equipment that is safe and durable, you don't need the Ralph Lauren baby sheet and comforter ensemble available for $125 at Nordstrom. Your baby will sleep just as soundly on the $14.99 version from J. C. Penney. Also, don't overlook your local consignment shop for baby equipment. There is a lot of barely used gear around—babies grow fast.

Dollars and Sense

Childcare expenses can be deducted when you file your income tax, but only if the provider is licensed. You need to report the provider's Social Security or tax-payer identification number to the IRS if you want to take the deduction.

As you probably know, childcare is expensive. If you're planning to go back to work after your baby is born, you'll need to carefully consider your options for finding someone to watch Junior. Unless you're lucky enough to have Grandma to watch the baby, you can plan on spending some serious dollars for good childcare. Don't wait until you're ready to go back to work to begin looking for reputable, reliable childcare.

The Least You Need to Know

- Your financial situation will be significantly affected by your life circumstances.

- Living single and bringing in a paycheck is a great time to save, but it's also a tempting time during which to spend.

- Living together without being married can affect your finances. Consider these effects before making a commitment.

- Getting married might involve changes to your taxes, insurance, bank accounts, and will.

- Everyone wants a great wedding, but you need to be sure you work within your budget.

- A baby is an expensive proposition, but there are ways to keep expenses under control.

Chapter 18

Not Your Father's Pension Plan: Retirement Funds in the Modern World

In This Chapter

◆ Why retirement savings are so important

◆ Knowing what kinds of plans are available

◆ Setting up a plan if you're self-employed

◆ Allocating your money inside a retirement account

◆ Penalties and regulations concerning early withdrawal

When *Money* magazine asked retirees what their biggest financial mistake had been, most of them said it was waiting too long to start saving for retirement. Gen Xers, who say they have little faith in the Social Security system, appear to be starting to save earlier than boomers did. A 2003 survey by Allstate Corp., in fact, showed that 71 percent of Gen Xers questioned reported that they are saving for retirement. Still, many people in all age categories aren't saving enough or saving at all.

Is Retirement Planning Your Top Priority? It Should Be.

It used to be that most people who worked had pensions that were provided by their employers. Between their pension checks and Social Security payments, retirees had enough money to live comfortably. Times have changed, though, and pensions are, for the most part, a thing of the past. In addition, the Social Security system is targeted for restructuring, and there have long been questions about the certainty of its future. To compound the problem, people are retiring earlier today than they used to, meaning they'll need to have more money saved to keep them going.

Studies show that most people will require about three fourths as much money to maintain their standard of living during retirement as they required before retiring. Of course, all kinds of factors go into that estimate (with the increase in prescription drug costs and Medicare supplement insurance premiums increasing at a rate much greater than inflation, this number may increase in the years ahead), and remember that it's an average. At this point, there is no way to know what your retirement years will bring. You can't know what your health will be like in 40 years or what other circumstances will be affecting your life.

Remember these two important facts about saving for retirement:

1. The earlier you start, the easier it is to accumulate all the money you'll need.

2. Little savings can add up over the years to make big savings.

If you find it hard to believe that a couple of years makes a big difference in what you'll be able to save, take a look at this example: If you invest $5,000 when you're 25 at an annual rate of return of 6 percent and let it sit until you're 60, you'll have $38,430. But if you wait until you're 35 to invest $5,000 at the same rate of return, you'll have only $21,459 when you turn 60. If you wait until you're 45 to invest the money, you'll have only $11,983.

The following sections discuss examples of how starting early is advantageous to your retirement's good health.

It Pays to Start Early

The following chart compares the profiles of two people who invest in diversified portfolios. The original investment made by Employee A was at age 21. Employee B didn't make his first contribution until he was 30. The results assume a 10 percent compound rate of return with a new $2,000 investment being made on January 2 of each year. Results are as of December 31 of each year.

	EMPLOYEE A	EMPLOYEE B
	Begins at age 21.	Begins at age 30.
	Invests $2,000 each year until he or she is 29, and does not put any more money in after that.	Invests $2,000 each year, and continues to do so until he or she is 65 years old.
	Total contributions made over 9 years: $18,000	Total contributions made over 35 years: $70,000
Age	EMPLOYEE A	EMPLOYEE B
22	$ 2,200	$ 0
27	16,974	0
32	36,146	4,620
36	58,210	16,970
41	93,746	40,766
46	150,977	79,083
51	243,147	140,794
56	391,587	240,179
61	630,652	400,238
65	839,396	658,015

As you can see, it makes more sense, and is, in the long run, much easier on your pocketbook, to start saving money as early as possible. Retirement seems eons away when you first start working, but the years pass by quickly and you'll have other financial commitments along the way.

Little Savings Can Mean a Lot

If you can't imagine that saving a couple of dollars here and there will make a difference, consider these fun facts from Fidelity Investments. The amounts are based on saving for 30 years at 9 percent interest:

◆ If you save $300 a year by exercising at home instead of joining a gym, you'll have $44,572.

◆ If you save $35 a month by collecting all your change, you'll have $64,557.

While many people aren't saving at all, or aren't saving enough for retirement, the increasing popularity of 401(k)s is improving the situation somewhat. Still, studies show that many people who have the opportunity to contribute to an employer-sponsored retirement plan such as a 401(k) do not take advantage of it.

Unfortunately, the IRS limits how much you can contribute annually to your 401(k) plan, although these limits are increasing and will continue to increase in the next several years. The 2004 limit is $13,000, increasing to $14,000 in 2005, and then increasing to $15,000 for years 2006 and after. Some employers also limit the amount of money you can contribute to the plan. Be sure you know if yours does.

The question is, then, if you have money to invest somewhere else, either instead of a 401(k) or in addition to your 401(k), where should you put it? The answer is that you should look at other retirement funds in which to invest your earnings. Why? Because of the tax advantages.

Pocket Change

Some experts say that questions concerning the future of the Social Security program and the proliferation of 401(k) plans are causing more and more Generation Xers to start saving. We say, "Whatever it takes!"

What's Out There?

In most cases, investing in retirement accounts is simpler than investing outside of retirement accounts. It tends to be less overwhelming because there are fewer options for investing, and you don't have to worry about tax factors because your investments aren't taxed until you make withdrawals from the accounts. 401(k)s are particularly easy because your employer does most of the work for you. But this chapter is about retirement funds other than 401(k)s, so let's have a look at what else is available.

Individual Retirement Accounts (IRAs)

As of the beginning of 2005, anybody who makes any money working can contribute up to $4,000 a year in an *individual retirement account* (IRA). An IRA is a tax-deferred type of retirement savings plan, meaning you don't pay taxes until you withdraw from the fund. Of course, this money can only be contributed if you work. If you make $4,000 a year mowing lawns and shoveling snow, but never report a penny of it, those earnings don't make you eligible to contribute to an IRA (they could, however, get you in trouble with the IRS). Currently, if you earn less than $4,000 a year, the maximum amount you can contribute is the amount you've earned. If you earn $1,650 scooping ice cream at Ben & Jerry's, for instance, that's the amount you can stash in an IRA. However, as of 2005, if you're married, but not working, your spouse can contribute up to $4,000 a year for you, or $8,000 total for the family.

IRAs used to be the hotshot investment vehicles. Things changed, though, when lawmakers got cranky and dumped all kinds of restrictions onto them in 1986. Back in the good old days, anybody could deduct his or her IRA contributions. Now the money you contribute might be tax deductible, but it might not be. Here's how it breaks down:

If you're single and do not have an employer-sponsored retirement plan, you can put up to $3,000 a year in an IRA. Under the recent income-tax revision, the $3,000 contribution limit of 2004 increases in stages until it reaches $5,000 for years 2008 and after. The full contribution is a dollar-for-dollar deduction from your taxable income on your income tax return.

The incremental increases are as follows:

Under Age 50	Over Age 50
2004: $3,000	2004: $3,500
2005-2007: $4,000	2005: $4,500; 2006-07: $5,000
2008 and beyond: $5,000	2008 and beyond: $6,000

Show Me the Money

An **Individual Retirement Account** is a retirement savings plan in which you can contribute up to $3,000 per year in 2004. This limit increases in stages until it reaches $5,000 for years 2008 and after. Funds can grow tax deferred until withdrawn at retirement. A **Roth IRA** varies from the traditional one in that the money you put in it is taxable, but the withdrawals are not. Roth IRAs are increasing in popularity.

After 2008, the limit will increase in increments of $500 annually to keep pace with inflation.

 ◆ If you're single, covered by an employer-sponsored plan, and your annual adjusted gross income is $44,999 or less in 2004, you can contribute up to $3,000 to your IRA and deduct the full amount. If your income is between $45,000 ($65,000 for joint filers) and $54,999 ($75,000 for joint filers), the deduction is pro-rated. If you make more than $55,000 a year, you can contribute, but you get no deduction. These cut-off numbers will gradually increase to $50,000 (take the full deduction) to $60,000 (take no deduction) by the year 2005.

> **Pocket Change**
>
> A person who has no income, but receives alimony, also is eligible to contribute to an IRA.

- If you're married and file jointly, have an employer-sponsored plan, and your annual adjusted gross income is $64,999 or less (thanks again, Uncle Sam), you can deduct the full amount. The figure is pro-rated from $65,000 to $74,999. After $75,000, you can't take any deduction.

- For workers over age 50, the 2001 tax bill provides a "catch-up" provision for those contributing to an IRA. In 2005, workers who are over age 50 can contribute an extra $500 (for a total of $4,500) to an IRA. The "catch-up" increases to $1,000 for 2006, 2007, and 2008 so that workers can contribute a total of $5,000 in 2006 and 2007 and then $6,000 in 2008.

- If your spouse doesn't have a retirement plan at work and you file a joint tax return, the spouse can deduct his or her full $3,000 contribution until your joint income reaches $160,000. After that, the deduction is pro-rated until your joint income is $180,000, at which time you can't deduct the IRA contribution.

> **Show Me the Money**
>
> A **tax-deferred** investment is one on which you'll pay no tax on income or gain until you withdraw the money. A **tax-deductible** investment is one that reduces the amount of your current taxable income.

Even if you can't deduct the contributions, they still help out with taxes because they're *tax deferred*. It's not as great as *tax deductible*, but it's the next best thing. IRAs are good savings vehicles, but if your IRA contributions aren't deductible, make sure you take advantage of the programs on which you can get a tax deduction, such as 401(k)s, first.

The Importance of Timing Your IRA Contributions

Most people start thinking about funding their IRAs when they meet with their accountants in April. While funding an IRA at that time of year is better than never, you should know that the earlier you stash some money in your IRA, the better.

If you fund an IRA in January or February, the funds begin to work, tax deferred, with gains starting immediately and accumulating for the entire year. You get twelve, maybe fifteen months of deferral by funding your IRA in January, rather than waiting until it's time to file your tax return. If it's not financially feasible to fund your IRA all at once, you might consider contributing some money each month, beginning in January.

Roth IRAs

This variation on your basic IRA has been popular since it was introduced in 1998. The *Roth IRA* is different from the traditional one in several ways, and many financial experts agree that it is better than the traditional IRA for people with the right circumstances.

For starters, your contribution to a Roth IRA is after-tax money, as opposed to the traditional IRA, in which your contribution is pre-tax money. Huh? Okay, when you contribute to a regular, deductible IRA, you put in $3,000 (or whatever) before you pay tax on that money. When you take your contributions and your earnings out at retirement, you have to pay taxes on that money. With a Roth IRA, your $3,000 contribution comes out of income you've already paid taxes on (that is, earnings). The funds contributed accumulate tax free, and if held for five years, you never pay tax on the money withdrawn. Yep, you heard it. If you follow the rules and hold the funds within the Roth for five years, you never have to pay tax on the account again. That means you get all the earnings on that $2,000, or $3,000 or $4,000 or $5,000 tax-free, which is a very appealing feature of the Roth. Contributions to a Roth IRA, however, are not tax deductible.

The new contribution limits for Roth IRAs are the same as for traditional IRAs (as stated above). So, by 2008 you could contribute $5,000 to a Roth IRA if your income is less than $110,000 (if you are single; $160,000 if you are married filing jointly).

Show Me the Money

A **Roth IRA** is an IRA in which the funds placed into the account are nondeductible. If held more than five years, the original funds withdrawn are received tax free, but the earnings are subject to a penalty if withdrawn before age 59.5.

Show Me the Money

There's also an IRA called an **educational IRA**. As the name implies, it's set up especially to fund education expenses.

> **Dollars and Sense** _____
>
> If you still have a traditional IRA instead of a Roth, you might want to consider switching it. You can do this if your income (single) is under $110,000. You'll be taxed on the money you're converting, but advisors say that you're still better off to move it, especially if you're under 50 years old. If you don't understand the implications, it would be a good idea to check with a financial advisor.

You can get your Roth money without penalty any time after you reach 59.5 years of age, but you're not required to take it out when you reach 70.5 as you are with traditional IRAs. You can just let that money sit there if you want to, continuing to grow, tax-free. You can even leave the money and *all* the earnings there to pass on, tax-free, to your heirs.

There are income limits to Roths, though. If your income is more than $110,000 and you're single, you can't get a Roth IRA. If you and your spouse have a combined income of more than $160,000, then you're not eligible for a Roth IRA.

Doing It on Your Own

Many Generation Xers are self-employed or working on a contract basis as free-lancers. If you're self-employed or have started your own business, you still need to think about saving for retirement. The good news is, you can set up a retirement plan that works for you, in your particular situation. The bad news is, you can set up a retirement plan that works for you, in your particular situation.

It really is both good and bad news. If done properly, designing your own retirement plan will give you exactly what you need. But it's going to take some careful consideration and a fair amount of work to figure out what you need and how to get it going.

SEP-IRAs

SEP-IRAs, which stands for Simplified Employee Pension Individual Retirement Accounts (talk about a mouthful!), are not very complicated and are a great deal for a person who's self-employed or owns a business with only a few employees. SEP-IRAs are designed for people who are self-employed or are owners of small companies who want to add more funds to a retirement account than they can with a traditional IRA. As with other types of IRAs, the interest you make in a SEP-IRA is not taxed until you take the money out.

If you work for yourself, you can contribute up to about 13.04 percent of your income, or up to $41,000, into a SEP-IRA every year. The money you contribute is deducted from your taxable income, so your contribution can save you a lot on federal and, depending on where you live, state taxes. You can open and contribute to a SEP-IRA up until the day of your tax-filing deadline.

SEP-IRAs are advantageous for people who need to save on their own. They might sound intimidating, but you can have a SEP-IRA anywhere you could have a regular IRA. It just requires a little paperwork. Ask your tax preparer or financial consultant about changing your IRA to a SEP-IRA.

> **Show Me the Money**
>
> A **SEP-IRA** is a retirement plan for self-employed persons or small company employers, in which contributions of up to $41,000 a year are permitted. A **Keogh** is a federally approved retirement program that enables self-employed workers to set aside up to $30,000, or 25 percent of their income.

Keoghs

Keoghs are another retirement plan for the small business owner. There are different types of Keoghs, and they can be tricky to set up because there's a lot of paperwork involved. It's a good idea to get a professional to help you with it. (See Chapter 21 for more information about finding the right financial person to help you.) Keogh plans must be set up by the end of the year, with contributions made by the tax-filing deadline, including exclusions. For Keogh purposes, the owner is considered an employer.

Keoghs have previously been the plans most frequently used by employers who have several employees. Recently, something called SIMPLE plans have been gaining in popularity for smaller companies, but they allow only $9,000 a year, per employee. That amount, however, is set to increase to $10,000 by 2005. Every employer should look at the advantages and disadvantages of various plans and decide what is best. For practicality purposes, you need at least 20–25 employees to efficiently offer a 401(k) plan—although there isn't any limitation by law. But even an employer with just one employee can set up a Keogh plan.

If you have your own business and have people working for you, you're required to provide coverage for your employees if you provide coverage for yourself. If you don't, you can be penalized by the IRS, which might even make your own prior contributions invalid. But don't put off starting a fund for yourself because you don't want to have to have one for employees. Some employees, such as part-timers and those who haven't worked for you long enough, can be excluded from the plans. All qualified employees, though, must be provided with plans that enable them to contribute a percentage of their income.

Simple IRA

Another IRA option for those who own or work for a small company may be a Simple IRA, which stands for Savings Incentive Match Plan for Employees. It's a traditional IRA set up by a person who owns a small company for the company's employees. The employee contributes, and the employer can make a matching contribution, based on a percentage of the employee's salary.

The maximum contribution an employee can make in 2004 is $9,000, but it's set to increase to $10,000 in 2005. After 2006, the limit will increase by $500 whenever inflation makes the raise necessary.

Simple IRAs are gaining in popularity, partly because the contribution limits are increasing, and partly because, as the name implies, they're simple to set up and implement.

Annuities

Annuities are a little confusing, and many financial advisors will advise you to look into other types of retirement investment vehicles first. Like nondeductible IRAs, annuities are tax-deferred investments, not tax-deductible. Because annuities are not tax-deductible contributions, you should consider them only if you have money to invest after investing in employee-sponsored plans or tax-deductible IRAs. Unlike IRAs, there's no limit to what you can contribute to annuities. You can plunk down $2,000, $5,000, or $100,000—the sky's the limit.

Show Me the Money

Annuities are tax-deferred investments that may offer, at retirement, a stream of equal payments at predetermined intervals.

Annuities are akin to life insurance in that if you stash your money in them and die before you get it out, your beneficiary (the person who receives your benefits) may be guaranteed to get your original investment. Annuities are contracts that are backed by insurance companies, so the similarities of annuities and life insurance policies make a little bit of sense. They can supplement IRAs when you reach retirement because you're not required to withdraw (and pay tax on) your money at age 70.5, as you are with IRAs. When you retire, you can leave your annuities alone while you use the money from your IRAs.

There are two kinds of annuities: fixed and variable. A *fixed annuity* is comparable to a certificate of deposit in that you receive a set interest rate on your investment over a set period of time. After that, the interest rate changes, based on the contract guidelines and an underlying fixed-income security. A *variable annuity* is invested in a series of mutual funds, similar to the funds within a 401(k). You can choose the funds in which you want to invest.

So Where Should My Retirement Money Go?

Once you decide on the type of retirement account you're going to use, you still have work to do. You need to decide where, within that account, you want your money to go.

If your money is in a retirement savings plan sponsored by your employer, then she'll provide the investment options for you. All you have to do is choose from the list. Most financial experts advise dividing your money between some of the stocks and bonds included in the options. How you invest depends on your risk tolerance and time horizon.

Try using this investment guideline: To find out what percentage of your portfolio should be invested in stocks, subtract your age from 100. If you're 25, for instance, about 75 percent of your investments should be stocks. That's because you have time to ride out a rough market if that should occur. Once you decide to invest in stocks, you need to choose what kinds of stocks. Chapter 20 handles that issue.

If your retirement fund is not set up by your employer, then you get to choose where your money goes. You can work with a reputable investment company, such as Vanguard or T. Rowe Price, which will assist you in applying for accounts and advise you in allocating your money in a manner that makes sense for you.

> **Pocket Change**
>
> There are lots of investment companies, but Vanguard, T. Rowe Price, and Fidelity are three of the most respected and well known. You can contact Vanguard by calling 1-800-662-7447 or online at www.vanguard.com. You can reach Fidelity at 1-800-544-8666 or at their website at www.fidelity. com, and T. Rowe Price at 1-800-922-9945 or www.troweprice.com.

An important thing to remember when you're trying to figure out this retirement account business is that you don't have to do it by yourself. If your plan is set up through your employer, there may be someone in the benefits office who can help you. Or you can ask advice from an investment company. Don't allow confusion or fear to make you give up on your retirement fund.

Early Withdrawal Penalties

Retirement savings plans have one major drawback. Once your money is in one, you normally can't get it out before you retire without paying a penalty. Requirements vary on different types of plans. For instance, as we told you in Chapter 13, there are penalties for taking money out of your 401(k) before you're 59.5 years old. The money you take out will be taxable and, in addition, you'll be charged a 10 percent penalty. But your employer might have a program where you can borrow from your 401(k) and pay back the money to your account. There's also something called a hardship withdrawal that applies to 401(k)s, but strict rules apply, and it has to be a genuine hardship, such as a serious illness.

With a traditional IRA, you must start withdrawing your money between the ages of 59.5 and 70.5 to avoid penalties—or, more precisely, before April 1st of the year following the one in which you turn 70.5 years old. You'll have to decide on a distribution schedule, which usually is based on your life expectancy. If you have a Roth IRA, you can tap into your principal after having the account for five years, and you don't have to start taking your money out of the account at any certain age.

With a nonqualified (post-tax) annuity, you don't have to begin withdrawing money at age 70.5. But if you try to get your money before you're 59.5, you'll get slapped with a 10 percent penalty on the interest you've earned from the IRS.

All these requirements, rules, and regulations concerning retirement savings plans are enough to cool anybody's enthusiasm for participation. Still, you have to look past the confusion and the red tape to the idea behind the plans. If you don't save now, you won't have anything later. It's that simple. But if you start saving now, when you have a lot of years to do so, you'll be able to plan for all those fun things you want to do when you retire at age 59.5.

The Least You Need to Know

◆ Most people don't start saving the money they'll need for retirement until it's too late, and many don't save at all.

◆ Various types of retirement savings plans are available, and they all have advantages and disadvantages.

◆ Always consider using a plan that is tax deductible first, and then go to one that is tax deferred.

◆ If you're self-employed, you can still set up a retirement plan.

◆ After you choose a retirement plan, you have to allocate your money within the plan.

◆ Make sure you understand the rules and penalties that apply to taking your money out of the plan early.

Chapter 19

Investing Beyond Retirement Accounts

In This Chapter

- ◆ When to start investing
- ◆ Figuring out what you're investing for
- ◆ Determining whether you're a high-risk, moderate, or conservative investor
- ◆ How investments can affect your taxes
- ◆ How to start investing
- ◆ Where to learn about investing

Investing money in the stock or bond market is incredibly exciting for some people and incredibly daunting for others. Regardless of how you feel about investing, it's an important part of your personal finances, and it won't become less important if you stick your head in the sand and ignore it. Even in times like this, with the market having its good days and its bad days, most experts say that long-term investment in the stock market is the surest way there is to make your money grow over time. For that reason, this chapter is important, because it will get you started toward wise investments—both now and in the future.

When Is the Best Time to Start Investing?

Before you move on, let's just make sure you understand that it's important to take care of basic business first. Before you even think about investing money, you need to be certain you're not carrying a lot of credit card debt and you're not behind on other expenses and bills. You also will need to have established an emergency fund and started saving for your retirement. Talk about what kind of investor you expect that you'll be.

What Are You Investing For?

Before you begin the investment process, you should sit down and identify just what it is you're investing for. Is it your first house? A beach house in 15 or 20 years? College money for your kids? Additional funds for your retirement years? Each investor has different goals that need to be considered before the investment process begins. If you're investing in hopes of sending your child off to Princeton in five years, for example, you'll probably invest differently than you would for your retirement 30 years down the road. What you're investing for should largely determine the type of investments you make.

"Investing" for the down payment of your house is not really investing, unless it's going to be a while before you'll be ready to make a down payment. If you're going to be staying in an apartment for a while, but you know that someday you want your own house, or maybe you've got grad school to finish first or need to advance in your job, then investing to earn a down payment is a good plan. In many cases, however, there's not enough time for investments to grow significantly enough to provide a down payment for a first home.

Emergency funds are short-term investments and shouldn't be placed in accounts that will be difficult to access in the event that you need the money. Accumulating money for your emergency fund, or a vehicle or home isn't really investing, it's really a form of saving. Once those things are taken care of, though, and you have some money you won't need any time in the near future, then it's time to begin investing.

What Kind of Investor Do You Want to Be?

Not all investors are created equally. Some are the aggressive, make-me-rich-quick kinds, who want to make a killing on their investments. They rarely do, or at least not for long, mind you, but they're sure willing to give it a try. This type of investor is the person at the amusement park who has to go on every roller coaster twice, except for the really big one that loops upside down. He has to go on that one three times.

Other investors are the middle-of-the-road kind. They want something that will be kind of exciting, but nothing too dangerous. They'll risk the tilt-a-whirl at the amusement park, but say "no, thanks" to the roller coasters.

Then there are those investors who just want a nice, safe place to put their money. They don't expect to get rich from their investments, but they want to feel confident that their money will do okay in them and the investments will provide some security down the road. These are the people at the park who love the carousel and think that the Ferris wheel is about as much excitement as there should be in life.

The following risk pyramid shows various investments and how the industry rates their risk of principal loss:

Each of these categories has risks and rewards. Let's have a look.

High-Risk Investors

People can be high-risk investors by choice, or as in most cases, they can be high-risk investors because they don't know enough about what they're doing. A high-risk investor is generally classified as someone who can live with losing about a quarter of his or her *investment portfolio* in a year.

An investment portfolio is the listing and value of all your investments. If you have $10,000 to invest, and the thought of losing $2,500 doesn't give you chills, you might qualify as high-risk. But even if you're a high-risk investor, you still have to do your homework and find out where your money has the best chance of earning you more. There's a big difference between high-risk and just plain stupid.

Show Me the Money

Your **investment portfolio** is the listing and value of all your investments.

Suppose an investor chooses to be high-risk. He jumps into the stock market and buys only investments with potential for very high returns. He got a hot tip from a buddy of his that a certain industry is about to take off, so he loads most of his money into that industry's stock. Even if this guy knows what he's doing, he's a daredevil. But if he's making high-risk investments because he hasn't done his homework and doesn't understand the importance of diversification or that his money should be spread around, he's risking catastrophe; he's speculating.

Speculating, like gambling, is taking chances and rolling the dice to try to make a killing in the market quickly. Getting a hot tip at a cocktail party and acting on it by putting down $5,000 is speculating. Investing is buying 100 shares of Microsoft stock after you've investigated exactly what the company does, the fundamentals (explained later in the chapter), and the company's outlook for the future.

Moderate-Risk Investors

If you're a moderate-risk investor, you won't bet the farm on a tip you overhear while you're getting your hair cut or sitting in the sauna at the health club. You're generally classified as a moderate-risk investor if you figure you can stand to lose up to 15 percent of that $10,000 in your portfolio. The thought of being out $1,500 doesn't make you jump up and down, but it won't keep you up every night either.

Conservative Investors

Conservative investors are the meat-and-potatoes people of the investment world. Keep your fancy appetizers, your cream sauces, and your puff pastry desserts. Just give these folks something they can depend on, something that won't give them any surprises, and something they don't have to worry about. They don't want to take any chances with their investments and will gladly give up even the possibility of high returns to know that their money will be there when they want it.

Conservative investors generally start having nightmares at the thought of losing even 5 or 6 percent of their portfolios over a year's time. The thought of losing $600 of that $10,000 investment sets their hair on end.

Your Timetable Is Important, Too

After you've figured out your investing personality, you need to think about your timetable. How long do you want to leave your money invested? One year? Three years? Ten years?

Your timetable has a lot to do with the way you should invest. Traditionally, investments with the potential for higher return are more likely to go up and down in value. That means you should be prepared to leave your money in those investments over a longer period of time. They're not short-term investments because you can't count on them being where you want them to be when you're ready to take your money out.

If, for instance, you're investing money that you want to use for your wedding the next year, you shouldn't buy volatile stocks that could go anywhere during the next 12 months. You'd want something safe that would allow your money to grow but wouldn't risk your principal. On the other hand, if you've just had a baby and want to put some money away for college, you know you have 18 years. That gives you a much better opportunity to ride out some storms and take advantage of the potential for high returns. As you can see, there are many variables when it comes to investments and investors.

Show Me the Money

If you're investing money that you'll need within two years or less, you're generally considered a **short-term investor**. Investing your money for two to seven years puts you in the **mid-term** range. If you won't need your money for more than seven years, you're considered a **long-range investor**.

One thing, however, is constant. Regardless of the type of investor you think you are, you need to know what you're doing. If you depend on an investment advisor to lead you by the nose through the world of stocks, bonds, and mutual funds, you'll never be in control of your financial situation. We're not suggesting that you'll never need help with investing or in other areas of your personal finance, but to hand all the responsibility over to someone else is to relinquish your control. Presumably, you've worked pretty hard to earn your money. Why would you let somebody else climb into the driver's seat and take off with it?

There are tons of good books on investing, and lots of other information is available, too. We'll list a bunch of resources later in the chapter; Appendix A of this book lists even more, so check it out.

You Can't Tax That! Can You?

We've already sung the praises of retirement accounts and the tax advantages they offer, and we hope we've sufficiently stressed that you should invest in any applicable retirement accounts before looking elsewhere. When you get into other types of investments, and you start earning on those investments, be prepared to pay taxes on your earnings.

To figure out how your investments will affect your tax situation, take a look at how much interest, or yield, you'll get from each investment. You must know your tax bracket, too (review Chapter 14 if necessary).

Say you're in the 25 percent marginal tax bracket in 2004. To refresh your memory, you're taxed at that rate if you make $29,050 to $70,350 as a single, or $58,100 to $117,250 if you're married and filing jointly. If you're keeping $5,000 in a money-market account that's earning 2 percent interest, you're earning only $100 a year on that money. This is the before-tax return on your investment. To add insult to injury, Uncle Sam takes 25 percent of your earnings ($25 in federal tax) leaving you with only $75 to spend. This is known as the after-tax return on an investment, and is your actual return. It's imperative that you're cognizant of the before- and after-tax returns of all your investments. Your $5,000 would be better invested in a tax-free money-market fund (a money-market fund for which income is not subject to income tax liability).

On the other hand, if somebody in the 15 percent tax bracket ($7,150 or less for a single earner) puts $5,000 in a tax-free money market with a .75 percent yield, he'll be earning $37.50 a year, tax-free. But if he put the $5,000 in a taxable account with a 2 percent yield, he'd earn $100 a year, less 15 percent tax. Because 15 percent of $100 is only $15, he's much better off after paying the tax than he'd be with the tax-free earnings.

> **Money Pit**
>
> Some people are attracted to the stock market because they think it's exciting—even glamorous. We're not discouraging you from Wall Street, but remember to put your financial house in order, first. If you don't consider all the advantages—and disadvantages (including taxes)—before you invest, you could be putting your personal financial situation at risk.

> **Pocket Change**
>
> Although we usually don't consider them as such, savings accounts are a type of investment. We'll talk more about different types of investments in Chapter 20.

Consider each investment carefully, but keep these general guidelines in mind:

◆ If you're in the 15 percent federal tax bracket, don't worry too much about the tax you'll have to pay on investment income. You'll probably come out further ahead than you would with lower-yield, tax-free investments.

◆ If you're in the 25 percent bracket, look carefully at the yield or interest before deciding whether to participate in the investment. You're likely to do better with taxable investments, but that might not always be the case.

◆ If you're in the 33 percent bracket or higher, stay away from investments that will give you taxable income. You have to hand over too great a share of your earnings. Look for investment vehicles that generate tax-free income instead.

Show Me the Money

Capital gains are the profit you make on an investment.

Once you understand the tax implications of investments, you can take a look at *capital gains*, your profits on an investment. Say that you purchased 100 shares of IBM stock at $50 per share, for a total of $5,000. You are able to later sell the same shares for $90 each. Good job! You've made a profit of $40 per share or $4,000. The profit you earned is the capital gain, and guess what? You're paying taxes on it. There's an upside to the tax thing, though. If your Nike stock nose-dives and you sell it at a big capital loss, you can use the loss to offset the taxes you'll be paying on your capital gain. Get it?

You can take an unlimited amount of capital loss per year as long as you have capital gains equal to or greater than the loss. If you don't, you can only deduct a max in capital losses of $3,000 in one year. If you have more than $3,000, the remaining losses are carried forward to future tax years.

Here are some more fun investment facts coming at you:

◆ If you hold an investment for less than one year, the gain or loss from that investment is considered short-term. Short-term gains and losses are netted against each other, and short-term gains are taxed at your regular tax rate. If you're in a 28 percent tax bracket, for instance, you pay a 28 percent tax on your gains. If you are in the 33 percent bracket, you'll owe a 33 percent tax on your profits. Short-term capital gains can be expensive.

◆ If you hold an investment for more than a year, the gain or loss is considered long-term. Long-term gains and losses are netted against each other, too. If you're in a 15 percent tax bracket, net long-term capital gains are taxed at 10 percent. If you purchased the asset after 1/1/2001 and held the asset for more than five years, the 10 percent capital gains tax falls even further to 8 percent. If you're in a 25 percent or greater marginal tax bracket, your capital gains are taxed at 20 percent. If you purchased the asset after 1/1/2001 and hold it longer than five years, the capital gains tax liability falls from 20 percent to 18 percent. Keep this in mind over the next several years! This tax advantage makes it desirable to hold assets for more than a year, particularly if your income is pretty high.

♦ After you've calculated the long-term gain or loss and short-term gain or loss, there is additional netting of the net amounts. Short-term losses can be taken against net long-term gains or net long-term losses can be netted against net short-term gains. Interesting, huh? Follow your tax program and know the final net figure; a gain could cost you money.

The tax implications concerning capital gains are important to keep in mind. However, you should never invest solely on the basis of tax considerations, nor should you sell stock only on the basis of capital gains or losses.

Before we leave this exciting topic, we need to cover one more area: capital gains on mutual funds. When you purchase shares in a mutual fund, you are now the proud owner of a piece of a pie. The pie contains many different stocks—shares of ownership in various companies. These stocks trade quite regularly. The turnover ratio (how often a stock trades within a mutual fund) is an important tidbit to learn about a fund before you buy it.

It's important to know, because almost every time a stock trades within an account, there is a capital gain or loss. Within the mutual fund, the gains are held in a separate fund and distributed out to shareholders as cash. This distribution normally occurs once a year, although sometimes it's done more often. This cash is taxed to the shareholders as short-term or long-term capital gains, or both. Usually, you'll be able to choose whether to reinvest the capital gains into more shares of the mutual fund or take them as a cash payment. Either way, you will owe taxes on the gains at the end of the year.

Pocket Change
Mutual funds used to operate based only on their performances, with no regard for the tax implications of the capital gains and losses they generated. A new crop of mutual funds is opening, however, that takes capital gains and losses into consideration, called tax-advantaged mutual funds.

Whew! That was pretty intense. We're hopeful that you have a handle on some of these tax matters, and you feel confident enough to move on.

Show Me the Way to the Investment Store

Beginning investors often are confused about exactly how to get started. Do you just walk into an investment firm and announce that you're ready to buy? Do you call an 800 number and commit your investments to a voice on the phone? Do you fill out an application, stick it in the mailbox, and hope for the best? Or do you jump online and throw your money into cyberspace? There are several ways to get started.

Buying Mutual Funds

Suppose you've saved $3,500, and you're ready to begin investing. You're thinking about getting into a mutual fund, and you heard the guys at work talking about a cool telecommunications fund. It sounds good, and you want to know more about it. Where do you go?

You have two choices:

◆ Call a stockbroker, a professional buyer and seller of investments, and ask about the fund.

◆ Go directly to the mutual fund. Either go to the library, check out the fund online at www.morningstar.com, or find the telephone number of the fund and let your fingers do the walking.

We'll talk about the different types of brokers a bit later in the chapter. For now, think about whether you know anything about this fund you're thinking of jumping into. How has it performed over the last five years? Is it considered risky? Find out everything you can about the fund before you decide whether to buy it.

Get a mutual fund directory and read about the fund. The report will have a toll-free number, which you can call and get information about the fund. This information usually comes in the form of a prospectus. After you have the *prospectus*, read it thoroughly and learn as much about the fund as you can. The prospectus is a detailed explanation on an investment. We'll get into more detail about it in Chapter 20.

There are several mutual fund directories, such as the Morningstar report or Value Line, which track and offer information on thousands of mutual funds. They are available

Show Me the Money

A detailed explanation on a particular investment is called a **prospectus**.

at your local library. They're also available online. Find Morningstar at www. morningstar.com, and Value Line at www.valueline.com.

Opening a new account with a mutual fund isn't exactly a stroll through the park. After you contact the mutual fund or the stockbroker, you'll receive a new account form. You'll need to provide all kinds of information, such as where you work, the name of your bank, your first transaction, your investment knowledge, your driver's license number and expiration date, your Social Security number, and many, many other things.

If you open an account online, you'll need all the same information, but the procedure is streamlined. Purchasing a mutual fund or stock online is almost as easy as buying a book on Amazon.com. Many mutual fund companies and online (discount) brokers provide a phenomenal amount of research information on their websites. Even if you feel you need to talk to someone on your first trade, at least review the data provided online.

If you're fairly financially savvy and willing to do your own research and make investing decisions, then an online broker probably is fine for you. Review the list of popular online funds in Chapter 13, but don't forget to do your homework before signing up with one.

Also, check out the online sites listed in the following:

- E*Trade at www.etrade.com

- TD Waterhouse at www.tdwaterhouse.com

- Charles Schwab & Co. at www.schwab.com

- Ameritrade at www.ameritrade.com

After you've handed over all the pertinent information and the mutual fund company has opened an account for you, all you have to do is tell them that you'd like to buy XYZ Mutual Fund. The person on the phone will tell you how much it will cost, and you state whether you want in and how much money you want to invest. After a verbal agreement is reached, you'll get a written confirmation. Always check the confirmation as soon as it arrives to verify that the transaction is correct. If it is, immediately send a check to the mutual fund to make the deal final.

After you've bought in to the fund, you'll either get a monthly or quarterly statement, showing you the value of the fund. It will also include what income has been paid out in the fund, whether more shares have been purchased, the price of the fund today, the share price of the fund when you purchased it (which some fund statements provide), and the like. You also will get an annual statement at the end of the year and a 1099 form to use when you prepare your income tax return.

Understanding Index Funds

An *index* is an unmanaged group of securities whose overall performance is used as a standard to measure investment performance. Most people consider the Dow Jones Industrial Average (known as the Dow) as the measure of the market. This measure is an index (group) of 30 large, industrial stocks.

While the Dow might be the most visible index, the S&P 500 (Standard & Poor 500) is a better measure of the market. This index is a grouping of corporations drawn from various industries by their size—the 500 largest U.S. corporations. These firms account for over 80 percent of the market capitalization (size) of all the stocks listed in the New York Stock Exchange.

An Index Fund is a passively managed mutual fund that seeks to parallel the performance of a particular market index. A mutual fund company sets up a mutual fund that mirrors the index by including shares of all the firms that make up the index. An investor can purchase an index fund, which seeks to match, rather than outperform, the return and risk of the market. The advantage to indexing is that there are minimal trading costs.

The grandfather of all index funds is Vanguard's Index 500 Fund. This fund was so successful that there now are myriad index funds. There are bond index funds, domestic stock index funds, international/global index funds, and even industry-specific funds.

When an investor calls a mutual fund company and instructs the firm to buy or sell fund shares, the trade is not made until the end-of-the-day pricing of the fund. On a wildly volatile day, you could call in an order at 10 A.M., only to have to sit and watch the market plummet or skyrocket all day.

To get around the end-of-the-day pricing, Wall Street invented exchange-traded shares, a group of securities that represent a mutual fund, but are traded in the stock market throughout the day, at the market value at that time. This way, an investor can own an index fund, and still be in control of market timing. The downside is that there's a brokerage fee associated with exchange-traded shares that doesn't occur with a regularly traded index fund.

Buying Stocks or Bonds

The way you buy stocks and bonds—which, as you'll learn in Chapter 20, are different types of investment vehicles—is very similar to buying mutual funds. You work with a broker to buy or sell stock.

There are a couple different varieties of brokers. You could use a full-service broker, who charges about 1 percent of the value of your investment. What are you getting for your money, you ask? Hopefully, the broker you'd be working with would have good knowledge and information concerning your particular investment, and you would benefit from his or her expertise.

> **Show Me the Money**
>
> The **U.S. Securities and Exchange Commission** is an independent, quasi-judicial agency that's responsible for administering federal securities laws. The agency calls itself "the investor's advocate."

Discount brokers are brokers who are paid a salary by the company for which they work, rather than working on commission. This makes them very attractive to many investors who recognize the potential for a conflict of interest among brokers who work strictly for commission.

Some analysts say you can save 50 percent or more by buying from the big discount brokers such as Charles Schwab or TD Waterhouse Securities, rather than from the traditional brokerage firms such as Merrill Lynch and Morgan Stanley. Full-service or discount broker? The choice is yours. If you feel you need advice and direction, look for a full-service broker. If you know what you want, or you have another type of financial advisor (more on financial advisors in Chapter 21), a discount broker should be fine.

The Least You Need to Know

◆ Make sure your savings, debt, and retirement funds are taken care of before you start thinking about investments.

◆ Just as there are different kinds of people, there are also different kinds of investors.

◆ Your investments can have a big effect on your taxes.

◆ You can buy stocks, bonds, and mutual funds on your own or enlist the help of a broker.

Chapter 20

Investment Options

In This Chapter

◆ Getting a handle on the basic terms

◆ You can own, or you can loan

◆ Understanding ownership and lending investments

◆ More about mutual funds

◆ Knowing which investments are safe

◆ Knowing which investments are risky

After you have a feel for the type of investor you'll be, and you've located some materials from which to learn more about investing, you're ready to start looking at some investment options. That doesn't mean that we're going to give you a list of stocks and tell you how many of each to buy. No way.

Just in case you've been living in Bolivia lately, the stock market, which was already shaky before 9/11, pretty much bottomed out after the terror-ist attacks on New York and Washington, D.C. It has rebounded a bit since then, and analysts are hopeful that the recovery will continue and the market will stabilize. Still, many financial advisors, and certainly we, would not at this point presume to give you a list of stocks and tell you that's where to put your money.

What we give you is a basic understanding of how the stock market works. We also talk about other investment options, such as bonds and mutual funds.

How Does the Stock Market Work?

Listen to the stock reports sometime, or try to read that impossibly tiny print they use to list them in most newspapers. They're filled with words and phrases like NASDAQ, the Dow Jones, blue chip stock, and composite index. It's enough to make any potential investor pack up his portfolio and go back to watching soap operas.

First, what exactly is the stock market? The *stock market* is a generic term that encompasses the trading of *securities*. This trading takes place in stock exchanges. There are three major stock exchanges in the United States:

◆ Formed in 1792, the New York Stock Exchange (NYSE) is the largest organized stock exchange in the United States.

Dollars and Sense

Check out your local newspaper's business page for a "stocks of local interest" column. Read these stock reports daily for a week or two to get a feeling for how the local companies are doing in the market. It's sometimes easier to understand something that can be confusing, such as the stock market, if you look at how it pertains to something with which you're familiar.

◆ The American Stock Exchange (AMEX) was known before 1951 as the American Curb Exchange. That's because trading was conducted on the curb of Wall and Broad streets in New York City. The American Stock Exchange has less stringent listing requirements than the NYSE, so it attracts many smaller companies.

◆ Another of the major stock exchanges, NASDAQ stands for the National Association of Securities Dealers Automated Quotation System. Unlike the NYSE and the AMEX, there isn't any physical location for the exchange; trading is done by computer. The American Stock Exchange and NASDAQ have merged, but maintain their own names and identities.

The overall performance of the stock market is evaluated in many different ways. The Dow Jones Industrial Average (DJIA) is one measure of the stock market, the standard we hear every day. It consists of three indices that include averages for utilities, industrial, and transportation stocks, as well as the composite averages. Each average reflects the simple mathematical average of the closing prices (prices at the end of the day) and indicates the day-to-day changes in the market prices of stocks in the designated index.

Okay, what does that mean? The DJIA is a composite (group) of 30 stocks with a daily average. Tomorrow, if the stocks as an average go up in price, the DJIA goes up. If the average value of these selected stocks goes down, the DJIA goes down. If market trends are moving increasingly upward, as they did in the latter part of the 1990s, it's called a *bull market*. Market trends that are moving continuously downward, such as they have since the middle of 2001, are called a *bear market*.

Now that you know the major exchanges and how the market is measured, let's get down to business. How do you make money on this deal? There are two kinds of investment returns: total return and yield. *Total return* on an investment is the current income, plus the capital gain or loss. *Yield* is the amount of dividends or interest paid on an investment. These returns can be very different, although many people lump them together as the same thing.

Every investment you make involves a certain level of *investment risk*, with the chance that you'll lose the money you invest or that the investment won't perform as well as you thought. Investments with the chance for higher returns carry greater risk than those without the return potential.

Show Me the Money

The **stock market** is the organized securities exchange for stock and bond transactions. **Securities** are investments that represent evidence of debt, ownership of a business, or the legal right to acquire or sell an ownership interest in a business.

Show Me the Money

When market trends move upward, it's called a **bull market**. It's a **bear market** when trends move continuously downward.

Show Me the Money

The **total return** on an investment is the current income (known as the **yield**) plus the capital gain or loss. When you invest, you take a chance that you'll lose money; that's the **investment risk**.

Although the terminology involved can be a bit baffling, the basic concept of investing isn't all that complicated. You can buy something with your money: a little piece of a company as shares of stock, or some real estate, or something else. Or you can lend your money to an organization and have it agree to pay you back, with interest, over a specified time. When it comes to investing, you can own, or you can loan.

When You Own

When you invest your money in a company, or in real estate, or in stamps, or Beanie Babies, you're buying a piece of something that you hope will increase in value and be profitable. While most people think mainly of the stock market in relation to investing, it's not the only investment opportunity.

Stocks are merely investments that represent a piece of ownership in a company. The more *shares* of stock in one company that you have, the bigger a piece of the company you own. Owning stock makes you a *shareholder* in the company. The word stock is commonly used interchangeably with the phrase *common stock*. There are different kinds of stocks, such as blue-chip stock, which refers to stock of well-established companies like General Motors and Exxon, and growth stock, which is that of companies on their way up.

All corporations have stock, but not all corporate shares are sold to the public. A company may sell stock, or little pieces of itself, to raise money. When it sells stock through an *initial public offering (IPO)*, it *goes public*. When a company goes public, it no longer controls who can purchase its stock.

Show Me the Money

When a company goes public, it offers its common stock for sale to the public. The first time it does so it's known as an **initial public offering**. After that, it's no longer a privately held company.

Shares of stocks are usually sold in **round lots,** which are groups of 100. Groups of less than 100 shares are called **odd lots.**

If you buy stock in the Disney Corporation, for example, you're buying a tiny, tiny piece of a huge company. Shares of stock usually are sold in groups of 100, which are called *round lots*. Groups of less than 100 shares are called *odd lots*. If you buy 100 shares of stock from a company that has a million shares of stock outstanding, you can figure that you own one thousandth of the company. Regardless of whether you buy 10 Disney shares or 10,000, you're still a shareholder in the company. As long as the company makes a profit, you're entitled, as a shareholder, to share and benefit from it.

Stocks can make money in two ways. As a shareholder, you may get annual dividends. Hopefully, the price of the stock will also increase so that if you wanted to, you could sell your stock for more than what you bought it for and make a profit. The amount of dividends a corporation pays out is a reflection of the type of company it is. The stock of a growing company will not pay out the dividends that, say, an electric company does. It's important to remember this difference if you're planning to buy shares of a company. Will you receive a good annual income from your stocks, or are you banking on profits that will occur a few years or more down the road?

What happens, though, if somebody comes up with something even more exciting than Mickey and Disney World that captures the collective imagination of the whole world? All of a sudden, people stop visiting Disney parks, watching and buying Disney movies and shows, and purchasing scads of Disney toys, clothes, and other merchandise. If that happens, your Disney stock will take a nosedive. The value will plummet faster than you can watch it fall, and you'll be left alone, wearing your Mickey ears and holding your stock certificates.

Stocks aren't the only type of investment that you can own. Many people buy investment real estate, which they rent out to receive an income or resell for a profit. Or, you can decide to invest in something else that you hope will increase in value, such as baseball cards or McDonald's Happy Meal collectibles. These are called "commodities."

Those are some of the opportunities you have to own your investments. Now, let's look at the type of investment in which you loan your money.

When You Loan

Ownership investments aren't the only option. You also can participate in a *lending investment*. A lending investment is when you loan your money with the understanding that you'll get it back—with interest—after a specified time.

We most commonly think of *bonds* as lending investments, and they are the most widely used. There are many flavors of bonds, including

> **Show Me the Money**
>
> A **lending investment** is when you loan your money with the understanding that you'll get it back—with interest—after a specified time. Think of a **bond** as an IOU. When you buy a bond, you're lending your money to the company or government for a specified period of time.

municipal bonds, general obligation bonds, revenue bonds, corporate bonds, high-yield bonds, savings bonds, and government agency bonds. But there are other lending investments as well. Some other examples are certificates of deposit, Treasury bills, and notes.

These are all investments in which you give your money to a particular entity with the understanding that you'll get it back at a certain time, with an agreed-upon amount of interest added. The entity borrowing your money varies from a bank,

> **Pocket Change**
>
> An important thing to remember about bonds is that when interest rates go up, the value of your bond goes down. When interest rates go down, the value of your bond goes up. When your bond matures, you get your money back.

which generally administers certificates of deposits, to the U.S. government, which offers bonds. Bonds are also offered by corporations. They borrow funds from you, in the form of a bond, giving you interest, which generates income for you.

The conditions, such as the length of time the money will be invested, the amount of interest paid, and so forth, are different for each of these types of lending investments. In most cases, bonds offer a fixed interest rate. That is, the rate remains steady throughout the life of the loan.

If you're holding a bond that pays 5 percent interest and the interest rate jumps to 7 percent, you lose on the value of your bond if you sell it. But if you're earning 7 percent interest on your bond and the interest rate drops to 5 percent, you're still entitled to 7 percent, the agreed-upon rate. In that case, your bond would have increased in value (known as a premium bond) compared to new bonds being issued. Either way, you'll get your initial investment back when the investment matures. Always make sure the bonds you buy have a clear maturity date so that you'll know exactly when you can get your money back.

Mutual Funds

We discussed mutual funds in Chapters 13 and 19, but they're such an important investment vehicle that we felt compelled to say a bit more about them. Mutual funds can be ownership or lending investments and, in some cases, are both. When you invest in mutual funds, your money can go into stocks, bonds, and other holdings, as well. Many people think of mutual funds as being strictly stocks, but they're not.

To better understand mutual funds, think about them as pies. When you put down your money for mutual funds, you're getting a slice of the pie. If the value of your mutual fund goes down, the pie (and your piece of the pie) gets smaller. If the value increases, the pie gets bigger.

We discussed the advantages of mutual funds in Chapter 13 and told you about load funds and no-load funds. As a refresher, load funds are those that charge you a sales commission when shares are purchased, and no-load funds are those that you can buy directly from a company, without paying a sales commission.

Another important mutual fund distinction is between open-end mutual funds and closed-end mutual funds. *Open-end mutual funds* are the huge pies that can continue to grow. Open-end funds can issue an unlimited number of shares to investors. The size of the fund can therefore continue to grow, as long as investors are willing to keep putting their money into them. The number of shares available to investors is limited to an initial set amount in *closed-end mutual funds*. Shares in these funds are sold like stocks and bonds.

Show Me the Money

Open-end mutual funds are those with no size limit. They can contain an unlimited number of shares and can continue growing as long as investors keep putting money into them. **Closed-end mutual funds** have a limited number of shares, which are sold like stocks and bonds.

Mutual fund companies offer different types of mutual funds for different types of investors. As with stocks and bonds, some types include more risk than others. The most common types of mutual funds are the following:

◆ Stock funds

◆ Bond funds

◆ Money-market funds

Stock funds are those that invest in stocks (you probably could have figured out this one yourself). There are different kinds of stock funds, and some involve higher risk than others.

Bond funds are those mutual funds that invest in bonds (see how easy this is?). They're usually less risky than stock funds, and some of them are tax-free. Bond funds contain many, many bonds, which normally are set up so they will mature periodically.

Money-market funds are those in which the value of your original investment normally does not change. They're not too different from savings accounts, but they have some distinct advantages, including historically higher yields and check-writing privileges. Some are tax-free. Money-market funds are the safest type of mutual fund.

Understanding the Risks

Everyone knows that investing money is never risk-free. The idea is for you to find the investments that offer the best chance for a good return, with the least amount of risk, and that takes some know-how. Some risk affects only a particular business or industry, and is called *unsystematic risk*. Risk that affects the entire market is called *systematic risk*. Both are to be managed by diversification.

First of all, there are all kinds of investment risk. The following are just some of the different types:

- **Business risk** This risk comes from the way in which the business that issued the security is managed. Will it be in business in three years? Does it have a marketable product? To get some perspective on business risk, talk to somebody who invested in a dot.com company back in the late 1990s. Many of those companies are now nonexistent or worth less than $5 per share of stock.

- **Financial risk** This risk is associated with the finances of the company. Does it have too much debt (the recent declaration of bankruptcy by Enron is a prime example), or does the company spend too much on new technology?

- **Purchasing power risk** This risk is the effect that inflation might have on the value of your holding. When your 30-year, $10,000 corporate note matures, how much will $10,000 truly be worth? If there's been high inflation over those 30 years, your bond won't be worth as much in current dollars as if inflation had been low.

- **Interest rate risk** This risk involves how changes in interest rates may affect your investment.

- **Market risk** This risk reflects the tendency for stock to move with the market or entire industrial group or for a particular security, as a result of factors such as economic, political, or social events—also known as systematic risk.

Show Me the Money

The type of risk that affects the entire market is called **systematic risk**. The kind of risk that affects only a single business or industry is called **unsystematic risk**.

♦ **Default risk**   This risk is the chance that the company you've invested in will be unable to service the debt.

♦ **Foreign currency risk**   This risk is that a change in the relationship between the value of the U.S. dollar and the value of the currency of the country in which your investment is held will affect your holding. This is an important risk for international investing. Just ask anyone who's had money in a Thai or Russian fund during the past year. Ouch!

Reading all those possibilities for risk can be scary, but you must understand as much about risk as possible. The key thing to understand is exactly how great these risks are and where they are most likely to occur.

For most beginning investors, until recently, the stock market has been a pretty tempting place. Now it's a pretty scary place. In the past, everybody knew stocks really paid off, right? In the long run, they usually do. Even when the stock market is down, as it was from 2000 to 2002, many financial advisors recommend buying stocks (either via individual stocks or via equity mutual funds) if you're planning to invest over a long period of time. If you can't leave your money invested for a long period of time, however, then stocks might not be the best investment for you.

The stock market is subject to some pretty significant fluctuations and involves many possibilities for risk. Just look at the way the market plunged after the 9/11 terrorist attacks, as investor confidence plunged right down to Ground Zero. Even now, four years later, the market is unstable due to war in Iraq, record-high worldwide oil prices, shaky job growth, and other factors.

Still, if you can put your money in and ride it out for the long haul, you'll probably do okay. But if you have a limited period in which to leave your money in stocks, you risk having to take it out at a time when the market is down, such as it is currently. If that happens, you'll lose money. Investments in real estate carry similar risks. The real estate market can be great, or it can drop pretty dramatically.

On the other hand, if you invest in something extra safe, you're almost assured to get a lower return, at least when interest rates are as low as they are today. Investors want to be rewarded

> **Dollars and Sense**
>
> Mutual funds often offer built-in diversification, which makes them an attractive option to many investors. As you get to know your way around the investment arena a little bit better, you can pick and choose your own diversified investments. When you're a beginning investor, however, mutual funds make good sense.

for the risks they take, so junk bonds must pay a higher yield than Treasuries and so forth. If it's feasible for you to have your money invested for a long time, then stocks are probably a better investment than low-risk, low-yield bonds.

Probably the best way of controlling risk, as far as your investments are concerned, is through *diversification*. When you diversify, you put your money into different investments so that if the value of some of them decreases, the value of the others is likely to be high enough to keep your investments stable.

Understanding Asset Allocation

No investor should be entirely invested in either stock or bonds. The process of determining the broad categories of assets in which you'll invest your money is called *asset allocation*, which is simply the process of dividing your funds between bonds, equities, and cash. The proportions should be based on your financial objectives and your risk tolerance.

A general rule of thumb is that an investor should never have less than 25 percent or more than 75 percent of his or her funds in common stock. The more aggressive an investor, the higher the ratio of stock to other investments will be.

Some advisors will recommend that you subtract your age from 100, and use that number as a guide for asset allocation. For instance, if you're 25 years old, by this rule, 75 percent of your portfolio should be in stock, and 25 percent in bonds and/or cash. If you're 38, then 62 percent of your portfolio should be invested in stock, and 38 percent in bonds. It was exciting in the late 1990s to watch the equity—or stock—portions of investors' portfolios grow. Nearly everyone, however, lost money when the stock market took a dive in the spring of 2000. Smart investors at that time kept a close eye on how their funds were allocated, and modified the allocations, as necessary. A financial advisor can be a valuable tool in helping you allocate your assets.

> **Show Me the Money**
>
> **Asset allocation** is the process of assigning your investment funds to different families of assets, using your financial objectives and risk tolerance as guides.

Where to Invest Your Money

We've told you a little bit about various investment vehicles and the risks and opportunities associated with them. Stocks generally have the potential for better returns, but they're riskier than bonds. Money markets are the safest, but you're not going to make a killing from them. So what's a new investor to do?

Safe, but Not Too Exciting

If we're talking safe, but not too exciting, we're talking bonds—dependable, safe, boring bonds. Well, that's not really fair. Bonds can be quite interesting, particularly long-term bonds with their fluctuation potential; they just don't share the glamour that we associate with stocks.

Even bonds, however, are not without some risk. When you buy a bond, you're agreeing to lend your money to a company or other agency for a certain amount of time, and they're agreeing to pay you a certain amount of interest after that time.

But what if you want to get your money back early? Or what if the company calls your bond in early? If a company is permitted to call in a bond early, there's nothing to stop it from waiting until the interest rates drop, calling in your bond, and reissuing it at a lower rate, which means you end up losing the future interest at a higher interest rate. You will be forced to reinvest at a lower rate. Companies only call in bonds when it is financially prudent for them to do so. They call in the higher-interest–rate bonds, and then reissue them at a lower rate to save money in the annual amount of interest they are paying to bond holders. This is similar to what you do when you refinance your mortgage. These are issues you need to inquire about before you purchase a bond.

Remember the bond rule: If the interest rate drops, the value of your bond increases. If the interest rate rises, the value of your bond drops. If the value of the bond increases, the bond is called a *premium bond*. If the value decreases, it's called a *discounted bond*.

> **Dollars and Sense**
>
> Always make sure that you know the interest rate on your bond and when it is due for maturity. In addition, make sure you know whether the company can call in the bond early. If it can, you might want to look around for something else or see if it makes sense to invest until the call date.

> **Show Me the Money**
>
> A **premium bond** is a bond whose value has increased. If its value has decreased, it's called a **discounted bond**.

If you loan the XYZ Company $10,000 at 6 percent interest for five years and the interest rate drops to 4 percent, the value of your bond will be somewhere around

$11,500. If the interest rate rises to 8 percent, though, your bond will be worth about $8,000.

Exciting, but Just How Safe?

Stocks keep your blood pumping with their potential for payoffs, but they can also give you an incredible, wake-you-up-at-night headache with their potential for loss. It's important to remember that there are different types of stocks, with different degrees of risk:

- **Growth stocks**   These stocks are reputed to be one of the easiest ways to make money because they're issued by companies that have higher-than-average earnings and profits. But they're volatile and can decrease in value, too. Be prepared to hold onto growth stocks in order to ride out any ups and downs.

- **Income stocks**   True to their name, income stocks pay dividends on a regular basis. They're not the flashy investments that growth stocks are, but they're more dependable and easier on the blood pressure.

- **Growth and income stocks**   These stocks offer the best of the two previous types of stocks. You can get capital gains from growth stocks as well as some dividends from the income stocks. Unfortunately, you might not get all the growth benefits that you would from pure growth stock.

Is Investing in Baseball Cards a Good Idea?

The answer to that question depends on how much you like baseball cards, or Happy Meal toys, or stamps, or antique furniture, or dolls, or whatever collectibles you're interested in. Investing in collectibles is not a sure thing, to say the least. For starters, you have to physically care for the stuff you're collecting. You have to do extensive research to know what to buy and what not to, and you have to work with dealers who are looking to make a profit off of you.

If you ask a financial advisor whether you should plow the nest egg money into baseball cards, you can pretty much count on a negative reaction. Collecting as an investment is risky, and, while no investment is ever 100 percent safe, there are much more certain ways to invest than piling your life's savings into baseball cards or other collectibles.

The Least You Need to Know

◆ There's a lot of jargon and confusing talk about investments, but if you get an understanding of the basics, it won't seem so overwhelming.

◆ Stocks are investments that you buy. Bonds are investments for which you loan money and get interest back in return.

◆ Mutual funds can contain ownership and lending investments.

◆ There are risks associated with all kinds of investments, but some types carry more risk than others.

◆ Stocks are generally considered higher-risk investments than bonds.

◆ Collectibles are fun, but they're not considered great investment vehicles.

Chapter 21

We All Need Somebody to Lean On

In This Chapter

- ◆ How to find someone to help you with your investments
- ◆ The right questions to ask before you hire a financial advisor
- ◆ Knowing who to stay away from
- ◆ Some cautions concerning your financial advisor

Probably the worst thing someone who knows nothing about his personal finances can do is go out and hire a financial advisor, assuming that she'll take care of everything and he'll never have to think about his finances again. On the surface, it sounds like it would be a good idea. The problem with hiring a financial advisor when you have no knowledge of your own finances is that you're placing a lot of trust, and some of your most valuable assets, in the hands of a person you may know nothing about. We've all read stories in the newspaper about shady, low-down scoundrels who bilk elderly people out of their savings through one scam or another. You've probably heard about some guy who convinces his friends and neighbors that he can get them the deal of a lifetime if they'll just hand over their money, only to go blow the savings of everybody he knows in some Atlantic City casino. This kind of stuff happens all the time.

It could also be that the financial "expert" you hire is not an expert at all. Basically, just about anybody can claim to be a financial advisor. Finances, investments, taxation, and the like are all very complicated topics that take years of education to acquire the knowledge to do the job well. Not everyone can be an expert, and it's imperative to find someone who has the knowledge that you're looking for.

Know Thy Finances, Know Thy Advisor

All of this gloom-and-doom financial advisor talk isn't meant to scare you off from hiring someone to help you with your finances. Nearly everybody can use some help sometimes. The point is, the more you know about your personal finances, the easier it will be for you to find a qualified, trustworthy *financial advisor*.

> **Show Me the Money**
>
> A **financial advisor** is a broad term for a professional whom you hire to help you make decisions about your finances. Anybody can claim to be a financial advisor, but that doesn't mean that person is qualified to do the job.

When you understand your finances, you'll be able to ask intelligent questions of those you're considering for the job and understand their answers. You'll know what they're talking about when they throw out phrases like "full-service broker" or "fee-only advisor." You won't feel stupid asking questions about your own money because you'll know that, generally, you know exactly what you're talking about. You'll work together with the advisor to put your money to the best possible use.

A financial advisor is called an advisor because it's his or her job to advise you on the best uses of your money. Ultimately, however, it's your money, and you're in charge of what happens to it.

> **Money Pit**
>
> Some unethical financial advisors try to take advantage of people who are emotionally distraught. If you're going through an emotionally trying time and you need financial advice, be careful. Seek all the advice you need, but try to avoid making any major decisions until you've had a chance to think clearly about them.

Do I Need a Financial Advisor?

There are many reasons why you might need a financial advisor. Maybe you're faced with a complicated financial situation regarding the sale or purchase of a property, or want some advice about which stocks and bonds to buy. Maybe you're setting up a college fund or getting really serious about your retirement fund.

The reason for and point at which you seek help with your finances is entirely up to you. Whether you're leaving a job and deciding what to do with a $5,800 401(k), or you've inherited $200,000 from your grandmother, you might feel that you need some financial advice.

The Who's Who of Financial Advisors

What are some of the different kinds of financial advisors? This issue can be a little bit complicated, because a financial advisor by any other name may, or may not, be a financial advisor.

Some of the common classes of financial advisors are explained in the following sections. Just remember that what type of advisor you need depends on your circumstances, and you should never hire someone just because he or she has a title that you think sounds impressive.

Financial Planners

The term "financial planner" often is used to describe anyone who offers financial advice or services. It also frequently is used interchangeably with "financial advisor."

Financial planners, as the name implies, are people who design financial plans of action. They may design and carry out the plan, or their clients may choose to execute the plans.

Financial planner is a very broad categorization, so if you're looking to hire one, make sure you know what credentials or other titles may come along with it. For starters, financial planners can be certified—or not.

Certified Financial Planners

There's a very large fraternity of people in this country called *certified financial planners*. What they have in common is that they've earned the Certified Financial Planning (CFP) credential, a national certification. Earning the CFP credential involves working through a home-study program and passing a cumulative, 10-hour test. Designees must have three years of financial work experience and promise to adhere to a code of ethics. Work experience should include financial planning, investments, or banking. CFPs are also required to take 30 hours of continuing education courses every two years to keep up-to-date on industry happenings.

Financial Consultants

Another type of financial planner are *financial consultants*, who provide an overview of financial information and options in order to enable you to choose the products that make the most sense for you. They generally will not produce a plan for your finances, only information and advice. The assumption is that the consultant is fee-only (he won't receive a commission on any products sold). Ask how your consultant will be paid.

Bank Customer Service Representatives

A bank *customer service representative* (*CSR*) is another type of financial planner—usually trained by the bank at which he's employed. His job is to bring deposits into the bank, either as CDs, money-market funds, trust accounts, or other types of accounts. He also is expected to direct clients' money to a subsidiary company that sells mutual funds, annuities, or one in which the bank receives either a commission or a percentage of the management fee. Unless you purchase a load fund—that is, one that charges a sales commission—you do not pay any fee to these consultants.

Certified Public Accountants/Personal Financial Specialists

More and more *certified public accountants* (*CPAs*) are becoming financial consultants all the time. The American Institute of Certified Public Accountants now has a special designation, called a *personal financial specialist* (*PFS*), for CPAs who have three years of financial planning experience and pass a six-hour test. Unless you purchase a product, CPAs usually are paid on an hourly basis. Many people depend on their CPA for financial help, regardless of whether or not the CPA is designated a PFS.

Insurance Agents

You may not normally think of an insurance agent as a financial planner, but some agents specialize in financial planning. They usually have either a CLU (Chartered Life Underwriter) or ChFC (Charter Financial Consultant) designation, or both. These are designations by the American College in Bryn Mawr, Pennsylvania, given to persons who complete and pass an eight-course program. Often, the program of study can be designed in the agent's area of expertise. CLUs and ChFCs need continuing education. The designations, though not mandatory to do financial planning, show a level of expertise and experience.

Money Managers

Finally, a *money manager* is a financial planner who, after reviewing your parameters, risk tolerance, and total financial picture, agrees to handle your funds, make trades on your behalf, and buy and sell stocks and bonds for you. A money manager normally is employed by investors who have a substantial amount of money. Money managers typically receive a percentage of the market value of their client's account as compensation (approximately 1 percent of the value of the assets on an annual basis). As an example, a money manager who has $200,000 under management and charges an annual fee of 1 percent, would earn $2,000 per year. He or she probably would charge the quarterly fee, which is $500. Most money managers have a CFA (Certified Financial Analyst) designation. Look for this designation when you're thinking about hiring a money manager.

Finding a Reputable Financial Advisor

A good way to find a financial advisor is by using your ears. Listen to people at work when they talk about money at the water cooler and make a note if somebody's raving about an advisor with whom he or she's been working. Do any of your friends have financial advisors? How about your relatives? If you have a lawyer or accountant, you can ask her for the names of some good financial advisors. If you keep hearing the same name in the context of good financial help, that person is probably worth checking out.

When you're with your prospective advisor, there are some questions you should ask. Let's get one thing very clear, though, before we start. Don't forget, even for a minute, that you're the person who will be hiring the financial advisor, and you'll be paying his fees. It's not the other way around.

> **Dollars and Sense**
>
> Just because your father has been working with the same financial guy for 25 years doesn't necessarily mean that you should work with him, too. Perhaps, though, that service record should point you toward the firm the guy works for, where you might find someone else that you'd like.

> **Dollars and Sense**
>
> It's important to find somebody who shares your views and philosophies on investments, so don't hire someone without first having a meeting to get to know that person. Remember that you should have some good financial information and understanding under your belt before the meeting, because you've been doing your homework and reading about investments and other financial matters that may affect you.

Many people are intimidated by professionals, because they feel stupid or uninformed around them. Hello! That's why you're meeting with the advisor in the first place. It's understood that he has more expertise in the finance area than you do, and hopefully you can benefit from his knowledge. That's the point, right? You don't need to impress the financial advisor; he needs to impress you. Some questions you should ask the financial advisors you consider are listed here:

♦ *How long have you been in this business?* As with most professions, experience is important. You want to find someone who fully understands the financial industry and all its nuances.

Pocket Change

When choosing a financial advisor, ask to see a Form ADV. This provides a person's background, and whether there has been any trouble in the past with the law or with investment regulatory offices. If an advisor refuses to make this form available, it should set off warning bells.

♦ *How have you prepared for this job?* You'll want to know about your potential advisor's education and previous job experience.

♦ *What was your job before you became a financial advisor?* Look for a logical progression, such as moving into a financial advisor position from a banking job. If the progression doesn't seem logical, be sure to ask for an explanation.

♦ *Can you give me the names of some other clients, please?* References are very important. If you talk to other clients and don't get all the information you're looking for, don't be afraid to ask the candidate for more names.

Pocket Change

Some financial advisors cater to particular groups of people, claiming they can better serve their needs with specialized advice. American Express has trained some of its advisors to handle the particular financial needs of gays and lesbians. Several large financial firms offer specialized advice for women, college students, nonprofit groups, and so forth. Some planners cater to ethnic groups such as African Americans or Asians.

Finding a Financial Advisor Online

There are lots of online brokers these days, with more and more showing up all the time. If you're going to use one, do your homework and compare what different brokers offer, not just what fees they charge. Look for quality trade executions, online newsletters and reports to keep you informed about what's happening in the financial world, 24-hour telephone service, personal access to representatives in case you need face-to-face service, and customized stock alerts to let you know when something is happening that might affect your account. Also, be sure to find out how you'll be able to access your accounts in the event that you don't have a computer handy. Is there an interactive voice response phone system? Or can you access through a PDA?

Some popular online brokers include Ameritrade at www.ameritrade.com, Datek Online at www.datek.com, Fidelity Investments at www.fidelity.com, Waterhouse Securities at www.waterhouse.com, and E*Trade at www.etrade.com.

Go With the Gut

There's one more important factor when you're choosing a financial advisor: your gut. Some people click, and others don't. Although you should never hire somebody just because you like him, you probably shouldn't hire somebody whom you just don't like.

If you like somebody, and you're assured that he's professional and good at what he does, then it sounds like you've got a match. You need someone who will take the time to talk with you, teach you, and be there for you. If you don't like someone, it probably will be very hard to work together effectively, even if he's the best financial advisor in the business. Ultimately, the decision is up to you. Consider all the factors, throw in your gut feeling, and go for it.

Places and People to Avoid

We don't need to tell you that if you see somebody operating as a financial advisor out of the trunk of his car, it's not a good plan for you to get involved with him. Just say "no." But there also are other, more subtle things to avoid when you're choosing a financial advisor: exorbitant fees, conflict of interest concerning products and services, less-than-notable track records, and a sleaze factor.

Too-High Fees

Unless you're a notable exception, you're a little short on money that you don't know what to do with. That's why you have to make sure up front what a financial advisor charges and what you get for that fee.

Find out whether the advisor is fee-only or whether she gets a commission for the financial products she sells. If you can, stick with someone who doesn't sell for a commission (more on that in the next section). Then find out what she charges as an hourly fee. Rates vary greatly, so be sure you shop around. You don't want to sign up with somebody and find out later that her rate is $250 an hour.

The following table compares a standard brokerage fee schedule and a discounted brokerage. Interesting!

Stock Commissions

	200 Shares	300 Shares	500 Shares	1,000 Shares
Full Service Brokerage	$130	$165	$225	$308
Discount Brokerage	89	96	107	124
Deep Discount Broker	35	41	58	90
Internet Trading	12	12	12	12

If the hourly fee seems too high (expect to pay between $100 and $150 an hour), call some other advisors in your area and compare rates. Remember that fee-only financial planners will charge you every time you ask for advice or information. That's how they make their living. If you choose a fee-only advisor, make sure you're billed regularly. That will let you know exactly what you're paying for and help you to decide whether the advice is worth the money.

Dollars and Sense

Always find out when you set up an initial appointment with a financial advisor whether the meeting is free. Many, but not all, advisors offer a free consultation for prospective clients.

If your financial advisor works on commission and receives a fee from the annuity company from which she gets the products she sells, you won't know how much she's earning on your investment unless you ask. Go ahead. She should tell you the price of her advice. If she doesn't, find another advisor. Even if you aren't actually paying the fee, you should know how much the advisor is making for the advice or help you receive.

Conflicts of Interest

If a financial advisor stands to make big money on commissions from selling certain types of financial products, then watch out. You might be pressured to buy products that are more beneficial to your advisor than they are to you. An advisor who does this is more salesperson than financial advisor, and that's not what you need. Some of the best financial consultants available are commissioned salespeople; you just need to understand how they are paid and ask if there is a product available with a smaller commission.

When you first meet with someone you think you might hire, ask whether he gets a commission from products he sells. If he says he doesn't, but you're getting a bad feeling, you can check him out. All advisors are required to register with the Securities and Exchange Commission (SEC) in Washington or their state SEC, and they all must fill out the Uniform Application for Investment Advisor Registration (try saying that before your first cup of coffee!).

Ask the advisor for a copy of that form, commonly known as Form ADV. If he says he doesn't have one, you can call the SEC to make sure he's registered. Every advisor also must be registered with his state SEC, and you should be able to get a copy of your advisor's registration form from that agency.

> **Dollars and Sense**
>
> You can contact the U.S. Securities and Exchange Commission at 1-800-732-0330 or by writing to 450 Fifth St. NW, Washington, D.C. 20549. Or contact it online at www.sec.gov.

I Know What You Did Last Summer

Form ADV contains information about whether an advisor has had problems in the past, such as being sanctioned, has been named in a lawsuit or had complaints filed against him, or has had his license suspended. If you want to check your advisor's track record, ask the SEC in Washington and your state SEC office if they have received any complaints concerning this advisor. You also could call the Better Business Bureau or even the insurance commissioner in your state.

> **Money Pit**
>
> Most financial advisors are diligent and honest, and want to do their best for their clients. As in any profession, though, you'll find some financial advisors who are out to make a quick buck. These are the people who bring the "sleaze factor" to the profession. If you keep in mind that the sleaze factor exists, you'll be more likely to avoid it.

Things Your Investment Advisor Should Never Do

There are some things your financial advisor might do that you don't like, such as take off every Friday afternoon to head for the beach or recommend that you put money in an investment that ends up in the tank. But there are some things your financial advisor should never, ever do. If he does, you need to find yourself a new advisor, and you might want to consider taking legal action.

Misrepresentation

If your advisor tells you the mutual fund you're buying carries no commission for him, but you find out later that he made big bucks by selling it to you, that's *misrepresentation*. It's also misrepresentation if the advisor tells you to go ahead and put your money in a particular investment because you're guaranteed to make 20 percent, and you end up losing most of your principal.

> **CAUTION**
>
> **Money Pit** _____
>
> Be on the lookout for an advisor who guarantees your investments or makes commissions off of sales that he told you carried no commissions for him. If he's doing just that, you can charge him with *misrepresentation*. Some shady advisors also move your investments all over the place, earning commissions at your expense. That's called *churning and burning*, and you don't have to stand for it.
>
> Another kind of misrepresentation is personal misrepresentation. If you find out your advisor has told you he's something or someone he's not, you should ask him about it, check out his most recent ADV, and if you still feel uncomfortable, find someone new.

If he would have said, "I think this might be a good investment for you. Why don't we try it?" you couldn't charge that you'd been a victim of misrepresentation. But an advisor should never tell you something is guaranteed unless he has a guarantee, in writing. Your advisor should always give you the pros and cons of an investment and tell you exactly how the risk relates to your objectives. If he doesn't, consider it a sign that he may be conducting less-than-ethical business.

Taking Custody of Your Money

Regardless of what type of advisor you have, he or she should never have custody—or personal access—to your money. Having custody means that the advisor would be able to move your money into his or her business account, after which who knows what might happen to it. You don't want your money in your advisor's account, even if only for a few days. Always make investment checks payable to the brokerage house, insurance company, or whatever, but never to your advisor.

Ignoring Your Wishes or Neglecting to Keep You Informed

If you read about a money-market fund that gives you just what you've been looking for and you call your advisor and tell him you want to put $3,000 in it, he should go ahead and complete the transaction. Unless he's a money manager (and he should do it anyway), your advisor is obligated to follow your instructions. Now, if he feels it is an inappropriate investment for you, he should tell you why, maybe even following up with a letter; however, he should still follow your instructions.

He may try to advise you not to put your money in that particular fund, and if you trust him, you'd do well to listen. Still, if you insist, he must place your money where you tell him. It is, after all, your money.

If you find out your advisor has been buying and selling your investments without your approval, you have a legitimate complaint. Terminate your relationship immediately. A money manager or broker has two types of investment relationships: discretionary and nondiscretionary. If your relationship is nondiscretionary, an investment should never be made without your agreement. If your advisor has discretion, you should have a formal agreement, and you should fully understand the discretionary relationship and what it costs.

> **Show Me the Money**
>
> **Arbitration** is the hearing and determination of a dispute between parties by a third party. The American Arbitration Association will send you materials you'll need to prepare your own case, if that's the route you choose. Call the American Arbitration Headquarters at 1-212-716-5800 to request the package, or write to the headquarters at 335 Madison Ave., New York, NY 10017-4605.

If your financial advisor always has an excuse to get out of a meeting with you, or doesn't keep you informed about what's going on, you need to ask why. Your advisor should meet with you either on a regular basis or certainly upon your request.

If you feel that your financial advisor has cheated you or has done something unethical, you can look for help by contacting a securities lawyer. Or you can seek *arbitration*, which is the hearing and determination of a dispute between parties by a third party. You can do this either by hiring an attorney to represent you in arbitration, or by representing yourself in arbitration. Before you hire an attorney, contact the NASD (the National Association of Securities Dealers) at 1-301-590-6500 or online at www.nasd.com. This website lets you file a complaint online with the NASD.

If you go into arbitration, you and your advisor will each present your side of the matter to an arbitration panel. A three-member panel will hear the case and then decide on a solution. Its solution is final and can't be appealed.

The Least You Need to Know

- ◆ Although you might be able to handle most aspects of your personal finances on your own, there are times you may need someone to help.

- ◆ You need to know what types of financial advisors are available and where to find someone you can trust before you can choose one.

- ◆ Don't be afraid to ask your potential advisor specific questions about his or her experience, qualifications, and references.

- ◆ Avoid advisors who overcharge, look for big commissions at your expense, have poor track records, or embody the "sleaze factor."

- ◆ Keep an eye out for the things your financial advisor should never do.

- ◆ If you feel you've been cheated by your financial advisor, you may have some recourse.

Part 5

So You're Thinking of Buying a House

Ten years ago, it probably never occurred to you that you'd be a home-owner someday. Sure, you figured that some day you'd have a house, but it wasn't something you thought about on a regular basis. But now it seems pretty important, and you find yourself thinking about it a lot. You can just imagine yourself in your own house, and you're pretty comfortable with the image.

Buying a house seems like a good idea. The problem is, it's a huge under-taking. You don't know much about getting a mortgage or paying it off once you have it. You'll need to find out about homeowners insurance, taxes, down payments, settlement, and all kinds of other house-buying–related things.

Buying a home is a huge move, there's no question about it. But don't worry. In Part 5, we cover the basics, and a lot of the particulars, of home buying. You'll feel a lot more comfortable with the idea of getting a house when you finish reading Chapters 22 through 26.

Chapter 22

There's No Place Like Home

In This Chapter

- To buy or not to buy
- Figuring out how much house you'll be able to afford
- Considering a down payment
- Choosing a real estate agent
- Looking for a house
- Other expenses associated with buying a house

People decide to buy their first home for many reasons. They get tired of paying out money for rent every month, or outgrow an apartment and decide to get a house instead, or think a house would be a good financial move. Or, and this is a biggie, they've embraced the *idea* of having a house. They imagine having friends over for a party on the deck on a hot summer night or picture the family gathered around the table on Thanksgiving Day, waiting for the turkey to be taken from the oven.

For whatever reason, many people buy homes for the first time each year, and maybe you think you're ready to become one of them. If so, you're on the verge of making a very important decision that will affect your life, and your finances, for a very long time. The first order of business is to figure out whether owning a home is right for you.

It's the American Dream—But Is It Right for Everyone?

Americans have this idea that everybody should have a home of their own, yet we probably all know people who really shouldn't be homeowners. Some people love the *idea* of having a house, but they hate the work that goes with it.

When you have a house, there's always something to be fixed, adjusted, or redone. Maybe you can hire somebody to do all those things for you, so it doesn't matter whether you enjoy doing them. More likely than not, though, you'll end up doing the bulk of those chores yourself. If you can't stand the idea of doing this kind of work or having to deal with the never-ending problems that come with owning a house, then maybe you should reconsider or look at a condominium. Condos provide home ownership with the outside work done for you, of course, for a monthly maintenance fee.

> **Pocket Change**
>
> Roper polls show that owning a house is the single item mentioned most often when people are asked what they require in order to be happy.

Another reason it might not be a good idea to buy a house is if you know your life situation will be changing soon. None of us can know what will happen in our futures, but if you have a clue—say, your boss told you that you'll be transferred in six months to a year—then it's not a good time to think about buying a home. The same thing applies if your marriage is on shaky ground, or if your job security is threatened, or if you've just learned that you'll need an advanced degree in order to keep your job.

Of course, lest we sound too pessimistic here, you should know that there are some very good reasons why you should consider buying a house:

- You'll build up *equity* in your house as you pay off your mortgage. You'll have something that is yours.

- Owning a home gives you good tax advantages. We discuss this issue in detail in Chapter 25, but be aware that it can save you a bundle.

- Owning a home makes you part of a community and gives you a stake in the well-being of that community.

Only you can decide whether owning a home is right for you. The implications of home ownership extend well past the financial ones, so you'll have to examine the whole picture and then make a decision.

If you decide, after checking out the financial and other relevant implications of home ownership, that you want to buy a home, congratulations! It's certainly an exciting time. Be prepared to do your homework and talk to a lot of people to get the best information you can. You'll have many important decisions to make.

Maybe after you carefully evaluate all the information concerning buying a home, you'll decide that now isn't the right time for you to do it. If that happens, you might feel disappointed, almost as if something has been taken away from you. Your images of the matching bedspread and curtains evaporate, along with your dream of Thanksgiving dinner in your dining room.

It's okay to feel like that, but remember that postponing home ownership doesn't mean you can never buy a house. If you decide that, for whatever reasons, you're not ready to own a home, you've probably done the right thing. There will be homes for sale next year, and the year after that, and 10 years down the road. When you're ready to buy, you'll find a house that you'll like.

> **Show Me the Money**
>
> **Equity** in a home is the difference between the current market value of the home and the money you still owe on the mortgage, plus any equity loans or lines of credit loans.

> **Dollars and Sense**
>
> If you're getting ready to buy a home, it's a good idea to set up a file to keep everything organized. You'll be collecting a lot of paperwork throughout the process, and you'll need to keep it all organized.

How Much House Can You Afford?

To buy a house, one of the first things you must do is determine just how much house you can afford. You need to know how large a loan, or mortgage, you'll be able to get. (We talk more about what a mortgage is and where you can get one in Chapter 23.)

Before you apply for a mortgage, you need to get your finances in order. To improve your chances of getting the mortgage you want, do the following things:

◆ Reduce your debt. Pay off as much debt as you can before you even start shopping for a mortgage. That includes credit cards, car debts, and any other debts you might have.

◆ Start getting some money together for a down payment. We discuss down payments in more detail later on. For now, we'll just say that the more you have for your down payment, the less you'll have to finance on your loan.

◆ Patch up any glitches on your credit rating or get some credit established—fast!

How Much Do You Make?

To determine how big a mortgage you can probably get, the first thing to look at is how much money you make, before taxes. This amount is your gross income. The recommended guideline is that you should spend no more than 28 percent of your gross monthly income on your mortgage payment. (If you're not sure exactly what your monthly income is, gather up your last couple of pay stubs and figure it out. Or divide your gross annual income by 12 to get the figure.) The mortgage payment includes the principal, interest, real estate taxes, and homeowners insurance.

Pocket Change

Some financial advisors, and many mortgage lenders, will tell you that it's okay to spend more than 28 percent of your monthly income on your mortgage. Many recommend not going higher than 33 percent—some may even go a point or two higher. Remember, however, that many people have made themselves "house poor" by buying a more expensive home than they reasonably could afford.

The principal of a mortgage is the amount loaned. If you borrow $120,000, that amount is the principal, and you are obligated to repay a portion of the mortgage amount each month. You pay principal each month based on the unpaid balance of the mortgage. The interest is the fee the lender charges you to use his money. Real estate taxes are the taxes assessed by the municipality and/or school district within which you live. They're based on the value of your home. And homeowners insurance fees are the cost of insurance to protect the property and its contents. The four things are normally figured into each payment you'll make on your mortgage, although the taxes and insurance are sometimes paid separately.

> **CAUTION**
>
> **Money Pit** _____
>
> Realtors sometimes will encourage you to buy a home that's more than you're comfortable handling financially. Their reasoning is that, while your mortgage payment will stay the same, your salary is likely to increase, so you're fine to buy a house with a bigger mortgage payment than you'd like. A high mortgage payment can put you into the category of "house poor," which could force you to cut spending in other areas.

Your Expenses

It seems that every time you turn around, your expenses have increased. When you're thinking about applying for a mortgage, you must pay close attention to your expenses as they relate to your income.

Although the recommended maximum for your mortgage payment is 28 percent of your gross monthly income, the recommended maximum for your total monthly debt is 36 percent of your income. That means that all your expenses other than a mortgage, such as your car payment, credit card bills, student loans, child support payments, and other bills, should total no more than 8 percent of your gross income.

> **Dollars and Sense** _____
>
> If you have very high monthly expenses because of high credit card or other debt, reduce the debt as much as you can before you go to apply for a mortgage. It will work against you on your application.

Your Monthly Mortgage Payment

Say you're earning $40,000 a year. That means, without going above 28 percent of your income, you could pay $11,196 a year for your mortgage, or $933 a month. To keep within the 36 percent limit for total debt payment, you could spend $14,400 a year or $1,200 a month on all of your debts. The following table gives you a better idea of how much you can afford to pay each month. Remember that a mortgage will typically include the principal, interest, real estate taxes, and homeowners insurance. There are additional payments for PMI (Private Mortgage Insurance), mortgage insurance, etc.

Maximum Amount You Should Borrow for Your Mortgage

Annual Income*	Annual Mortgage Payment	Monthly Mortgage Payment
$ 20,000	$ 5,600	$ 466.67
25,000	7,000	583.33
30,000	8,400	700.00
35,000	9,800	816.67
40,000	11,200	933.33
45,000	12,600	1,050.00
50,000	14,000	1,166.67
55,000	15,400	1,283.33
60,000	16,800	1,400.00
65,000	18,200	1,516.67
70,000	19,600	1,633.33
75,000	21,000	1,750.00
80,000	22,400	1,866.67
85,000	23,800	1,983.33
90,000	25,200	2,100.00
95,000	26,600	2,216.67
100,000	28,000	2,333.33

Gross Income

You should have an idea of how high the property taxes, also called real estate taxes, are in the areas in which you're looking at homes. The tax rate can vary greatly, depending on the makeup of the area. For instance, an area that contains affluent businesses and industry will normally offer a lower tax rate for residents, because the industry provides a strong tax base. An area that is almost entirely residential, however, generally has a higher tax rate. The tax rate can make a difference when you're deciding whether you'll be able to afford a particular home.

Show Me the Money

Lenders often require **private mortgage insurance (PMI)** to protect them against losing their money if you should default on your loan.

If you have a mortgage, you're required to have homeowners insurance. If you put down less than 20 percent of the value of the home, you'll need *private mortgage insurance (PMI)*, as well. Lenders often require this type of insurance as protection against borrowers who may default on the loan.

Try to get an idea of what the cost of homeowners insurance runs in the areas in which you're looking at homes. Your insurance agent or a company in the same general area will be able to give you estimates. We discuss homeowners insurance in more detail in Chapter 26.

The All-Important Down Payment

Another very important factor in figuring out how much house you can afford is the down payment. A down payment is the amount of money you're required (or have available) to pay up front on a house. The rest of the payment for the house is financed through a mortgage. You're normally required to put down between 5 and 20 percent of the price of the home you want to buy, though some lenders will go as low as 3 percent. That's somewhere between $4,500 and $30,000 on a home that costs $150,000.

If you don't have the greatest credit record in the world, but you have a sizable down payment, many lenders will give you more serious consideration than you'd get without a substantial down payment. The bigger the down payment you make, the less your monthly mortgage payment will be. This can work in your favor in two ways:

Show Me the Money

Don't apply for a mortgage and then start trying to scrape together a down payment. Have your down payment in place well before you apply.

- You can lower your monthly payments and have more money to invest or to use for other purposes.

- You could afford a more expensive house with a bigger down payment, because you'll be financing less of the cost of the home. If you buy a $100,000 home and make a $5,000 down payment, you have to finance $95,000. But if you make a $20,000 down payment on the same house, you'll be financing only $80,000.

The following tables show examples of how down payments and interest rates factor into determining how much house you can afford.

Monthly Payment on $100,000 Home—6.5% Interest Rate, Different Down Payments

Down Payment Amount	15-Year Mortgage	20-Year Mortgage	30-Year Mortgage
$ 5,000	$ 815	$ 694	$ 585
10,000	772	658	554
15,000	729	621	523
20,000	686	585	493

The interest rate isn't a factor in how much you need to borrow to buy the house. It's a factor in how much you'll have to pay for borrowing the money. With interest rates currently at historical lows, individuals can afford to purchase a great deal more house than ten years ago because the monthly repayment amount is so much lower than when interest rates are higher.

Monthly Payment on $100,000 Mortgage—Varying Interest Rates, Varying Mortgage Terms

	6.5%	9%	12%
15 year	$ 857	$ 1,014.27	$ 1,200.17
20 year	731	899.73	1,101.09
25 year	660	839.20	804.63
30 year	616	1,053.23	1,028.62

If your mortgage application is turned down because you don't have enough of a down payment, you can either come up with more money or look for a less-expensive house. Hopefully, you've planned for your down payment and have enough money saved. If not, you'll want to accumulate money as quickly as possible.

Perhaps you could cut expenses to save more, or borrow from your 401 (k). You could consider withdrawing funds from your IRA or borrowing money from a relative. Or you may be able to find a mortgage insured by a government agency that requires no or little down payment.

Choosing the Right Real Estate Agent

After you've decided you're going to buy a house and you've figured out about how much you'll be able to spend, it's time to look for a real estate agent. Some first-time buyers decide to do their house hunting and buying on their own without the experience and expertise of a professional real estate agent. We don't recommend this. Unless you're knowledgeable about the ins and outs of real estate, there are just too many legal and financial factors involved to try to go it alone. You could end up spending much more than you have to, or worse, finding out after the fact that you're in some kind of legal trouble. If you do decide to buy or sell a property on your own, good luck. The least you should do is have a real estate lawyer review any agreements before you sign them.

Real estate agents are abundant in almost any given area. Try these tips to find one who will look out for your interests:

- Get personal recommendations. If your friends just got a good deal on the cutest house and they raved about their real estate agent the entire time they worked with her, you should hear some bells ringing. A reference like that is very valuable, and you shouldn't overlook it. On the other hand, if your friends just endured a terrible experience with a real estate agent, you probably should look for somebody else.

- Check 'em out. Do an interview. Ask the agent for names of clients they've worked with in the past four or five months. Don't be afraid of appearing pushy. A good real estate agent will not be offended. Rather, he or she should appreciate the fact that you want the best help you can get when buying your home.

- Call your local board of real estate agents and ask for recommendations. Or ask your local chamber of commerce to recommend a real estate agent.

Show Me the Money

Be sure to stand firm when working with a real estate agent. Don't let her talk you into something that you don't want or don't think you can afford. Remember, real estate agents work on a commission basis and benefit from you buying a house that might be more than you can comfortably afford.

As with any other profession, there are great real estate agents, good real estate agents, mediocre real estate agents, and those who shouldn't be real estate agents. You and your real estate agent will spend a lot of time together during the months that you're house hunting, arranging for a mortgage, and getting ready to move. You want someone that you get along with, but it's also important to have someone who is a professional and knows how to get the best deals possible for you.

Consider the following when you're looking for someone to help you buy a home:

- Experience

- Diplomacy and communication skills

- Honesty

- Understanding

- A feel for the areas to which you're considering moving

- Knowledge of various mortgage companies, inspectors, and other people you might need

The Great House Hunt Begins

An important rule to remember when you're house hunting is to keep an open mind. Don't refuse to look at homes anywhere outside of the three-block area you have your heart set on, because you're sure to miss out on some good properties. The house of your dreams might be just on the other side of the creek you've set as your boundary, or on the other side of town, or the county.

Money Pit

Hunting for a house can become nearly an obsession, if you're not careful. Determine ahead of time just how many hours a week you can spend house hunting and stick to it.

Real estate prices vary tremendously, based on the location of the home. You may be able to afford a townhouse in the "in" neighborhood or a much larger single home with an acre of land in another area. It's a matter of getting your priorities and your finances straight.

For many people, house hunting gets to be like a sickness. Those infected by the house hunt fever are often seen frequenting Sunday afternoon "open houses" or skulking around neighborhoods at various times of the day and night, checking out houses with "for sale" signs in the front. Consider yourself warned.

Building a House vs. Buying a House

Building vs. buying an existing house is a personal choice that should be based on availability, preference, tolerance, and, of course, your finances. Certainly, there are advantages and disadvantages to both options. When you buy a house that someone else has lived in, you're stuck—at least temporarily—with their tastes, which may be far from your own. On the other hand, buying an existing home allows you to get a sense of the area in which it's located, potential neighbors, traffic, and so forth.

If you decide to build a new home, you get to pick your own colors and styles—within your budget, of course. While you won't end up with patterned wallpaper and shag carpet, you may have to do some serious upgrading to get the quality of carpet, paint, cabinets, and so forth that you want. And be prepared to be on call when it comes time to choose carpet colors and other options. If you decide to build a home, you need to know that it's a big commitment and be willing to keep a close watch on its progress. Hopefully, you'll work with great developers and builders and everything will be done right and on time. Often, however, new construction brings with it some glitches, making it advantageous for you to be alert and watchful.

Dollars and Sense

Consult the National Home Warranty Association website at www. hwahomewarranty.com for a local firm and costs.

If you decide to buy an existing home, you should have it inspected first by a certified home inspector. And a home warranty is highly recommended. A home warranty, which normally costs between $400 and $750, is a service contract that covers unexpected repairs during the first year after a house is purchased. A seller or real estate agent often will pick up the cost of a home warranty in order to speed a sale. If not, you should consider paying the cost.

If you decide to build a new home, make sure some of the money to go to the builder is kept in escrow until you're satisfied that everything has been finished the way it's supposed to have been. You may have to make settlement on the house before all the little finishing touches are completed to your satisfaction, but don't be talked out of an escrow fund, which provides some incentive for the builder to complete all the work. Once the jobs are complete, the escrow can be refunded.

How About a Fixer-Upper?

A "fixer-upper" is a home that, because it needs some improvements, can be purchased at a lower price than if the house were in good condition. Fixer-uppers are great for those who love to work around the house, or are lucky enough to have friends or family members who do. There are some great houses out there at great prices, just waiting for some TLC. If you're inclined to spend your weekends sanding, painting, and doing other projects, a fixer-upper might be for you.

If you do decide to buy a fixer-upper, though, be sure you're not getting in over your head, or buying a house that needs improvements you won't be able to afford. Having to scrape and paint the exterior of the house is one thing, while having to replace the entire roof and electrical system is another. If you can't do the work yourself, you'd be wise to get some estimates before you agree to buy the house, to assure you'll be able to afford the necessary improvements.

Single, Double, Townhouse, Duplex, or Condo?

There are so many different kinds of homes; how will you ever find the one you want and can afford? Let's start with single dwellings. Many people who think about buying a house consider only single dwellings. To them, a single dwelling is the only option that truly is a house; the rest are somehow something less.

> **Pocket Change**
>
> Americans not only love to buy homes, we love to buy stuff to put in those homes. According to the National Association of Home Builders, the size of the average house has increased nearly 40 percent, even though the average family size has decreased. Guess what we're using all that extra space for …

True, single homes tend to be larger than nonsingles and generally come with more land. So people with large families, or the need for a multi-acre garden, might require a single. But not everyone does. If you're set on a single home, go ahead and check them out. Just remember that they're not the only game in town.

A double house is a structure with two homes that are side-by-side, sharing a common wall. Each dwelling in a double home can be quite large, and each half often includes some property. They generally are less expensive than single homes and can be a good value.

A townhouse is an attached home, commonly called a row home. These homes are generally less expensive than singles, unless they're in an extremely trendy area.

Townhouses offer advantages such as security, community, and financial value. As with double homes, only you know how you feel about living in close proximity with your neighbors.

A duplex is another example of nonsingle-family housing, but in this case, one complete living unit is above another complete living unit. Duplexes are popular investment properties, and the owner will often live either upstairs or downstairs and rent the other unit.

When you buy a condominium, you own it and part of everything else in the community. That means you normally have shared costs for maintenance and other expenses. Condos are great for people who have no time or interest in the upkeep involved with a single home and property.

There Goes the Neighborhood

People choose the neighborhoods they live in for many different reasons.

Regardless of why you choose the neighborhood you do, be sure to check it out thoroughly before buying a home there. If you visit a home in a particular neighborhood during the day, be sure you go back at night to see what's going on. Noises you might never notice in the daytime can be annoyingly loud at night. Is there a train track near the neighborhood? If so, how many trains will pass through while you're trying to catch some Zs?

Early morning is another good time to visit. What's the traffic like? If you're near a school, consider bus traffic. Do trucks use your street as a thoroughfare?

> **Dollars and Sense**
>
> Always ask the person who's selling his home why he's moving. If he gives you a reason, but you suspect there's something he's not telling you, press a little bit harder for a more honest answer. There could be a problem you're not hearing about.

Don't Forget to Check Out the Schools

I know. You don't have any kids. Maybe you're not even married. The locations and qualities of the surrounding schools are of little concern to you. For now. A lot can change in three or four years, and life often moves quickly and without much advance notice. The schools may be insignificant to you now, but they'll probably become important a bit further down the road. Your real estate agent should be able to get you information concerning particular schools and districts, and you should factor this information into your decision. In addition to coming in handy if you happen to have some kids, being in a good school district makes your house easier to sell when you decide it's time to move on.

Time to Buy Some Furniture

An important financial consideration when you're thinking about moving is what you're going to need to buy once you've purchased the home. Make sure you think about this before you decide to buy, or you could be in for a big shock later. If you absolutely can't stand the wallpaper in the living room, you'll have to factor in the cost of redoing the room or having somebody else redo it. Are you going to need new rugs? What about furniture? If you're moving from a small apartment to a fairly large house, you're apt to have some empty rooms.

Be sure to find out what stays in the house. Appliances like stoves and refrigerators (known as attached appliances) are often required to be included in the sale. Curtains, drapes, and custom-made furniture that fit in a particular spot are usually extras. Attempt to negotiate to retain as many items from the seller as possible. This will enable you to replace the items as you can afford to, not immediately.

CAUTION **Money Pit** _____

Many people are very emotional when it comes to home buying, and don't sufficiently consider the practical matters. We know someone who fell in love with a home, bought it, and moved in, only to discover the windows were really old and extremely difficult to open and close. She spent a fortune on replacement windows, and her finances suffered because of it for years. Be sure you know what you're getting and what you'll need to buy before signing the sales agreement.

You've just committed to spending a huge amount of money for the next 15 or 30 years, and now you realize you need furniture for three empty rooms! What's a new homeowner to do? Consider these tips:

♦ Accept that you can't buy everything you want as soon as you move in.

♦ Check out the second-hand shop for some bargains.

♦ Adopt a minimalist philosophy and a less-is-more mindset.

♦ Be patient.

The Least You Need to Know

- ◆ Not everyone is cut out to be a homeowner.

- ◆ If you want to buy a house, you'll need to figure out how much you'll be able to pay.

- ◆ The amount of money you put down will affect your mortgage payment and is a key factor in how expensive a home you'll be able to consider.

- ◆ It's very important to get a real estate agent you trust professionally, as well as one you like and can work with effectively.

- ◆ When you start looking for a house, remain open-minded concerning the type of structure and the location.

- ◆ You need to consider after-moving costs, such as the cost of furniture and home repairs, when you think about buying a house.

Chapter 23

We'd Like to Borrow Some Money, Please

In This Chapter

◆ Understanding the concept of a mortgage

◆ Finding out about different types of mortgages

◆ Determining which mortgage makes sense for you

◆ Where to get a mortgage

◆ Bettering your chances of getting the mortgage approved

◆ Defining settlement

Owning a home is the American dream, right? The home you buy will be your very own. You can paint the walls whatever color you'd like, invite your friends over for parties, and plan to raise a family there. Of course, you have to pay for your piece of the dream, and it's probably the biggest chunk of change you'll ever put down for anything.

Just What Exactly Is a Mortgage?

The costs of homes vary tremendously, depending on where you live or want to live. Even within a 25-mile radius, location can have a great effect on the costs of homes. The cost varies even more from region to region, across the country. If an area is desirable, due to proximity to a main travel route or certain area, historical significance, or other factor, real estate prices will be higher than in a less desirable location. The median home price in America in 2002 was $161,043, according to the Federal Financial Institutions Examination Council. But $161,043 will buy you a lot more house in some areas of the country than others.

Regardless of whether we pay $100,000 or $280,000 for a house, the great majority of us cannot plunk down the entire amount at one time. So we do the next best thing. We borrow. No, we don't go to Uncle Marvin and ask him for a big, fat loan. (You could, if you had an Uncle Marvin with a lot of money to spare, but most of us don't have Uncle Marvins who will graciously offer to loan us thousands and thousands of dollars.) We do something a little different; we get mortgages.

> **Dollars and Sense**
>
> Remember that the three most important words in real estate are location, location, and location.

> **Show Me the Money**
>
> A **mortgage** is a loan for the cost of your home, minus the down payment.

A *mortgage* is a loan that you get from a bank or other lender. You borrow the difference between the cost of the house and the money you have for a down payment, and agree to pay it back over a specified period of time and at a specified rate of interest. On one hand, mortgages are great, because most of us couldn't buy houses without them. On the other hand, they can be financially crippling if not managed properly.

In this chapter, we look at various topics associated with mortgages. It's important to understand what's involved with mortgages so that you can get the one that's best for you, and make sure you'll be able to handle it financially. When you borrow money for your house, the mortgage lender has a big piece of collateral—your home. The lender holds a lien on your home, just in case you default on, or don't pay, your mortgage. If you don't pay, the lender can take your house. This collateral usually means the interest rate you pay for the mortgage is lower than for other loans.

Because you're going to be stuck with your mortgage for a long time, usually between 15 and 30 years, it's important to understand the different kinds of available mortgages and to get the one that makes the most sense for you. Because you're paying back such a large amount of money over a long period, the interest rate you get is extremely important. A couple of percentage points make a huge difference when you're talking about $125,000 paid back over 30 years.

When you decide on the house you want, consider how much you'll owe and whether you'll have to make any lifestyle changes to make the payment. If you're going for a huge house, you'll probably need a huge mortgage that will consume all of your income. If you want a house, you have to be willing to give up some of the things you were able to afford before the mortgage.

And don't forget that there are other costs associated with a mortgage. You pay much more than just the price of the house. You'll have to consider fees for inspections, legal fees, points, and the like. All these have to be factored in when you're figuring out what you can afford.

Maybe you've always dreamed of owning a perfectly restored eighteenth-century, New England farmhouse with lots of land, and maybe you'll be perfectly happy to spend every bit of your income on the mortgage for that house. But if you want the house, and you want to buy and keep horses in the barn, continue to take two expensive vacations each year, have dinner a couple of times a week in trendy restaurants, and hire somebody to make custom curtains for every window in the house, you'd better take a close look at your income versus your expenses. Now that you've had your frugality lecture, let's get back to mortgages.

> **Money Pit**
>
> First-time homeowners frequently get themselves into trouble by buying a house that's too expensive for their incomes and lifestyles. Many first-time buyers try to get their dream house immediately, instead of getting a starter home and waiting until their incomes can support the dream house.

> **Show Me the Money**
>
> **Refinancing** your mortgage is trading in your old mortgage for a new one. People refinance to get better interest rates, and thus lower their monthly payment, and/or shorten the term of the loan, or to change their mortgage from one type to another.

Getting the Mortgage That's Best for You

The two most common types of mortgages are fixed-rate and adjustable-rate. There are some other kinds that we'll mention briefly, but fixed-rate and adjustable-rate are the big two.

Fixed-Rate Mortgages

Fixed-rate mortgages are the most common kind of mortgages—sort of the industry standard—and they're the easiest to understand. You agree to pay a certain amount of interest on your mortgage for as long as you have it. If you pay 7 percent interest the first month, you'll pay 7 percent interest the last month, too. The rate doesn't change and neither does your monthly payment. You'll receive a schedule of payments, and you'll know exactly how much you'll pay each month. So if you like to know exactly how to plan your long-term budget, you'll probably like fixed-rate mortgages. It removes the guesswork.

Show Me the Money

A **fixed-rate mortgage** is one where the interest rate remains constant over the life of the loan. An **adjustable-rate mortgage** is one where the interest rate normally stays the same for a specified amount of time, after which it may fluctuate.

Interest rates a lender charges on a mortgage, or any loan, change because of the general economic environment, usually dependent on inflation. Interest rates are controlled by the Federal Reserve, through the interest rates that this federal agency charges to banks. If the Feds charge banks high interest, your mortgage rate will be high; if rates are low, a mortgage you take out should have a low rate.

A problem with fixed-rate mortgages, though, is that if the interest rates drop dramatically, you're still stuck paying the higher rate. You can *refinance* your mortgage to take advantage of low rates, but this process requires time and involves significant expense for things such as appraisals, title insurance, points, and the like. These fees can easily add up to $3,500 or $4,000. When you refinance your mortgage, you're basically trading it in for a new one. Still, there are reasons why more people have fixed-rate mortgages than any other kind. They're easy to keep track of, and you can count on a specific payment you'll make each month. Let's have a look at how the other kinds compare.

Adjustable-Rate Mortgages

Adjustable-rate mortgages (*ARMs*) are different from fixed-rate mortgages because the interest rate doesn't stay the same for the entire term of the loan. Because of that, your monthly mortgage payment varies. Homebuyers generally are attracted to ARMs because they offer initial savings. You often can get an ARM without paying *points*, which are the fees (actually prepaid interest) you pay your mortgage lender to cover the cost of completing the mortgage application. (We'll talk more about points a little later on in this chapter.) Also, the beginning interest rate of an ARM is normally lower than the rate for a fixed-rate mortgage.

You generally agree to pay a fixed interest rate for a certain amount of time, after which your rate and monthly payment may start to fluctuate. The interest rates for ARMs are tied into various indexes, which determine how they'll rise or fall. The indexes used for the interest adjustment are based on the current interest rate scenario evident at the time the ARM rate is adjusted. Whatever index is used will be specified by the lender. Most ARMs also include annual caps, so your interest rate can't keep increasing forever. You could, however, end up paying hundreds of dollars more on your monthly payment down the road than you do initially if the interest rates rise dramatically. On the other hand, if interest rates stay low, an ARM can be a good deal.

During the last several years, interest rates dropped to a 45-year low, and ARMs aren't as popular right now as they were when interest rates were higher. The difference between an ARM and a fixed-rate mortgage is minimal these days, compared to as much as a 4-point difference back in the days when mortgage rates were up at around 9 percent.

The following are two of the more common types of available ARMs:

♦ A 7/1 ARM has an initial rate that's locked in for seven years. The rate can change every year after that.

♦ In a 3/3 ARM, the initial rate is locked in for three years, then the rate can be adjusted every three years. It can be raised 2 percent at a time, with a 6 percent increase cap for the life of the loan.

Fortunately for the buyer, most ARMS offer caps that protect against really huge increases in payments. There are different kinds of caps:

♦ A lifetime cap limits how much the interest rate can rise over the life of the loan.

♦ A periodic rate cap limits how much your payments can rise at one time.

♦ A payment cap limits the amount that your payment can rise over the life of the loan.

The initial savings of an adjustable-rate mortgage over a fixed-rate mortgage can be tempting. Don't get sucked into an adjustable-rate deal, however, unless you fully understand how it works and are willing to take the risks.

Which Is Better: Fixed-Rate or Adjustable?

If you're trying to decide between a fixed-rate or adjustable-rate mortgage, it's good to get all the information you can about each. After you have a pretty good understanding of the differences between the two types of mortgages, ask yourself these questions:

♦ How long do you plan to live in the home you're buying?

♦ How often does the ARM adjust and when is the adjustment made?

♦ How high could your monthly payments get if interest rates were to rise?

If you're only going to live in the house for a few years, an ARM might make more sense than a fixed-rate mortgage. Remember, the initial interest rate usually is lower with an ARM, and you might be able to avoid paying points. If you're only going to live in the house for three years, and your interest rate can't be adjusted within that time, you may be able to get a good deal with an ARM.

Pocket Change
More than three quarters of the people who get mortgages choose fixed-rate mortgages.

After the initial, fixed period, during which time the interest rate on an ARM can't change, most ARMs adjust every year on the anniversary of the date you closed on the mortgage. A 3/3 ARM means you'd have the initial payment for three years, after which it can be adjusted every three years. You're normally notified of your new rate about 45 days before it takes effect.

Suppose you have an ARM with a cap that allows your interest rate to jump 2 percent a year, with a lifetime cap of 6 percent. If you have a $100,000 mortgage, and started with an interest rate of 5.75 percent, your monthly payments could jump more than $400 by the time your lifetime cap kicks in. Quite a hammering, isn't it? In that case, and that's a worst-case scenario, you'd be better off having a fixed-rate mortgage. Economists and financial experts who study these things say that if you can get a good fixed rate, you're probably better off with it, even if you don't plan to stay in the house too long.

The following table shows the different monthly mortgage payments and the differences in total income paid for mortgages at different interest rates. Quite a difference!

Sample Adjustable Rate Mortgage Payment Differential

2% adjustment, permitted 4 times (6% maximum increase in rate)		
5% rate	$ 402.62/month	$ 4,831.44/year
7% rate	498.98/month	5,987.76/year
9% rate	603.47/month	7,241.64/year
11% rate	714.25/month	8,570.91/year

Before you choose a fixed-rate or adjustable-rate mortgage, you need to determine how comfortable you are with risk. If you choose an ARM, and your interest rate zooms up, will you be able to afford the higher payments? Do you have an emergency fund you could borrow from if you had trouble? Are you likely to be incurring additional expenses soon? Do you need to buy a new car, or are you planning on starting a family? Are you sure your income will continue rising, or is it possible that it will decrease?

These are all questions you'll have to think about and answer before making a decision. An ARM can pay off, but it's a gamble. Sometimes there's a lot to be said for something that's safe and dependable, like a fixed-rate mortgage.

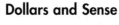

Dollars and Sense

Before assuming an adjustable-rate mortgage, figure out what the highest possible, worst-case scenario payment could be. If you don't think you could swing it, go for a fixed-rate mortgage.

Knowing When to Refinance Your Mortgage

Although interest rates in the summer of 2004 were beginning to creep up, there still is opportunity to refinance your mortgage. Refinancing your mortgage is when you replace your current mortgage with one that has a lower rate. Lenders will tell you that it makes sense to refinance your current mortgage when rates have fallen 1.5 percent or more below what you are currently paying. If that applies to your mortgage and you plan to stay in your home for a period of time, you might want to think about refinancing.

Some lenders claim it makes sense to refinance when rates are less than 1 percent below your current rate, but, depending on closing costs, the length of time you are planning to stay in your home, and other factors, it's questionable. Ask the lending agent to run the numbers for you, considering these factors: the interest rate to be charged on the loan, closing costs, and how long you will be in the house. The numbers should tell you what is best for your situation.

Other Types of Mortgages

Remember we mentioned earlier in the chapter that fixed-rate and adjustable-rate mortgages aren't the only games in town? Here's a look at some of the other types of available mortgages:

- ◆ **Hybrid mortgage** As the name implies, this type of mortgage is a mixture of fixed-rate and adjustable-rate models.

- ◆ **Balloon mortgage** Another type of hybrid mortgage is a balloon mortgage. With this type of mortgage, you make payments with lower-than-normal interest rates for a while, and then you're expected to pay off the principal balance of the loan all at once! You normally have between 3 and 10 years before your lump-sum payment is due. This type of mortgage isn't a good idea unless you're absolutely sure you'll have money available to pay off the balance.

- ◆ **Jumbo mortgage** This type of mortgage doesn't apply to the great majority of us. A jumbo mortgage, as the name implies, is one that exceeds the limits set by Fannie Mae and Freddie Mac. The 2004 limit was $333,700.

Dollars and Sense

While researching mortgages, you're likely to hear the terms *Fannie Mae* and *Freddie Mac.* These aren't mortgage lenders from Arkansas; they're publicly chartered corporations that buy mortgage loans from lenders. This ensures that mortgage money is available at all times, everywhere across the country.

- ◆ **Assumable mortgage** This is when the buyer of a home takes over the mortgage from the seller. It can be advantageous if the owner got the mortgage at a terrific interest rate, and the rates have increased significantly. Also, assumable mortgages rarely have the fees associated with standard mortgages.

- ◆ **Seller financing** The seller of the home provides financing to the buyer, and the buyer pays back the seller instead of a mortgage lender.

- ◆ **Biweekly mortgage** We'll get into more detail about this kind of mortgage in our next chapter, so for now we'll just tell you that the monthly payment is split into two, and you pay half of it every two weeks. This shortens the length of the loan dramatically. We'll tell you how in the next chapter.

As you can see, there's a lot to think about when choosing a type of mortgage. Try to get as much information as you can, and then make an intelligent, informed decision. But wait! There are other things to consider before choosing one.

Thirty-Year vs. Fifteen-Year Mortgages

Mortgages can be paid back over varying amounts of time, depending on the terms you agree on. The two most common payment periods are 30 years and 15 years. A 30-year mortgage has the advantage of lower monthly payments, because your loan is spread out over a longer period of time. However, you end up paying thousands of dollars more in interest on a longer-term mortgage.

With a 15-year mortgage, you have a higher payment each month, but you can usually get an interest rate that's one quarter to one half of a percent lower than on a 30-year mortgage. Paying off the loan at a lower interest rate and in half the time results in big savings, as the following chart shows:

Total Interest Paid over Life of Mortgage

7% Loan	
15-year Mortgage Loan	$ 46,350
30-year Mortgage Loan	104,632
9% Loan	
20-year Mortgage Loan	$ 86,951
30-year Mortgage Loan	142,249

As you can see, your interest savings are tremendous. Something to be considered, though, is how paying off a mortgage affects your taxes. The interest you pay on your mortgage is 100 percent tax-deductible, which reduces your after-tax cost. With a 30-year mortgage, more of your monthly payment is for interest, and you have a larger deduction than with a 15-year mortgage.

Some people choose 30-year mortgages even though they could afford the higher monthly payments of a 15-year mortgage, because they'd rather take the difference and invest it. They figure that in a good market, it pays off to invest rather than shorten the length of your loan and decrease your interest.

So what will it be? A 30-year fixed-rate mortgage? A 15-year adjustable? Before you decide, there's one more thing to consider: points.

Points

We've told you that points are fees (or actually prepaid interest) that amount to 1 percent of your loan. The tricky thing is that lenders charge different numbers of points on different mortgages. Usually, the lower the interest rate is, the more points you'll be charged and vice versa. If you want to lower your monthly payment, you probably will pay more points to do so.

Because points are prepaid interest, the more interest you pay initially means you pay less throughout the term of the mortgage via a lower interest rate. An example of this is a 6.7 percent mortgage with 3 points: If you don't want to pay the points, you can obtain a 7.45 percent mortgage, with no points. You pay the interest one way or the other. Which scenario is best for you depends on how much cash you have available to pay points. Ask your lender how the points affect your total loan interest payment, and then decide what is best for you.

You can either pay the points up front, at settlement, or you can finance them as part of your loan. For instance, if your mortgage is for $100,000, each point is worth $1,000. If your lender charges you 3 points, and you finance them, you'd have to increase your mortgage to $103,000—or, pay no points but pay a higher interest rate. Sound confusing? Just remember to compare the total interest to be repaid. This is the bottom line for you. When you choose a mortgage, you can usually lock in your interest rate by paying a commitment fee equal to 1 point at the time of application.

Alternative Types of Mortgages

There are some government programs available to help people who don't have a lot of money for down payments and closing costs. Most, although not all, of these programs are aimed at first-time buyers. These programs are intended to provide affordable housing for middle- or low-income families, who may not qualify for other types of mortgages. There are several of these programs available.

Federal Housing Administration Loans

The name of this type of loan is confusing, because the Federal Housing Administration (FHA) doesn't actually lend the money. Private lenders make the loans, and the government guarantees them and pays off the loans in full if the borrower defaults.

Typically, a buyer can't get as large of a mortgage if it's administered by the FHA as he could otherwise, but an FHA loan requires a low down payment and offers a lower interest rate than a standard mortgage. FHA mortgages can be for 15, 20, 25, or 30 years.

Veterans Administration Loans

Available to those who have served or are currently serving in the U.S. military, Veterans Administration (VA) loans also are guaranteed by the U.S. government. VA loans, which usually carry lower interest rates than other mortgages, require no down payment and are available both as fixed-rate or adjustable-rate mortgages. The fixed-rate mortgages can be for either a 15- or 30-year term, and the adjustable-rate mortgage is for 30 years.

Community Home Buyer's Program

This program is offered in partnership with Fannie Mae, a publicly chartered corporation that buys mortgage loans from lenders. The Community Home Buyer's Program (CHBP) requires only a 5 percent down payment, and 2 percent of that can be a gift from family or friends. Money that's considered a gift doesn't show up on a credit report, and doesn't count as debt that you owe. People seeking CHBP loans are required to attend educational programs regarding personal finances and issues regarding home ownership.

Fannie Neighbors

Also in partnership with Fannie Mae, a Fannie Neighbors loan requires that the property being purchased is located in an area designated for low- to middle-income housing. Fannie Neighbors loans, which are fixed-rate loans, require lower down payments than conventional mortgages and less cash for closing costs.

While these types of loans come with restrictions concerning the amount of income a borrower may have, the geographic area in which the borrower wants to buy a home, the length of the loan, and so forth, they are good alternatives for people who don't qualify for standard mortgages.

Where to Go to Get Your Mortgage

Once you decide what kind of mortgage you want and the length of your loan, you'll need to find a lender. Mortgages, like most products, vary in cost, making it necessary to shop around to find the best value. Getting a mortgage that carries an interest rate of just half a percent less than another rate will save you thousands of dollars over the life of your loan.

Lots of places offer mortgages. Although the number and variety means there's lots of competition—and that competition often results in lower rates for you—it can make finding the right lender a bit of a chore. But you can do it.

You can get an idea of the mortgages available by checking out your Sunday newspaper's real estate section. It should include rates from various banks and other types of lenders. If your paper doesn't list mortgage rates, just get the paper from any good-size town. Don't assume, though, that the rates listed are the only ones available or the best ones.

Large banks are able to advertise their rates, but that doesn't mean they're the best ones around. Check out the smaller banks in your area, too. They might have lower rates than the big boys. And don't forget about mortgage bankers, who do only mortgages. Stay away from slick salesmen, who fast-talk you into thinking their deals are the best, when they're not even close.

Dollars and Sense _____

The Internet has some cool sites that make it easy to get the lowest up-to-date interest rates. Here are a few to get you started:

Compare interest rates at www.compareinterestrates.com

Mortgage Rates in Your State at www.interest.com/rates

LoanWeb at www.loanweb.com

HSH Associates at www.hsh.com

Some people prefer to get their mortgage with a local company or bank. This is fine, as long as you don't end up paying higher rates. There's an advantage of using a local company when it comes to making payments because you can hand-deliver them and know that they're credited to you for that very day. If you have to send your payment 3,000 miles across the country, you have no control over when your payment is credited, and that can subject you to late fees.

Lenders also charge other fees, charged up front and supplemental to the mortgage amount, in addition to the actual mortgage, so be sure you find out what they are and how much they add up to. Fees for things like appraisals, copies of your credit report, and loan applications and processing can add up to thousands of dollars that you'll need to pay up front. Consider that information when choosing your lender.

If you think you can't get the best mortgage on your own, you can hire a mortgage broker to do it for you. You have to pay for his services, but if you just don't have time to shop around, or you feel intimidated by it all, it might be worth your while to have a broker. If you apply for a mortgage and are turned down, then you should call a broker.

Online Mortgage Lenders

As with many other services, you now can acquire a mortgage from Internet companies. And some of their rates are very competitive. If you're looking for a mortgage, check out some of the websites listed below.

Lendingtree.com

Eloan.com

Loansearch.com

Lowquotemortgage.com

Bankrate.com

If you decide to use an Internet lender, you'll receive the paperwork necessary to make everything official. Be sure that the contract matches the quote you receive online, and be sure to read everything carefully before signing. Many online scams are related to mortgage lending due to excess fees, higher interest rates than quoted, and so forth. A point in fees or interest can cost you thousands in interest payments. It's not unheard of for closing costs and interest rates to show up differently at the time of settlement than they did in a quote.

Getting Your Mortgage Approved Faster

After you've located a lender and decided on the type of mortgage you want, you have to fill out an application and then wait patiently while the lender takes his good old time deciding whether to approve your loan. You'll probably meet with a mortgage officer, who will help you with the application.

To speed up the mortgage process, take the following items to your appointment. Having this information ready will save time and speed up your application:

- Your W-2 forms from the previous year.

- Documents showing two years of residence and employment history.

- A current paycheck to prove your salary.

- A copy of your credit report with any necessary corrections.

- Your employer's name, address, and telephone number.

- Any financial statements for your personal assets and proof of income if you are self-employed.

- Tax returns from the last three years.

- Lists of all your assets, including loans and deposit account numbers. Also, take the last monthly statement available on each account.

> **Pocket Change**
>
> Most lenders will give you a copy of your credit report if you ask. They'll probably charge you for the copy, but they'll do it. You can get a free copy of your credit report from TRW, one of the large credit agencies. Call TRW at 1-888-503-0048.

If you suspect you're on shaky ground for getting your mortgage approved, try to come up with some more money for a down payment. This will greatly improve your chances, and will make your mortgage payments less, as well.

What Happens at Settlement?

After your mortgage has been approved, you've found the house of your dreams, and the seller has agreed to the sale, you're in business. The only thing standing between you and moving into your new dream house is settlement. But what is this mysterious thing, and what goes on there?

Settlement is the final closing of the sale of your home. It's when the bank (the lender) pays the seller your mortgage funds. You'll drink coffee, sign about a million papers, wait around while people make copies, and then sign some more papers. In addition to taking up your time, settlement will cost you money. Costs for things such as a 1 percent transfer tax, notarization fees, a check to make sure your taxes are paid, a check to see whether your house is in a flood plain, title insurance, and a fee to prepare the deed will be tallied up and presented to you during settlement.

Show Me the Money

The final closing on your house purchase is called a **settlement**.

The number of complaints from homeowners who say they were slapped with fees that they were never told about before settlement is on the increase. When you make an offer on a house, the real estate agent is obligated to give you a good-faith estimate of the money you'll need at settlement. Be sure you ask, and ask your real estate agent to be as specific as possible about what fees to expect.

Money Pit

Beware of hidden fees that can affect your settlement. Tacking on extra fees at settlement has become so common that federal housing and finance officials are pressing for legislation to stop them. Be sure you know what fees you're expected to pay, and question any that you didn't hear about prior to settlement.

The Least You Need to Know

♦ A mortgage is a loan for the cost of the house, minus your down payment.

♦ There are various types of mortgages, but the two most popular are the fixed-rate and adjustable-rate mortgages.

♦ Most people get mortgages that they agree to pay back over 15 or 30 years.

♦ It pays to shop around when looking for a mortgage lender because rates can vary greatly.

♦ You can improve your chances of getting your mortgage approved and speed up the process by doing some simple preparations.

♦ You should be aware of settlement costs and be on the lookout for any extra fees.

Chapter 24

Paying It Off, Little by Little

In This Chapter

- ◆ The benefits and drawbacks of paying off your mortgage early
- ◆ Where your mortgage money goes
- ◆ Missing a payment or two
- ◆ The importance of private mortgage insurance (PMI)
- ◆ Putting money in an escrow account

If you're thinking you might like to speed things along a little bit and make an extra payment or two on your mortgage, or are wondering about a biweekly mortgage payment, you're at the right place.

This chapter examines the issues related to paying mortgages. You'll learn about making extra payments on your mortgage and exactly what parts of your mortgage your payments are applied to throughout the life of your loan. We'll also see what happens if, for some reason, you can't make a mortgage payment or are late with a payment. We'll also have a look at the pros and cons of escrow accounts.

How Quickly Should You Pay Your Mortgage?

Mortgage payment periods vary. Some people pay off their debt over 15 years; others take 30 years. There's no right way or wrong way to pay a mortgage; you just have to decide what makes the most sense for you. While the two most common mortgages are 15-year and 30-year plans, less common types are 10-year, 20-year, and 25-year mortgages.

One thing that most financial experts agree on, though, is that, if you can, paying off your mortgage early makes sense. If you make extra payments, you'll reduce what you'll pay over the life of the loan, and increase the *equity* in your home all that much sooner. Increasing the equity in your home means you'll have more money to invest in your next home. Not everyone agrees, mind you. Some experts would tell you it's better to take the extra money, find yourself a good investment with a potential for big returns, and go for it. That's the way to go, they say, especially if you'll get a tax break, as with a retirement account. Decide what is right for you, invest or prepay. Calculate the total return of both scenarios, and then, *do it!*

Show Me the Money

Equity is the net value of your house. It's the market value, less the balance of your mortgage and any equity loans or lines of credit. If your house is valued at $100,000 and you have an $80,000 mortgage, you have equity of $20,000 in your home.

If you do decide you want to pay extra on the mortgage, there are several ways you can do it. You can pay a little bit extra every month, or you can make periodic lump-sum payments. Most financial experts agree that if you're going to prepay your mortgage, it's better to do it sooner, rather than later. For instance, instead of making a lump-sum payment once a year, make smaller monthly payments. Why? Because the more you pay on your mortgage, the more interest you save, and the more equity you have.

Home equity is important for several reasons. It's *collateral* you can use for a car or other loan. If you ever want to get a home equity line of credit, this line will be based on the amount of equity you've built up in your home. The more equity in your home, the more money you'll get to keep if you sell the house, giving you a larger down payment if you decide to buy another house.

When you first get your mortgage, the lender will give you an *amortization schedule*. The schedule will show the amount of your mortgage month by month based on regular payments, with no prepayments. If you pay exactly what is required each month, you'll stay on the schedule. You pay interest on your mortgage, which is calculated each month on the remaining balance of the loan. Every time you pay extra on your principal, you're reducing the amount of your loan and the amount of interest you'll have to pay.

Show Me the Money

Collateral is the assets pledged as security for a loan. It's something that the lender holds as assurance of payment.

An **amortization schedule** is the schedule of repayments you're required to make to your lender over a specified period of time.

Once you start paying off your mortgage, you'll make the payments according to the amortization schedule your lender will provide. The following is an example of an amortization schedule:

Amortization Schedule

Mortgage Amount	Interest Rate	Monthly Payment
$75,000	6.625%	$658.50

Payment Number	Interest Payment	Principal Payment	Principal Balance
2	$ 412.71	$ 245.79	$ 74,509.77
3	411.36	247.14	74,262.63
4	409.99	248.51	74,014.12
5	408.62	249.88	73,764.24
6	407.24	251.26	73,512.98
7	405.85	252.65	73,260.33
50	338.37	320.13	60,968.99
51	336.60	321.90	60,647.09
52	334.82	323.68	60,323.41
53	333.04	325.46	59,997.95
54	331.24	331.24	59,670.69
96	246.10	412.40	44,164.02
97	243.82	414.68	43,749.34

continues

Amortization Schedule (continued)

Mortgage Amount	Interest Rate	Monthly Payment
$75,000	6.625%	$658.50

Payment Number	Interest Payment	Principal Payment	Principal Balance
98	$ 241.53	$ 416.97	$ 43,332.37
99	239.23	419.27	42,913.10
100	236.92	421.58	42,491.52
143	124.30	534.20	21,981.35
144	121.36	537.14	21,444.21
145	118.39	540.11	20,904.10
146	115.41	543.09	20,361.01
147	112.41	546.09	19,814.92
177	14.34	644.16	1,952.51
178	10.78	647.72	1,304.79
179	7.20	651.30	653.49
180	3.61	653.49	0.00

Extra payments on your mortgage don't have to be regular, and they don't have to be for the same amount each time. If you have some extra money at the end of the month, add it to your mortgage payment. The mortgage payment above is $658.50. If you rounded that up to $675 every month, you'd be adding $16.50 per month, or $200 more per year to principal (in other words to the mortgage loan), probably without even thinking much about it. If you increased the payment to $700 every month, you'd be prepaying $41.20 each month, or $500 per year. You'd be surprised at how that extra money would cut the payment time on your mortgage and save you some big bucks in the long run. Prepaying doesn't have to be anything formal or planned in advance. But you do need to make sure the lender realizes that the extra money is a prepayment on your principal (so state the extra amount in a note with the check), not extra money to be put into an escrow account for taxes (more on escrow later in this chapter).

Show Me the Money

Some mortgages include prepayment penalties that could force you to pay 2 or 3 percent of your total loan if you pay it off early. Be sure to ask whether your mortgage includes this. It's something that might just slip by and could end up costing you thousands of dollars.

How Much Extra Do I Have to Pay?

You don't have to pay a great deal extra to make a difference in paying off your mortgage. Adding just $25 a month to a $100,000, 30-year, fixed-rate mortgage at 8 percent will save you $23,337 in interest before taxes over the life of the loan. If you can swing $100 extra a month, you'll save $62,456.

You can see that it makes sense to pay extra. So how can you do it? Review Chapter 10 for tips on saving money and tack the savings onto your mortgage payment. You can easily spend $25 a week on extras. If you cut down and apply the saved money to your mortgage, you'll see a big difference in the long run. Or you could designate a bonus or your income tax refund as an extra payment.

What About Biweekly Payments?

Nearly all biweekly mortgages are set up through banks, savings and loans, or credit unions. That's because these types of institutions have access to your accounts and can make automatic withdrawals from them. Mortgage companies normally can't make these withdrawals, so they're unable to offer biweekly mortgages.

Let's have a look at how biweekly mortgages work. Instead of paying 12 large monthly installments each year, you pay half of your monthly payment every 14 days. It's not as painful as it sounds, because the money is deducted automatically from your checking or savings account. Because you pay every 14 days, you end up making 26 payments a year, not 24.

By making biweekly payments, you can pay off a 30-year mortgage in a little less than 23 years, and a 15-year mortgage in less than 14 years. That's the good stuff on biweekly mortgages. The downside is that not all lenders offer this option, so if you're sold on it, it could limit from whom you can get your mortgage.

The following table shows the savings in interest paid and when the mortgage term is decreased. It sure is interesting to see how paying extra cuts down the interest paid over the term of the loan.

> ### Pocket Change
>
> For some people, the primary benefit of a biweekly mortgage is that it's deducted automatically, saving them the task of sending the payment to the lender. Another potential benefit is that you make smaller payments more than once a month rather than having to come up with the funds to make one large monthly payment.

Biweekly vs. Standard Mortgage Payment Comparison

$100,000 loan @ 6 percent

Term	Mortgage Payment	Interest Paid	Interest Saved	Shortened by
15 year (180 months)	$ 843.86	$ 51,895		
15 year biweekly	421.93	45,144	$ 6,751	1.33 years
30 year (360 months)	599.55	115,838		
30 year biweekly	299.78	91,260	24,578	6.83 years

Critics of the biweekly mortgage say it's of little benefit to the consumer, but of great benefit to the lender. There's often a fee to switch your payment plan over to the biweekly system, and it can be quite hefty. A fee of between $250 and $400 is not unusual. There can also be a transaction fee of $3 or $4 for every payment you make, in addition to the one-time charge.

You should be able to find financial institutions that provide biweekly mortgages but don't charge a fee. High fees defeat the purpose of prepaying your mortgage, so just say "no" to lenders who charge them.

Be wary of critics of the biweekly payment plans. Is the information they provide influenced by their not being able to offer biweekly plans? Comparison shop at several financial institutions before you choose the payment format that is best for you.

If you decide to go with biweekly payments, make sure that the payments are credited to your mortgage when they're deducted from your checking account. There are biweekly payment plans that withdraw the funds but hold them aside until the mortgage company has one month's total mortgage payment, at which time they make the payment. While withdrawing funds biweekly and holding them until you have a full payment from your checking account is easier to manage than one monthly withdrawal, it's more advantageous to have the money turned over to the mortgage company whenever the funds are withdrawn from your account. Paying on your mortgage every two weeks is better than paying only once a month.

CAUTION

Money Pit

Multiply a $4 transaction fee by 26 payments, and you'll find you're paying $104 a year for the privilege of having a biweekly payment. If you save that money instead of spending it on fees, you could apply it to your mortgage!

Critics also say that telling people that paying biweekly reduces the interest payments over the loan is confusing. It makes consumers believe they're getting a better interest rate on their mortgage, when the interest rate doesn't change. In the end, they say, you'll do just as well by making one extra payment a year on your own, without the benefit of the bank's biweekly mortgage plan.

That sounds good, but we all have a lot of places we could spend our money. What happens if it's time to make your extra payment, but you've just surprised your wife with plane tickets to Italy to celebrate your fifth wedding anniversary? If you don't think you have the discipline to put aside the extra money for the payment, it probably makes more sense for you to add some extra money to your payment each month.

Put Your Money Where Your Mortgage Is

Your mortgage payment has four main components:

1. Principal, which is the amount you borrow from the lending institution

2. Interest, which is the fee you pay the lender to borrow money

3. Tax, which is the money you pay to your city or county, based on the value of your property

4. Insurance, which is the amount you pay for homeowners insurance (which is required by most lenders)

Tax and insurance costs may or may not be included in your mortgage bill, depending on your lender. Be sure you know ahead of time if those expenses are figured into your mortgage or if you'll need to pay for them on your own. If these costs are part of your mortgage payment, they're held in an escrow account (for more info on escrow accounts, read the section "Putting Money in an Escrow Account").

During the first year of a typical 30-year mortgage, you pay over 10 times more in interest than you do on the principal of your loan. Although the bulk of your mortgage payment is applied to interest during the first few years, eventually your payments kick in and start reducing your principal. Less and less of each payment goes toward the interest, and you start to build up equity (value) in your home. By the time you get about two thirds through your mortgage payments, about the same amount will be going to principal and interest with each payment. The amount of principal you're paying will increase each month until your mortgage is paid off.

By the time you've made your mortgage payment for 30 years, it's likely that you will have paid double the cost of your original loan. Pretty amazing, isn't it? It's good to know where your mortgage payment goes, but don't dwell on it. There's no point in making yourself crazy.

What If I Can't Make a Payment?

Gasp! The mortgage payment is due, and you don't have the money to pay it! Will the bank take your house? Put you in jail? Send big, nasty-looking creditors over to beat it out of you? Harass you with sarcastic phone calls? What will you do?

Relax. Probably none of these things will happen. Okay, you might get a phone call, but you won't lose your house for being late or missing one payment. Granted, missing a mortgage payment is serious business, and it's not at all good for your credit rating, but it's not the end of the world.

If you know you can't make this month's payment, call the lender.

Tell him or her why you can't make the payment: You lost your job, your son's medical bills are outrageous, or whatever the reason is. Just tell the truth. Then work together to come up with a reasonable plan to begin paying again. Make whatever payment you can to show that you're acting in good faith. It's important that you be up front with your lender. Don't say you'll be able to catch up on your payments the following month if you're not going to be able to. If you've had a financial catastrophe or you've just gotten in over your head, make sure you tell the lender what's going on.

Be honest with yourself, too. Will the situation get better, or will you eventually need to sell your house? These are all things that will have to be considered as you work with the lender. Remember that honesty is the best policy.

Late Penalties

If your payment is late, you'll probably be hit with a penalty. The amount of the penalty is set by the mortgage company or bank, and is zapped on you whether your payment is one day late or 30. If paying late gets to be a habit, you can be sure it will show up on your credit report, which is not a good thing! Late fees are considered a deduction for income tax purposes, but that's not enough reason to pay them. Do everything you can to pay your mortgage bill on time.

A potential problem with making your mortgage payment is the postal service. You might think you mailed your payment in plenty of time for it to get to that post office box in Georgia by the due date. The problem is that you're at the mercy of the U.S. Postal Service, as well as the mortgage company's payment-processing speed.

If you're close to the payment due date for your mortgage and your check isn't in the mail, send the payment by overnight, two-day, or priority mail or pay online. It will cost extra, but not as much as a late penalty.

If the lender charges you a late fee in error, call the lender immediately. Tell the lender when you mailed the check. Often, the lender will refund the fee, but don't ask too often. A once-sympathetic lender can turn nasty when pressed too hard.

> **CAUTION**
>
> **Money Pit**
>
> Another downside to being late with your mortgage payment is that it makes the next payment seem like it's due within days of the previous one. If you're two weeks late with your August payment, that September bill is going to be coming in before you know it.

The best way to avoid late penalties is to have your monthly or biweekly payments withdrawn from your checking or savings account automatically each payment period. Like magic, the payment is made, even if you forget to send it or are away when the payment is due. To do this, however, you need to be sure that there is sufficient money in your account to cover the payment. The best thing is to have the monthly or biweekly payment made the day, or the day after, you get paid. You don't want to incur overdraft charges while paying your mortgage.

Private Mortgage Insurance

Your lender didn't just fall off of the cabbage truck. Lending companies are well aware that people miss mortgage payments. There have been many, many instances in which people have gotten a payment or two behind and stopped paying altogether. They *default* on their mortgages.

That's why you'll hear from your lender if you miss just one payment. People who have been in the lending business for any amount of time know that once you fall behind on your payments, it's easy for a snowball effect to begin. When that happens, a little problem easily becomes a big problem.

Show Me the Money

To **default** on your mortgage is to not repay the debt as agreed to in the terms of the mortgage. It is a failure to live up to the agreement.

Private mortgage insurance (PMI) is insurance that protects the lender against a default on his loan.

Because many people do default on their mortgages, lenders have to protect themselves with something called private mortgage insurance. Purchasing *private mortgage insurance (PMI)* protects the lender against any default on the loan. The lender usually requires it if you have less than 20 percent of the cost of the home for a down payment. PMI charges normally amount to about one half of 1 percent of the loan.

So if you put down 10 percent on a $100,000 house, your mortgage will be for $90,000. The lender multiplies the amount of the mortgage by .05 percent and comes up with $450. That's the annual cost of your PMI, which breaks down to $37.50 a month.

If you do default on your mortgage, look out. It takes years for your credit rating to recover from something like that. Go ahead, default on your mortgage, and then just try getting a car loan. You'd better pump up the old bike tires.

Your lender will cash in on the private mortgage insurance policy you've been paying for, along with the rest of your mortgage payment, and be on his merry way. You, meanwhile, will have lost your home and ruined your credit. In case you didn't know, if you don't pay your mortgage, you are forced to sell your home. The bank doesn't let you stay in it just because you put that pretty wallpaper in the bedroom.

Dollars and Sense

Keep track of your payments on the principal of your mortgage. When you have reached an 80 percent debt/equity ratio, which means you've paid 20 percent of the cost of your home, notify your lender. In most cases, you'll no longer be required to carry PMI. Legislative changes back in 1998 required that the PMI automatically be dropped when your mortgage amount drops to 78 percent (or your equity is 22 percent) of the original price of the house or the original appraisal, whichever is lower. Once your mortgage is paid off, you may qualify to get some of your PMI payments back. Contact the U.S. Department of Housing and Urban Development at 202-708-1113 for more information. Or check out its website at www.hud.gov.

If you are forced to sell the home and it's sold for less than the remaining mortgage owed to the lender, your mortgage insurance will cover the difference. You will lose your down payment, though. You are responsible for all fees incurred by the lender concerning paying off the mortgage. If the home is sold for more than what is due the lender, you get the difference back. Hopefully, the amount you get back will be more than you put down on the house originally.

Most people who can't make their mortgage payments try to sell their homes themselves, rather than foreclosing and/or going through a sheriff's sale. There are hefty fees for *foreclosures*, which are when lenders take back properties that have been defaulted, and most people are pretty mortified to have their names listed among those with properties up for public auction at a *sheriff's sale*. If you see trouble down the road with keeping up with your mortgage payment, make a plan. Many state and city housing agencies offer counseling to people who are in danger of defaulting on their mortgages. Don't wait until you're several months behind on your mortgage to look for help.

Show Me the Money

A **foreclosure** is legal action by the lender to take back the property on which the loan has been defaulted. The lender can resell it privately, or offer it for public auction at a sheriff's sale. A **sheriff's sale** is for the purpose of recouping debts on the property—or it can also be done for delinquent taxes or water bills, even if the mortgage is up to date.

Putting Money in an Escrow Account

Most lenders, but not all, require you to put money into an *escrow account* to cover taxes and insurance if you owe more than 80 percent of the value of your home. That means, if you don't have at least a 20 percent down payment and your lender requires an escrow account, you'll have no choice in this matter. Some lending institutions require that you have an escrow account regardless of how much you have for a down payment.

When you reach the point where you've paid at least 20 percent of the value of the home, you can decide whether to continue paying the tax and insurance money and having it go into escrow or to pay the taxes yourself. Many people prefer to have that money put into escrow, knowing it will be available when the tax or insurance bill comes due. It's a comfort to a lot of people to not have to worry about putting money aside for those bills. Others, though, want to keep control of their money and use it any way they want until the payments are due.

If your money is put in escrow, you pay part of your homeowners insurance and taxes each month. One twelfth of your yearly bill is paid off each month. When you escrow, you, as the homeowner, are responsible to send your tax bills to the lender for payment. Your homeowners insurance company should bill the lender directly; however, it is wise to verify that the payment has been made. Mark the date your premium is due on your calendar. Then, call your lender about 15 days before the due date and verify that the payment is due. You are ultimately responsible for making the payment, so it's worth the time to make sure mistakes don't occur—at your expense.

> **Show Me the Money**
>
> An **escrow account** is an account set up for a particular purpose. The money put into an escrow account is to be used only for the designated purpose, such as paying for insurance or taxes.

> **Pocket Change**
>
> If you go the escrow route and forego the interest you could make on your money, just consider it a service charge you have to pay the bank for keeping track of your payments.

If you feel strongly about not having to put money in an escrow account, you can hunt around until you find a lender that doesn't require it. Or you can start with an escrow account, and then pay your own insurance and taxes after you've got more than 20 percent of the cost of your home paid off. Remember that you'll have to request that the escrow account be closed and that you pay the bills on your own. The lender doesn't have to notify you when you've reached the 20 percent mark.

Shock occurs the first time you receive notification that your mortgage payment is increasing. How come? You have a fixed-rate mortgage, right? Well, your mortgage didn't increase, the escrow payment did. Either the homeowners insurance premium or the real estate taxes increased, and that means that the lender needs more from you each month to cover the cost. The lender should review escrow accounts annually so that you don't get too far behind with the funds in your account.

The Least You Need to Know

◆ If you decide you want to repay your mortgage ahead of schedule, there are several ways you can do it.

◆ Biweekly mortgages are highly regarded by some and scoffed at by others.

◆ Your initial mortgage payments go almost entirely toward paying interest, but eventually they shift over to paying mostly the principal.

◆ Being late or missing a mortgage payment is likely to result in a penalty, and it can damage your credit rating.

◆ Many lenders require you to put money in an escrow account to pay for insurance and taxes on your home.

How Owning a Home Affects Your Taxes

In This Chapter

- ◆ Understanding how owning a home can reduce your taxes
- ◆ Knowing what deductions you can claim
- ◆ Coping with property taxes
- ◆ Understanding home equity loans and taxes
- ◆ Weighing the tax advantages and disadvantages

Owning a house—regardless of whether it's a five-bedroom Colonial, a mobile home, a condo, or a town home—gives you significant tax advantages, but it also means you have to pay property taxes, which can be quite high. To make things a little more confusing, although you have to pay property taxes, you may get to deduct the full amount, if you itemize on your tax return. Being able to deduct the taxes isn't as good as not having to pay them in the first place, but it sure makes it a little easier to bear.

Tax Benefits of Owning a Home

When you buy a house, Uncle Sam gives you a little housewarming gift (he's real generous with the gifts, isn't he?). You get to deduct two of the biggest owning-a-home expenses from your federal income tax:

1. The interest on your mortgage

2. Your property taxes

Dollars and Sense

If you refinance your mortgage, the points you pay can be deducted from your taxes over the life of the loan, but you don't get a one-time deduction for the entire expense.

There are other, one-time deductions, such as the points you pay at closing, but interest and property taxes are the long-term biggies.

These deductions are great news for homeowners. When paying the mortgage bill every month starts to seem like more than you can bear, remember that, come April, you'll be happily filling out Schedule A, which is a part of your federal income-tax return (see Chapter 14). If you itemize deductions, the interest and taxes paid on your loan lowers your tax liability.

Deductions, Deductions

If you remember from Chapter 14, tax deductions can be itemized and subtracted from your adjusted gross income (commonly known as AGI), if they're greater than the standard deduction allowed by Uncle Sam. The deductions and personal exemptions are subtracted from your income before you figure out how much tax you have to pay on it. If your total income is $45,200, but you have $7,500 in deductions and two exemptions totaling $6,200, you'll pay tax on only $31,500.

When you become a homeowner, you get the privilege of taking some pretty hefty deductions. If you haven't itemized your deductions before buying the house, make sure you find out all the deductions you're entitled to before you pay this year's taxes. Mortgage interest and property taxes are both expensive, and they can take quite a large chunk out of your income when you total them up for tax purposes. That's good news for your wallet on April 15. Take a look at lines 10–14 on the Schedule A in this chapter. This will give you an idea of where the deductions are used. Also, if line 28 is greater than your standard deduction, you'll save money at tax time.

Interest and taxes are the biggest mortgage-related deductions, but there are others. You also can deduct the points you pay at settlement, but you can only get this deduction in the year that you first get the mortgage.

Points usually are the responsibility of the buyer, but a seller that really wants to sell can sometimes be convinced to assume responsibility for paying some, or all, of the cost of the points. If you can convince the seller to pay the points, you win in two ways. One, you don't have to pay the points. Two, you can still deduct them from your income tax. If you and the seller split the points, you still get to deduct the total amount.

Dollars and Sense

To get a quick idea of how much you'll save on taxes as a homeowner, add up the amounts of your property taxes and your mortgage interest if you itemize, and multiply that amount by your marginal federal tax rate. It's not an exact formula, but it will give you a good idea of the savings you can expect.

Be aware that if you buy a home late in the year, you won't see too much tax advantage the first year. People often buy homes in September or October and are convinced they'll get great tax breaks when it comes time to file. But remember that the standard deduction for a married couple filing jointly is $9,700. You can't itemize things such as your mortgage interest and property taxes until your deductions add up to more than the standard deduction. So if you buy your home in October, you might not have enough time to build up deductions that will total more than $9,700.

If you don't take the deduction for points the same year you buy the house, you can amortize, which means you gradually take the points over the period of the loan. So if you have a 20-year mortgage and your itemized deductions didn't reach more than $9,700 (if you are married), you can take a deduction for some of the points you pay up front on your mortgage each year for the number of years that you have the mortgage. For example, if you have a 15 year, $100,000 mortgage with 3 points, $1/15$ of the $3000 in points is taken as a deduction each year.

In addition to deducting mortgage interest and points, you can deduct some of the property taxes and other expenses that are finalized at settlement. Some of the expenses you pay at settlement can be deducted from your income tax, and some of the other expenses are considered *capital expenses* when you sell your home. Capital expenses are expenses used toward the "basis" of your property, which are considered part of the cost.

Show Me the Money

Capital expenses are those currently nondeductible expenses that can be deducted against your profit. This is considered part of the cost basis of your house, and it's used to lower any capital gain liability when you sell your house at a profit.

Capital Gains Exclusion

You've just moved into your house, so this section on capital gains might be a little premature. This information will be helpful someday, though. A *capital gain* occurs when you sell your home at a profit. Say you buy it for $100,000, keep it for a while, and then sell it for $200,000. You've made a $100,000 profit or capital gain. Most profits, such as those on many investments, are taxed for capital gains purposes. A portion of the capital gains from selling your home, however, is not.

Show Me the Money

Capital gains are the profits from the sale of an investment or asset. Tax on this gain is usually due the year the asset is sold.

Pocket Change

The 1997 Taxpayer Relief Act was great news to persons under age 55 who wanted to sell their homes and buy smaller ones. Before this act, people who owned their homes for many years often had to pay high capital gains taxes at sale time.

Show Me the Money

A capital gains exclusion is an exclusion to the practice of taxing capital gains. It applies to those who sell their homes and are within the parameters set by the government: up to a $500,000 sum if married, $250,000 if single.

Capital gains used to be bad news for taxpayers, who saw a big bite taken out of the money they made on the sale of a house. Fortunately, the Taxpayer Relief Act of 1997 made big changes in the capital gains taxes you pay on the sale of your house. The 1997 law says you can take a $500,000 exclusion on your income tax if you're married and filing jointly, or a $250,000 exclusion if you're single.

You can file for the *capital gains exclusion* every two years at any age, as long as you've used the property as your principal residence for at least two of the last five years. If you only own your house for one year, you can take a partial (50 percent) exemption. If you have to move because of unexpected or uncontrollable reasons, such as a job transfer or health reasons, you get to take the total exemption. It won't be prorated, even if you haven't lived in the house for two years.

Don't rush out and sell your house now that we told you about the $500,000 exemption. It sounds like a huge amount to be sure, but you'd be surprised at how quickly costs add up. Always save any receipts associated with fixing up or improving your house. This is smart in case you need them for an insurance claim. Saving the receipts also gives you a record of capital improvements for the calculation of any gain for your state income tax return. Note that although the IRS allows a $500,000 exclusion for capital gains on a house sale, your state's allowable exclusion may be considerably less.

Pocket Change

The principal residence capital gains exclusion was especially good news for taxpayers, who had long complained about paying the tax or waiting until they were 55 to sell their homes. After all, no allowances were made (and still aren't) on tax returns for capital losses when selling a home. So if you made money on the sale of your home, you were expected to pay taxes. If you lost money—tough break, buddy.

You Wanna Play House? You Gotta Pay Taxes

As we mentioned in the beginning of the chapter, it's not all good news concerning taxes and owning a home. There's this pesky thing known as *property taxes*, and it can be a real strain on the old pocketbook.

It varies, but your property taxes usually run somewhere about $1\frac{1}{2}$ percent of the value of your property. Because paying property taxes can be prohibitive, many lenders require that homeowners pay money into escrow accounts to cover the cost of the taxes when they come due. See Chapter 24 for more information about escrow.

In most areas, you pay local property taxes (also known as your school tax), county taxes, and sometimes some oddball *municipal* taxes, too. Taxes can vary, depending on the quirks, wishes, and wealth of the municipal boards that impose them. The majority of property taxes you'll pay will go toward funding your local school district. A portion goes to the borough or township in which you live, and some goes to your county. You normally pay your taxes to a local tax collector, who distributes them to the proper places.

You can be assessed for your taxes once a year, twice a year, or even more often. Property taxes have gotten so high in some areas that officials are allowing residents to pay their taxes quarterly, in order to relieve the burden of huge lump sums.

Many property owners and legislators agree that property taxes are not an equitable means of raising money to support public education and other services. Elderly people whose

Show Me the Money

Property taxes are taxes levied by the municipality and/or school district within which you live. They're based on the value of your property.

Show Me the Money

A **municipality** is a zoned area, such as a city, borough, or township, that has an incorporated government.

children graduated from high school 40, 50, or 60 years ago still pay property taxes if they own homes. And people who don't own property enjoy the same services without having to pay the high property taxes. Property tax is an issue in almost every state, and movements are underway in some states to reform the tax.

The really annoying thing about property taxes is that the municipality imposing them can raise them by reassessing your home. Every now and then, municipal governments rampage and declare a major property reassessment. When that happens, look out. The municipality, at this point, has probably reached its upper allowable tax limit and is looking for a way to make more revenue. If it can't up your tax rate, it can reassess your home.

If you think the assessment on your home is too high, you can challenge it. You'll need to know the assessments of the other homes in your neighborhood, and your appeal might be denied. But if your property taxes seem out of line with those that others in your neighborhood are paying, it might be worth a fight. If you get an appeal, make sure you're prepared. Know the number of rooms in your house and how your home compares to others with lower assessments.

Obviously, there are expenses other than taxes involved with owning a home, and you can expect to pay various taxes in addition to your property tax. You might be charged additional taxes for streetlights, fire hydrants, trash collection, sewage, water, and the like. Unfortunately, these taxes are not tax-deductible.

This means you have to be careful when breaking down your expenses for your tax return. The bank might pay $1,000 to your municipality for your taxes, but only $850 of the $1,000 is deductible on your taxes. It's a good idea to keep copies of all your tax bills to use at income tax time.

Home-Equity Loans and Lines of Credit

Again, this information might be a little premature if you haven't been in your house very long. But there's another neat tax advantage that comes with home ownership, and it's called a *home-equity loan*. If you get one of these handy little (or big) loans, you're allowed to write off 100 percent of the interest charges up to $100,000.

> **Show Me the Money**
>
> A **home-equity loan** is a loan that's taken against the equity you've built up on your home.

Home-equity loans and home-equity lines of credit can be very convenient. In fact, they can be lifesavers if you have unexpected expenses or expenses you just can't cover. These types of loans are taken, as the name implies, against the equity you've built up in your home. Your equity is used as collateral on the loan. Always remember, though, that there's a big risk associated with home-equity loans. If you default on the loan, you lose your home.

There are several types of home-equity loans. The first type is a line of credit. This means you're given approval from the lender to borrow up to a specified amount of money against the equity in your home. You don't get the money in a lump sum, but it's there for you to borrow, if you need it. This kind of loan can be extremely useful in the event of an emergency or unexpected expense. You don't have to pay interest on the money until you use it, so if you don't use it, it costs you nothing. The interest rate on this type of loan is variable—that is, it fluctuates with the current interest rates.

Because current interest rates are low, these loans are popular. The problem, though, is that the rates will increase as the *prime rate*— a sort of starting point for banks—increases. The higher that interest rates are in general, the higher the rate your loan will be charged. If you borrow using a line of credit, be certain you can afford to pay higher payments in case the interest rates increase significantly.

Show Me the Money

Prime rate is the interest rate that banks charge their most creditworthy customers. All other borrowers are typically charged at some rate above prime, depending on their risk.

The other kind of home-equity loan is a fixed-rate loan. Your equity is calculated, and you borrow money against it. You repay the loan on a fixed schedule at a fixed rate of interest. You can always pay more on the loan than is required, but don't pay less than the fully required amount. This is a loan, not a line of credit.

There usually aren't as many fees associated with home-equity loans or line-of-credit loans as there are with a mortgage, but be assured, there are some. You'll probably have to pay a mortgage application fee, an appraisal fee, a fee for a credit report, and possibly processing fees. You won't have to pay points, however. If you're in line for a home-equity loan, go to the first meeting prepared, as you would be if you were applying for a mortgage (see Chapter 22). The application and processing time will be shortened considerably if you're well prepared.

Home-equity loans make sense in many cases. For instance, if you want to borrow $20,000 for a new Honda, you can take a car loan. Back in the good old days (before the tax law revamping in 1986), you could have even deducted your car loan interest.

CAUTION

Money Pit _____

  Lenders have been getting fee-happy lately when it comes to home-equity loans. If your lender tries to tell you that you have to pay points, however, tell him to take a hike, and go elsewhere.

Not now. If you get a home-equity loan, however, and use it to pay for the car, you can deduct the interest and save yourself some money. But we can't stress how important it is to understand the risks of home-equity loans.

Especially with a home-equity line of credit, use caution. It's like having a huge credit card to use whenever you want. The problem is, if you don't control the spending, it's your house that's on the line.

The Least You Need to Know

◆ One of the advantages of owning a home is the amount of deductions you may get to claim on your federal taxes.

◆ The interest on your mortgage and your property taxes are often two of your biggest deductions.

◆ Property taxes can be prohibitive, but it's possible to challenge the amount you're paying.

◆ You can use home-equity loans to your tax advantage, but be careful with them; the stakes are high.

◆ Generally speaking, it's a good idea to own a home—not only for tax purposes, but also for less tangible reasons, such as comfort, security, and pride.

Chapter 26

Homeowners Insurance

In This Chapter

- ◆ Yes, you really do need homeowners insurance
- ◆ Insuring your home
- ◆ Insuring your stuff
- ◆ Covering damage to other people and their property
- ◆ Protecting yourself against natural disasters
- ◆ Shopping around for a homeowners policy

Getting and maintaining good insurance policies that will protect your home and its contents takes some planning and follow-through, but the peace of mind it will provide is well worth the trouble. We discussed homeowners insurance briefly in Chapter 15, but if you own a home, homeowners insurance is too important to just skim over. In this chapter, we look at how much insurance you need and the types of coverage you should have. Then we figure out some of the best places to buy insurance. First, let's look at why homeowners insurance is so important.

Nobody Should Be Without Homeowners Insurance

Your home is probably the biggest investment you'll ever make, and unlike a mutual fund, it involves much more than your money. Your home is where you live, and it's a part of who you are. It's where you should feel safe and able to escape from the world. It's the place that holds the people and things that are most important to you and where you can put aside pretenses and impressions and just be yourself.

> **Pocket Change**
>
> The Insurance Information Institute reports that the average cost of home insurance per year is right around $600. When you think of all the unnecessary things you buy throughout the year, probably costing far more than $600, that doesn't sound like too bad of a deal, does it?

If your mutual fund takes a nosedive, you lose money. If your house burns down, however, you lose much, much more. To protect your home, you buy *homeowners insurance*. Although homeowners insurance can't replace your wedding pictures and the antique clock that belonged to your great-grandmother in the event of a fire or other catastrophe, it can at least enable you to rebuild your home and make a new start. It can't protect your emotional investment in your home, but it can protect your financial one.

The question, then, is how much of this insurance should you have? What kind? What should you do about deductibles? Exactly what will it cover?

Briefly, most insurance companies offer six basic types of homeowners policies. They're known in the industry as HO-1 through HO-6, and they cover a variety of different *perils*, or potential dangers. Some of the perils covered under the six basic policies are fire, damage caused by falling objects, an explosion in your heater or air conditioner, riots, vandalism, and hurricanes. There are also expanded versions of these policies, such as HO-3000, and they're all based on various coverages that different people need.

> **Show Me the Money**
>
> Homeowners insurance covers your home and its contents against perils. **Perils** is the insurance industry's word for every bad thing that could possibly happen. Homeowners insurance includes **personal property coverage** for the contents of your home and **liability insurance** for the damage you do to other people and other people's property.

The perils covered under any of the six policies might vary from insurer to insurer and from state to state. For instance, in Pennsylvania, damage to your home from wind is covered under your normal policy. But in Texas, which is considered a high-risk tornado area, wind damage is not covered under the normal policy; you need additional coverage.

In addition, not all insurers offer every type of policy. That's why it's so important to know exactly what your policy covers and doesn't cover. Be sure to ask your agent to explain the entire policy, and don't be afraid to ask questions.

How Much Homeowners Insurance Do You Need?

Homeowners insurance is designed to repair or replace your primary residence if it's somehow damaged or destroyed. Coverage usually is based on the sale price of the home when purchased, but remember that the sale price includes the value of the land. If your entire property is valued at, say, $175,000, but your house would cost only $85,000 to rebuild, then you don't need homeowners insurance based on the entire value.

The part of your homeowners insurance that covers your house (the structure, that is) is called *dwelling coverage*. Dwelling coverage isn't based on how much you paid for your house or how much money you borrowed to buy it. It's based on how much it would cost you to rebuild your house if it were completely destroyed.

The cost to rebuild is normally based on the square footage of your home, the type of home you have, and when it was built. If you have an older home with lots of details, such as a wooden staircase, stained glass above the doors, or ornate plaster work, your insurer is likely to tell you that that sort of detail could not be matched if your house had to be replaced. You can expect to pay more for your homeowners insurance if you have a lot of "extras" in your home, such as garbage disposals, ceiling fans, spas, French doors, fireplaces, and so forth.

Look for a Guaranteed Replacement Provision

If your home costs more to rebuild than the limits of your insurance policy, what will you do? Pay the extra yourself, or leave your home unfinished? Some insurance policies pay off your mortgage if your home is destroyed, but don't pay to rebuild the home. Or they'll pay you the amount of your policy coverage, but not the replacement amount for your home. Guess you could always pitch a tent on that lot you own.

> **Dollars and Sense**
>
> We can't stress enough how important it is for you to closely examine your insurance policies and know exactly what coverages you have and don't have. It can be financially devastating to assume you're covered for something, only to find out after a catastrophe that you're not.

If you have a *guaranteed replacement provision*, you won't have to pay for construction, leave your home unfinished, or pitch that tent; the insurance company will pay for the rebuilding, even if it ends up costing more than your policy limits. Most insurers will give you up to a certain amount more than your policy's limits. For example, if it costs $150,000 to rebuild your home, and your policy limit is $100,000, your insurer might give you 25 percent over your limit. That means you'd get an extra $25,000, but you'd still be $25,000 short of the actual construction costs.

> **Show Me the Money**
>
> The part of your home-owners insurance that covers the structure in which you live is called **dwelling coverage**. If that structure is damaged, and your policy has a **guaranteed replacement provision**, the insurance company will pay for the rebuilding, even if it ends up costing more than your limits.

> **Show Me the Money**
>
> A **rider** on an insurance policy is extra coverage added to your basic policy. An **inflation rider** is a rider specifically designated to cover the increased costs due to inflation (increased cost of living).

To make sure that your replacement cost provision will truly cover the full cost of rebuilding your home, your policy must provide coverage for the entire amount of the coverage you need. If your home is valued at $100,000, and your policy's limit is $50,000, you're underinsured. What you want in your coverage is a policy that guarantees the cost of construction, regardless of whether it costs $100,000, $150,000, or $200,000 to rebuild your current home.

There's a lot to think about regarding replacement cost provisions, but they're definitely worth paying extra for. You should have a replacement cost provision to cover your *personal property*, as well. Be aware, however, that the definition of guaranteed replacement cost varies from insurer to insurer. Be sure to clarify your guaranteed replacement cost coverage with your insurer.

Personal Property Coverage

It's amazing how much stuff we accumulate. Walk around your house some time and take a good look at everything in it.

You can't be certain that nothing will ever happen to these things. If it does, the fact is that some of them will be irreplaceable. Remember though, as hard as it is to lose things you care about, they're still only things. If there is a fire or other catastrophe, consider yourself very lucky if you and your family manage to escape unharmed.

Dollars and Sense

Cleaning out some of your stuff and donating it to a charity such as Goodwill Industries can be beneficial in several ways. It will help when tax time comes around (charitable contributions are tax-deductible if you itemize deductions), it will reduce the total value of your property and make your insurance cost less, and it will relieve some clutter in your home. So which closet will you clean out first?

Some things you will be able to replace. You can go out and buy furniture, clothing, kitchenware, and most of the other things you use every day. What you need to make sure of is that your insurance policy will adequately cover the cost of these things.

The best kind of personal property coverage includes *replacement cost guarantees*, which means you'll be reimbursed for what it costs to replace the damaged, stolen, or destroyed items at today's prices. Without replacement cost guarantees, your insurance company will give you about half of what you paid five years ago for that sofa you liked so much. If you do have the replacement cost guarantee, your insurer will pay you today's price for the sofa, and you'll be able to go out and find one that's similar to what you had, only newer.

The amount of personal property coverage insurance companies provide is usually based on the amount of your dwelling coverage. Your personal property usually is insured for 50 to 75 percent of your dwelling coverage, depending on the insurance company. The premium for replacement cost insurance increases the cost of your personal property insurance by about 13 percent a year, but it's worth it.

Exactly What Should You Insure?

You should insure all the property you would need to replace if it were destroyed or stolen. Your furniture, dishes, electronic equipment, washer and dryer, and all the other things in your home should be covered by insurance.

Be aware that some policies limit your coverage for certain items if they are damaged or stolen. You may have to purchase special riders to cover these things, and be aware that this extra coverage will increase your annual homeowners premium. The list varies from insurer to insurer, so be sure to inquire.

Dollars and Sense

Most insurance companies require that you replace the item that's been damaged or stolen. Your insurer won't hand over a check for $400 for you to buy a replacement TV, for instance, and let you use the money instead to upgrade your computer. You have to come up with some proof (a sales receipt) that you did, indeed, purchase a TV.

Make Sure You Know What You Have

We're going to ask you to do something that might make you uncomfortable. We simply want you to think about something: If your house burned down today while you were at work, and it and everything in it were completely destroyed, how would you prove to your insurance company what you lost? Would you even be able to identify everything that you lost?

Would it even occur to you to inform the insurance company of these things, or would you think about them six months down the road, long after your claim had been completed and settled?

Dollars and Sense

After you've inventoried and documented your personal property, be sure you store the documentation somewhere out of your home or in a secure, fireproof box or safe. It will do you no good to go to all the trouble of documenting your possessions if the documentation is destroyed along with your property.

What you need to do is document the property that you have. The best way to do it is to take photographs or videotapes of your stuff, write a brief description of each thing, and estimate each thing's value. You also should keep receipts for major purchases. Sounds like a lot of work, doesn't it? Most people will never do this because they think it's too much trouble. But if you need to file a claim to recover the value of personal property, you'll be very, very glad that you made the effort to document your possessions.

Keep in mind that personal property insurance doesn't cover only the items that are inside your house. It also covers property in your possession that might be damaged or stolen while you're traveling.

Liability Insurance

The other big part of homeowners insurance protects you from liability (that means lawsuits) for accidental damage. This coverage applies in the event that the following occurs:

- Someone is injured in your house or on your property.

- Someone is injured by you or a family member, anywhere.

- Someone else's property is damaged or destroyed by you or a member of your family.

- Someone claims you've slandered him or her.

How much liability coverage should you have? That's a tricky question. You should have at least enough to cover your financial assets; it's preferable to have enough to cover them twice. This liability coverage pays for the cost of defending you in court and any court awards up to the limit of your policy. You are covered not just in your home, but anywhere.

If you have all kinds of cash, you might have to purchase an umbrella liability policy, or personal catastrophic policy (PCAT), to cover your many assets. These types of policies give you additional liability insurance over the liability limits of your home-owners policy, which is added to the coverage you already have. They're usually sold in one-million–dollar increments, which might sound excessive. Remember, though, many people are sued for more than that. If you have a swimming pool, a pit bull, one of those big trampolines that are the cause of so many accidents, or anything else that could cause trouble above and beyond the norm, you probably should carry extra liability coverage. Personal umbrella coverage is available at a very reasonable price, usually $200 to $350 for $1 million of additional liability protection.

Dollars and Sense _____

Liability insurance covers only unintentional incidents. Intentional incidents are more likely to get you to the police station than to your insurance company.

Insurers say that there's always a big jump in applicants for flood or earthquake insurance after a flood or earthquake has hit an area. Typically, though, many homeowners will cancel their policies or not renew them if another disaster doesn't occur in the following few years. Once you have the insurance, you should do yourself a favor and keep up the policy!

Insuring Against Natural Disasters

A typical homeowners policy will protect you from damage caused by fire or rioting, but it won't help you out if your home is flooded or your foundation cracks during an earthquake. You have to buy extra coverage for those things if you live in an area considered to be at high risk for them.

Even if you don't live in an area considered high-risk for earthquakes, floods, and other natural disasters, it's good to explore the possibility of getting even minimal insurance, just in case. Check to see exactly what coverage you have, and talk to your agent about what you may need to get and how much it will cost.

Dollars and Sense

If you don't live in a flood plain, you can't buy flood insurance.

If you live in a flood plain, but your community hasn't adopted a flood plain management ordinance, lobby your local officials to do so. You can't be eligible for federally subsidized flood insurance if they don't.

Flood insurance is available through the National Flood Insurance Program for communities that have adopted and enforced flood plain management ordinances. This federally subsidized program is administered by the Federal Insurance Administration, which is part of the Federal Emergency Management Agency. You can call the National Flood Insurance Program at 1-800-638-6620.

Many homeowners in Florida had a rude, collective awakening in 2004 when three hurricanes hit the state in short succession, flooding and otherwise damaging or destroying hundreds of thousands of homes. It turned out that some homeowners had coverage through their insurance companies that predated guaranteed replacement cost. After the hurricane had come and gone, they found out their policies left them in a huge lurch, and were unable to rebuild their homes.

The Government Will Take Care of Us

Uncle Sam is getting tired of bailing out (no pun intended) people who live in flood plains but don't have flood insurance. There are moves underway to get more people to buy flood insurance so that the government won't have to keep putting out federal relief funds. You can't always count on federal funds in the event of a flood or other natural disaster, though. Less than 50 percent of flood sites are declared federal disaster areas, a designation necessary in order for them to be eligible for federal funds.

Even if you can get federal disaster relief funds, most of them are low-interest loans, not giveaways. Flood insurance program people say the interest you'd have to pay back on your federal loans would cost more than the approximately $300 yearly fee for flood insurance. And, they note, if you receive federal funds, you have to buy flood insurance afterwards to be eligible for any more funding. To be sure, $300 is a lot of money, but a flood can effectively wipe out your home and everything you own along with it.

The Best Places to Buy Homeowners Insurance

Shop around when you're looking for homeowners insurance, because coverages and costs vary for different properties. Find a good agent who will be able to tell you exactly what coverages you need for your circumstances, and who will help you with claims. Sure, go ahead and get some quotes from Internet sites; they'll give you a good starting point with which you can compare the quotes you get from an agent. Working with an agent is recommended, however, to ensure that you get the coverage that you really need. The following companies have good reputations for claims-handling and customer service:

- Nationwide Mutual

- Allstate

- Erie Insurance

- Liberty Mutual

You can call a local agent who sells these brands, or you can find the company's toll-free number in the phone book and call for information.

Dollars and Sense

The Insurance Information Institute offers the following brochures at no cost: "Twelve Ways to Lower Your Homeowners Insurance Costs"; "Insurance for Your House and Personal Possessions: Settling Insurance Claims After a Disaster"; "Am I Covered"; and "Home Inventory." To get one or all of them, just send a self-addressed, stamped envelope to the Insurance Information Institute, 110 William St., New York, NY 10038, or check it out online at publications@iii.org. You also can call the institute for advice at 1-800-331-9146.

Don't forget to ask if you qualify for any special discounts. Insurers look kindly on your extra protective measures, such as home security systems, dead-bolt locks, fire extinguishers, smoke detectors, and even having your auto coverage (called a multi-line discount) with the same company. If you have these things, or others, you may qualify for a discount. Also, be sure to compare rates from several companies. The most important thing to take from this chapter is that it is vital for you to be very familiar with your insurance policy.

The Least You Need to Know

◆ All homeowners need homeowners insurance.

◆ Dwelling coverage is the insurance you have on your home, while personal property coverage insures the things in your home.

◆ Make sure you have guaranteed replacement cost insurance; it's worth the extra money.

◆ Liability insurance protects you from lawsuits if something bad happens to someone while they are on your property, or if you or a family member accidentally injures someone else.

◆ Natural disasters happen. You should be insured against them.

◆ Shop around and check out the available discounts to save money when buying homeowners insurance.

Additional Resources

Now that you're into personal finance, here are some other books you might want to check out. The ones that contain the most information for fledgling financial wizards are listed first. The books get more complicated as you move down the list. Run over to your favorite bookstore or hop on the Internet to order a couple of these books. Better still, go to your local library and borrow the book. Borrowing instead of buying is a great way to save money!

Everything You Need to Know About Money and Investing: A Financial Expert Answers the 1,001 Most Frequently Asked Questions by Sarah Young Fisher and Carol Turkington

The Complete Idiot's Guide to Managing Your Money, Fourth Edition by Robert K. Heady and Christy Heady

The Complete Idiot's Guide to 401(k) Plans by Wayne G. Bogosian

The Complete Idiot's Guide to Making Money on Wall Street by Christy Heady

The Complete Idiot's Guide to Getting Rich by Larry Waschka

The Complete Idiot's Guide to Doing Your Income Taxes by Gail A. Perry and Paul Craig Roberts

1001 Ways to Cut Your Expenses by Jonathan P. Pond

Keys to Investing in Common Stocks (Barron's Business Keys) by Barbara Apostolou and Nicholas G. Apostolou

The Consumer Reports Money Book: How to Get It, Save It, and Spend It Wisely, Third Edition by Janet Bamford, Jeff Blyskal, Emily Card, Aileen Jacobson, and Greg Daugherty

Building Your Nest Egg With Your 401(k): A Guide to Help You Achieve Retirement Security by Lynn Brenner

The First Book of Investing: The Absolute Beginner's Guide to Building Wealth Safely by Samuel Case

Dictionary of Finance and Investment Terms by John Downes and Jordan Elliot Goodman

The Motley Fool Investment Workbook by David Gardner and Tom Gardner

The Truth About Money: Because Money Doesn't Come with Instructions by Ric Edelman

Investing from Scratch: A Handbook for the Young Investor by James Lowell

The Wall Street Journal Guide to Understanding Personal Finance by Kenneth M. Morris and Alan M. Siegel

10 Steps to Financial Success: A Beginner's Guide to Saving and Investing by W. Patrick Naylor

The 9 Steps to Financial Freedom by Suze Orman

The Green Magazine Guide to Personal Finance: A No B.S. Book for Your Twenties and Thirties by Ken Kurson

10 Minute Guide to the Stock Market by Diane Vujovich

Making the Most of Your Money by Jane Bryant Quinn

How to Buy Stocks by Louis Engel

The Complete Idiot's Guide to Being a Successful Entrepreneur by John Sortino and Susan Shelly

No B.S. Time Management for Entrepreneurs by Dan Kennedy

Working From Home: Everything You Need to Know About Living and Working Under the Same Roof by Paul Edwards and Sarah Edwards

The Secrets of Wealth by Fabio Marciano and Mike Litman

The Beginner's Guide to Investing by Richard Croft

Beating the Paycheck to Paycheck Blues by John Ventura

The following books cover more advanced and complicated topics regarding personal finance, especially investing. Don't rule them out, though. You have a good basic understanding of personal finance, and these books may serve to greatly expand that knowledge:

Capital Ideas: The Improbable Origins of Modern Wall Street by Peter Bernstein

Bogle on Mutual Funds by John C. Bogle

Big Profits from Small Stocks: How to Grow Your Investment Portfolio by Investing in Small Cap Companies by Samuel Case

The Sophisticated Investor by Burton Crane

Buying Stocks Without a Broker by Charles B. Carlson

New Guide to Finding the Next Superstock by Frank Cappiello

Mutual Fund Superstars by William Donoghue

The Motley Fool Investment Guide: How the Fool Beats Wall Street's Wise Men and How You Can Too by David Gardner and Tom Gardner

You Have More Than You Think: The Motley Fool Guide to Investing What You Have by David Gardner and Tom Gardner

How to Retire Rich: Time-Tested Strategies to Beat the Market and Retire in Style by James O'Shaughnesy

The Mortgage Book (Consumer Report books) by John R. Dorfman

The Common Sense Mortgage by Peter G. Miller

The Banker's Secret by Marc Eisenson

Wall Street Journal Guide to Understanding Money and Investing by Kenneth M. Morris

Retirement Countdown by David Shapiro

The Morningstar Guide to Mutual Funds: 5-Star Strategies for Success by Christine Benz

Challenge Your Taxes: Homeowner's Guide to Reducing Your Property Taxes by James E. A. Lumley

The following websites might interest you as well. Please remember that we don't endorse these sites. The authors of the sites are responsible for their content.

American Express: www.americanexpress.com

American Stock Exchange: www.amex.com

Bloomberg News: www.bloomberg.com

Current Budget: www.efmoody.com/planning/budget.html

Family Money: www.familymoney.com

FinanCenter: Budgeting Center: www.financenter.com

Household Budget Management: www.netxpress.com

Investorama: www.investorama.com

John Hancock: www.jhancock.com

Meta-Site: Consumer World: www.consumerworld.org/pages/money.htm

Morningstar, Inc.: www.morningstar.com

The Motley Fool: The Fribble, A Foolish Budget, by George Runkle: www.fool.com/Fribble/1998/Fribble980409.htm

National Association of Investors Corporation: www.better-investing.org

NASD Regulation: www.nasdr.com

North American Securities Administrators: www.nasaa.org

S&P Equity Investor Service: www.stockinfo.standardpoor.com

Securities and Exchange Commission: www.sec.gov

USA Today Money: www.usatoday.com/money/mfront.htm

Wall Street Research Net: www.wsrn.com/

Yahoo! Finance: www.quote.yahoo.com

The following financial publications contain all kinds of information you might find useful. Check them out at your local newsstand or access them at the websites listed here:

Barron's: www.barrons.com

Business Week Online: www.businessweek.com

The Economist: www.economist.com

Money Online: www.money.com

The New York Times: www.nytimes.com

Reuters News and Quotes: www.reuters.com/news

Wall Street Journal: www.wsj.com

Show Me the Money Glossary

401(k) plan   A retirement plan into which you can contribute a portion of your current salary (usually before taxes). Contributions can grow tax-deferred until they are withdrawn upon retirement.

adjustable-rate mortgage   A mortgage set up with an interest rate that can change at specific intervals, as determined under the initial contract.

adjusted gross income (AGI)   Your gross income, less certain allowed business-related deductions. These deductions include alimony payments, contributions to a Keogh retirement plan, and, in some cases, contributions to an IRA.

adjuster   An individual who inspects damage as reported on an insurance claim and determines a settlement amount for the claim.

aggressive growth fund   A type of mutual fund where the primary objective is seeking capital gains. It is understood that the potential for above-average returns in such an investment is countered by above-average risks.

amortization   Reducing the principal of a loan by making regular payments.

amortization schedule   A schedule of regular payments with which to repay a loan. The schedule indicates to the borrower the amount of each payment that is principal, that which is interest, and the remaining balance of the loan.

annual dividend   A share of a company's net profits that are distributed by the company to a class of its stockholders each year. The dividend is paid in a fixed amount for each share of stock held. Although most companies make quarterly payments in cash, dividends also may be made in other forms of property, such as stock. Dividends must be approved by the company's directors before each payment is made.

annuity   A stream of equal payments, as to a retiree, that occur at predetermined intervals (for example, monthly or annually). The payments may continue for a fixed period or for a contingent period, such as the recipient's lifetime. Annuities are most often associated with insurance companies and retirement programs.

arbitration   The hearing and determination of a dispute between parties by a third party.

asset allocation   The process of determining the assignment of investment funds to broad categories of assets. For example, an individual allocates funds to bonds and equities, with the proportions based on financial objectives and risk tolerance. An investment manager may allocate clients' funds to common stocks representing various industries.

balanced mutual fund   A mutual fund where the primary objective is to buy a combination of stocks and bonds. These middle-of-the-road funds balance their portfolios to achieve both moderate income and moderate capital growth. These funds tend to be less volatile than stocks-only funds. Balanced funds tend, on average, to be invested as 45 percent bonds and 55 percent stocks.

bear market   An extended period of general price decline in the stock market as a whole.

beneficiary   The person who is named to receive the proceeds from an investment vehicle, trust, or contract. A beneficiary can be an individual, a company, or an organization.

beta   A mathematical measure of the risk on a portfolio or a given stock compared with rates of return on the market as a whole. A beta of less than one is less volatile than the general market. A beta above one is more volatile than the market.

blue-chip investment   A high-quality investment involving a lower-than-average risk. Blue-chip investment is generally used to refer to securities of companies having a long history of sustained earnings and dividend payments.

bond   A debt instrument. The issuer promises to pay the investor a specified amount of interest for a period of time and to repay the principal at maturity.

bond fund   A mutual fund that invests in bonds and passes current income to its shareholders, with capital gains as a secondary objective. Some bond funds purchase long-term securities providing a relatively high current yield, but varying substantially in price with changes in interest rates. Other funds choose short-term securities having lower yields but fluctuating little in value.

broker   A person who earns a commission or fee for acting as an agent in making contracts or sales.

budget   A schedule of income and expenses, commonly broken into monthly intervals and typically covering a one-year period.

bull market   An extended period of generally rising prices in the market as a whole.

capital expenses   Expenses spent to improve property.

capital gain   Profits from the sale of an investment or asset. Tax on this gain is usually due when the asset is sold.

capital gains exclusion   An exclusion to the practice of taxing capital gains that applies to the sale of real estate.

capitalization   The sum of a corporation's long-term debt, stock, and retained earnings—also called invested capital.

capitalized cost   In leasing, the cost a leasing company pays for a vehicle.

cash-value life insurance   In this insurance, part of the premium is used to provide death benefits, and the remainder is available to earn interest. Cash-value life insurance is a protection plan and a savings plan that charges significantly higher premiums than term insurance.

certificates of deposit (CD)   A receipt for a deposit of funds in a financial institution that permits the holder to receive interest plus the deposit at maturity.

certified financial planner (CFP)   A professional financial planner who has completed a series of correspondence courses and passed a 10-hour examination in subject areas such as insurance, securities, and taxes. The designation is awarded by the College for Financial Planning in Denver, Colorado.

certified public accountant (CPA)   An accountant who has met certain state requirements as to age, education, experience, residence, and accounting knowledge. Accountants must pass an extensive series of examinations before becoming CPAs.

chartered financial consultant (ChFC)   A professional financial planner who has completed a series of 8 courses and examinations in subject areas such as economics, insurance, real estate, and tax shelters. The designation is awarded by the American College of Bryn Mawr, Pennsylvania.

churning and burning   To trade securities very actively in a brokerage account in order to increase brokerage commissions rather than customer profits. Brokers may be tempted to churn accounts because their income is directly related to the volume of trading undertaken by the customers. Churning is illegal and unethical.

collateral   Assets pledged as security for a loan. If a borrower defaults on the terms of a loan, the collateral may be sold, with the proceeds used to satisfy any remaining obligations. High-quality collateral reduces risk to the lender and results in a lower rate of interest on the loan.

commercial bank   Financial institutions, either chartered by the federal or state governments, that take deposits and loan money, and provide other services to individuals or corporations.

common stock   Shares of ownership of a company; a class of capital stock that has no preference to dividends or any distribution of assets.

compound interest   Interest paid on interest from previous periods in addition to principal. Essentially, compounding involves adding interest to principal and any previous interest in order to calculate interest in the next period. Compound interest may be figured daily, monthly, quarterly, semi-annually, or annually.

consumer price index (CPI)   A measure of the relative cost of living compared with a base year (currently 1967). The CPI can be a misleading indicator of inflationary impact on a given person because it is constructed according to the spending patterns of an urban family of four. Used as a measure of inflation.

co-payment   The amount the insured is responsible to pay at each time of service under a health insurance contract.

corporate bond   A bond issued by a corporation, as opposed to a bond issued by the U.S. Treasury or a municipality.

credit history   The record of an individual's past events that pertain to credit previously given or applied for.

credit union   A nonprofit, cooperative financial institution providing credit to its members who share a common bond. Credit unions often pay slightly higher rates of interest on passbook-type savings accounts, and charge lower rates on consumer loans.

creditor   A person or agency to whom money is owed under the terms of an agreement, promise, or law.

customer service representative (CSR)   A front-line bank employee who opens checking and savings accounts, certificates of deposit, and so forth. They know the products their financial institutions provide.

cyclical stock   Common stock of a firm whose earnings are heavily influenced by cyclical changes in general economic activity. As investors anticipate changes in profits, cyclical stocks often reach their high and low levels before the respective highs and lows in the economy.

deductible   The amount the insured must pay before an insurance company pays a claim.

deduction   An expenditure permitted to be used in order to reduce an individual's income tax liability.

default   Failure to live up to the terms of a contract or to meet financial obligations. Generally, the term is used to indicate the inability of a borrower to pay interest or principal on a debt when it is due.

defensive stock   A stock that tends to resist general stock market declines, and whose price will remain stable or even prosper when economic activity is tapering.

defined benefit plan   A qualified retirement plan that specifies the benefits received rather than contributions into the plan, usually expressed as a percentage of pre-retirement compensation and the number of years of service. The responsibility for the benefit is on the company, not the employee.

defined contribution plan   A qualified retirement plan that specifies the annual contribution to the plan, usually expressed as a percentage of the employee's salary. Contributions can be made by the employer, the employee, or both.

disability insurance   Insurance intended to cover the loss of income due to a disability.

discretionary expenses   Expenses that are incurred for nonessentials; money spent as a person chooses.

disposition charges   Expenses charged to lessee at the end of the lease for selling the vehicle or property leased.

diversification   The acquisition of a group of assets in which returns on the assets are not directly related over time. Proper investment diversification, requiring a sufficient number of different assets, is intended to minimize risk associated with investing.

dividend   A share of a company's net profits, distributed by the company to a class of its stockholders. The dividend is paid in a fixed amount for each share of stock held. Dividends are usually fixed in preferred stock; dividends from common stock vary as the company's performance shifts.

dividend reinvestment plan (DRIP)   Stockholders may automatically reinvest dividend payments in additional shares of the company's stock. Instead of receiving the normal dividend checks, participating stockholders will receive quarterly notification of shares purchased and shares held in their accounts. Dividend reinvestment is normally an inexpensive way of purchasing additional shares of stock because the fees are low or are completely absorbed by the company. In addition, some companies offer stock at a discount from the existing market price. Normally, these dividends are fully taxable, even though no cash is received by the stockholder.

dollar cost averaging   Investment of an equal amount of money at regular intervals, usually each month. This process results in the purchase of extra shares during market downturns and fewer shares during market upturns. Dollar cost averaging is based on the belief that the market or a particular stock will rise in price over the long term and that it is not worthwhile (or even possible) to identify intermediate highs and lows.

Dow Jones Industrial Average (DJIA)   One of the measures of the stock market that includes averages for utilities, industrial, and transportation stocks, as well as the composite averages. *See* index.

down payment   Funds the purchaser puts down when property is bought. Remaining funds for the purchase are borrowed.

dwelling coverage   The part of your homeowners insurance that covers the structure in which you live.

dwelling insurance   *See* renters insurance.

earned income   Salary, wages, and self-employment income derived as compensation for services rendered. Unearned income includes the return you receive from your investments.

emerging growth fund   The common stock of a relatively young firm operating in an industry with very good growth prospects. Although this kind of stock offers unusually large returns, it is very risky because the expected growth may not occur, or the firm may be swamped by the competition.

emerging market stock   The term that broadly categorizes countries in the midst of developing their financial market and financial economic infrastructures.

enrolled agent   A designation given by the IRS, showing that a tax preparer has adequately passed required testing.

equity   The value of your ownership in property or securities. The equity in your home is the difference between the current market value of the home and the money you still owe on the mortgage. Equities are used interchangeably with stocks.

escrow   The holding of assets (for example, securities or cash) by a third party, which delivers the assets to the grantee or promisee on the fulfillment of some condition. Some parts of mortgage payments are held in escrow to cover expenses like taxes and insurance. Down payments are also held in escrow until settlement.

exchange-traded shares   A group of securities representing a mutual fund that are traded in the stock market throughout the day at the market value at that time.

fair market value   The price at which a buyer and a seller willingly consummate a trade; the prevailing price of a security or property.

Fannie Mae   A security issued by the Federal National Mortgage Association (FNMA) that is backed by insured and conventional mortgages. Monthly returns to holders of Fannie Maes consist of interest and principal payments made by homeowners on their mortgages.

Federal Home Loan Mortgage Corporation (FHLMC)   A government organization established in 1970 to create a secondary market in conventional mortgages. The FHLMC purchases mortgages from federally insured financial institutions and resells them in the form of mortgage-backed, pass-through certificates. All income on securities issued by the FHLMC is subject to federal, state, and local taxation.

Federal National Mortgage Association (FNMA)   A privately owned profit-seeking corporation that adds liquidity to the mortgage market by purchasing loans from lenders. It finances the purchases by issuing its own bonds or by selling mortgages it already owns to financial institutions.

financial advisor   A professional who guides individuals to arrange and coordinate their financial affairs.

financial planning   The process of defining and setting goals to achieve financial security.

fixed-income assets   Assets that produce income, such as certificates of deposit, fixed annuities, and most bonds.

fixed-interest rate loan   A loan that has a set rate throughout the period of the loan. Payments are usually set at a specified, equal payment throughout the loan.

fixed-rate mortgage   A mortgage in which the annual interest charged does not vary throughout the period of the loan.

foreclosure   When a lender claims a property on which the loan has been defaulted.

Freddie Mac   A security issued by the Federal Home Loan Mortgage Corporation that is secured by pools of conventional home mortgages. Holders of Freddie Macs receive a share of the interest and principal payments made by the homeowners.

front-end load   *See* load fund.

gap insurance   Insurance purchased to pay the difference between the value your auto insurance will pay if a leased vehicle is stolen or totaled and the amount required to terminate the lease.

global fund   A mutual fund that includes at least 25 percent foreign securities in its portfolio. The value of the fund depends on the health of foreign economies and exchange rate movements. A global fund permits an investor to diversify internationally.

Government National Mortgage Association (GNMA)   A government-owned corporation that acquires, packages, and resells mortgages and mortgage purchase commitments in the form of mortgage-backed securities.

government obligations   A debt that is backed by the full taxing power of the U.S. government. Direct obligations include Treasury bills, Treasury bonds, and U.S. savings bonds. These investments are generally considered to be of the very highest quality.

government securities   Bonds, bills, or notes sold by the federal government to raise money.

gross income   All income except as specifically exempted by the Internal Revenue Code.

group insurance   Insurance offered only to members of a group, such as employees, often for only as long as they remain members of the group.

growth fund   An investment company whose major objective is long-term capital growth. Growth funds offer substantial potential gains over time, but vary significantly in price, depending on general economic conditions.

growth stock   The stock of a firm that is expected to have above-average increases in revenue and earnings. These firms normally retain most earnings for reinvestment, and therefore, pay small dividends. The stocks, often selling at relatively high price-earnings ratios, are subject to wide swings in price. The objective of investment is capital appreciation and long-term capital growth.

guaranteed replacement cost provision   An insurance provision that promises to pay the total cost to replace property upon loss or damage.

high-yield/junk bond   A high-risk, high-yield debt security issued by corporations or municipalities that are of lower quality. Junk bonds have a greater risk of default than higher-rated bonds. These securities are most appropriate for risk-oriented investors. They usually pay a higher interest rate than higher-rated bonds.

home equity loan   A loan in which property is used as collateral. Usually involves a second mortgage on a property.

homeowners insurance   Insurance obtained by a property owner to protect the property and contents. It also provides liability coverage for accidents that occur on the property.

hybrid fund   A mutual fund that has characteristics of several types of securities. An example would be a convertible bond, which is a bond that has a conversion feature, which permits the investor to convert the security into a specified number of shares of the company's common stock.

ILYA (incompletely launched young adults)   The acronym for the group of 65 million people between the ages of 18 and 34 who still live with their parents.

income fund   An investment company (mutual fund), the main objective of which is to achieve current income for its owners. Thus, it tends to select securities such as bonds, preferred stocks, and common stocks that pay relatively high current returns.

income stock   A stock with a relatively high dividend yield. The stock's issuer is typically a firm having stable earnings and dividends, and operating in a mature industry. The price of an income stock is heavily influenced by changes in interest rates.

index   The measurement of the current price behavior of a representative group of stocks in relation to a base value set at an earlier point in time. The best-known indexes are the Dow Jones Industrial Average and Standard & Poor's 500 index.

index fund   A mutual fund that keeps a portfolio of securities designed to match the performance of the market as a whole. The market is represented by an index such as the Standard & Poor's 500. An index fund has low administrative expenses; it appeals to investors who believe it is difficult or impossible for investment managers to beat the market.

indexing   An investment strategy that seeks to match the return and risk of the market by holding all securities that make up the index. This is known as passive management.

individual retirement account (IRA)   A retirement savings plan in which you can contribute up to $2,000 per year. Funds can grow tax-deferred, until they are withdrawn at retirement. Contributions may or may not be tax-deductible depending on the income level and participation in other retirement plans.

inflation   A general increase in the price level of goods and services.

inflation rider   Additional insurance coverage that is purchased to provide that the underlying policy coverage increases with inflation.

initial public offering (IPO)   A company's first sale of stock to the public. Securities offered in an IPO are often, but not always, those of young, small companies seeking outside equity capital and a public market for their stock. Investors purchasing stock in IPOs generally assume very large risks for the possibility of large gains.

interest   The cost for the use of borrowed money.

interest-sensitive stock   A stock that tends to move in the opposite direction of interest rates. Interest-sensitive stocks include nearly all preferred stocks and the common stocks of industries, such as electric utilities and savings and loans. A common stock may be interest-sensitive because its dividend is relatively fixed (as with an electric utility) or because the firm raises a large portion of its funds through borrowing (as with a savings and loan).

international fund   A mutual fund that invests only outside of the country in which it is located.

investment   The process of purchasing securities or property for which the stability of value and level of expected returns are somewhat predictable.

investment return   The return achieved on an investment, including current income and any change in value during an investor's holding period; also known as "total return."

itemized deduction   An expenditure permitted to be used to reduce an individual's income-tax liability.

Keogh   A federally approved retirement program that permits self-employed people to set up to $30,000 (or up to 25 percent of their income) aside for savings. All contributions and income earned by the account are tax-deferred until withdrawals are made during retirement.

large-cap stock   Stocks in companies with over $10 billion in capitalization—the largest companies.

lease   A contract under which someone obtains the use of an object, such as a vehicle or property, for a specified time and amount of money.

lending instrument   A debt instrument; companies borrow money from investors and agree to pay a stated rate of interest over a specified period of time, at the end of which the original sum will be returned.

liquidity   The ability to quickly convert assets into cash without significant loss.

load fund   A mutual fund with shares sold at a price including a sales charge (typically 4 to 9.3 percent of the net amount invested). Thus, load funds are sold at a price exceeding their net asset value, but they are redeemed at their net asset value.

marginal tax rate   The percentage of extra income received that must be paid in taxes, or the proportional amount of taxes paid on a given income or the given dollar value of an asset. If the tax is calculated on the basis of total income, it is the average tax rate. If the tax is calculated only on extra units of income, the rate is the marginal tax rate.

market value   The prevailing market price of a security or property; an indication of how the market as a whole has assessed the security's or property's worth.

maturity   The termination of the period that an obligation has until maturity; mortgages have a date of maturity, when they are due to be repaid in full.

mid-cap stock   Stocks in companies with $1 billion to $10 billion capitalization.

misrepresentation   To represent a financial product incorrectly, improperly, or falsely.

money manager   A person who is paid a fee to supervise the investment decisions of others. The term is usually used for the management of individual portfolios as compared to institutional funds. *See also* portfolio manager.

money purchase plan   A qualified employer retirement plan in which the employer makes an annual contribution to an employee's individual account. The amount of the contribution is determined by a pre-set formula, based on a fixed percentage, or is a flat monetary amount.

money-market fund   A mutual fund that sells shares of ownership and uses the proceeds to purchase short-term, high-quality securities such as Treasury bills, negotiable certificates of deposit, and commercial paper. Income earned by shareholders is received in the form of additional shares of stock in the fund (normally priced at $1 each). Although no fees are generally charged to purchase or redeem shares in a money-market fund, an annual management charge is levied by the fund's advisors. This investment pays a return that varies with short-term interest rates. It is relatively liquid and safe, but yields and features vary.

mortgage   A conditional conveyance of property to a creditor as security for the repayment of money.

mortgage life insurance   Term insurance that will pay the outstanding balance on the insured's home loan should he or she die.

municipal bond   The debt issue of a city, county, state, or other political entity. Interest paid by most municipal bonds is exempt from federal income taxes and often from state and local taxes. Municipal bonds with tax-exempt interest appeal mainly to investors with significant amounts of other taxable income.

municipal bond fund   A mutual fund that invests in tax-exempt securities and passes through tax-free current income to its shareholders. Some municipal bond funds purchase long-term securities, providing a relatively high current yield, but varying substantially in price with changes in interest rates. Other funds choose short-term securities having lower yields but fluctuating little in value.

mutual fund   An open-end investment company that invests its shareholders' money in a diversified group of securities of other corporations. Mutual funds are usually professionally managed.

net income   The income you have after you've paid taxes and any and all other liabilities, expenses, or charges against it.

net worth   The amount of wealth calculated by taking the total value of assets owned and subtracting all liabilities.

no-load fund   A mutual fund sold without a sales charge. No-load funds sell directly to customers at net asset value with no intermediate salesperson charging a fee.

nondiscretionary expenses   Expenses, such as mortgage payments and utility bills, that an individual must pay.

nonroutine expenses   Budgeted expenses, such as a furnace repair or unexpected medical expenses, that are not regular or customary.

nontaxable income   Income specifically exempted from taxation. On federal income tax returns, interest from most municipal bonds, life insurance proceeds, gifts, and inheritances are generally nontaxable income.

nonvariable expenses   Expenses that remain constant in amount from month to month, such as rent, a mortgage payment, fees for a class or club, car payments, and so forth. You pay the same cost each month for these expenses.

odd lot   Less than 100 shares of stock.

pension plan   An employer-sponsored retirement plan in which a retiree receives a fixed periodic payment made in consideration of past services, injury or loss sustained, merit or poverty, and so on.

personal finance   Every aspect of one's life that deals with money.

points   Prepaid interest paid as a fee to a mortgage lender to cover the cost of applying for the loan. One point is one percent of the loan's value.

portfolio   A group of investments assembled to meet an investment goal.

portfolio manager   A person who is paid a fee to supervise the investment decisions of others. The term is normally used in reference to the managers of large institutions such as bank trust departments, pension funds, insurance companies, and mutual funds.

preferred provider organization (PPO)   Health insurance coverage that rewards you for using providers from a specific list of care providers. The difference between an HMO and a PPO is that a PPO will pay for the services of a nonspecified provider, but an HMO usually will not pay for such services.

preferred stock   A security that shows ownership in a corporation and gives the holder a claim prior to the claim of common stockholders on earnings, and also generally on assets in the event of liquidation. Most preferred stock issues pay a fixed dividend set at the time of issuance, stated in a dollar amount or as a percentage of par value. Because no maturity date is stipulated, these securities are priced on dividend yield and trade, much like long-term corporate bonds. As a general rule, preferred stock has limited appeal for individual investors.

premium   The amount paid, in one sum or periodically, for a contract of insurance.

prenuptial agreement   A written agreement by a couple to be married in which financial matters, including rights following divorce or the death of one spouse, are detailed.

price/earnings ratio (P/E ratio)   A common stock analysis statistic in which the current price of a stock is divided by the current (or sometimes the projected) earnings per share of the issuing firm.

principal   The capital sum, as distinguished from interest or profit.

private mortgage insurance (PMI)   Insurance required by mortgage lenders for persons borrowing more than 80 percent of the value of a property. This insurance guarantees the lender repayment of the entire loan value in case of default.

profit sharing plan   An arrangement set up by a company for its employees that lets its staff share in company profits. The plan contribution, usually based on a participant's compensation and other factors such as corporate results, can vary annually. No minimum contribution to participant accounts is required.

property taxes   Taxes assessed on real estate. Most common are municipal and school taxes. Also called "real estate tax."

prospectus   A formal written document relating to a new securities offering that delineates the proposed business plan, or the data relevant to an existing business plan. Investors need this information to make educated decisions about whether to purchase the security. The prospectus includes financial data, a summary of the firm's business history, a list of its officers, a description of its operations, and a mention of any pending litigation. A prospectus is an abridged version of the firm's registration statement, filed with the Securities and Exchange Commission.

qualified retirement plan   A plan sponsored by an employer and designed to meet retirement needs.

rate   The amount charged to borrow money.

refinancing   Reapplying for a new mortgage, usually to receive a lower interest rate. Refinancing is done for consolidation or additional funding.

renters insurance   Similar to homeowners insurance, it provides insurance protection for a resident's personal property, along with liability coverage.

replacement cost guarantee   A provision of homeowners insurance that guarantees that the full cost of rebuilding, replacing, or repairing a home is covered in the policy. It also applies to replacing personal property within the house.

residual value   The value of a vehicle when it comes off a lease; the value you need to pay to acquire the vehicle.

rider   An addition or amendment to a document.

risk   The chance that the value or return on an investment will differ from its expected value. Business risk, financial risk, purchasing power risk, interest rate risk, market risk, default risk, and foreign currency risk are all types of risk associated with investments.

Roth IRA   Introduced in 1998, an individual retirement account in which the funds placed into the account are nondeductible. If held more than five years, all funds withdrawn are received tax-free.

round lot   The standard unit of trading in a particular type of security. For stocks, a round lot is 100 shares or a multiple thereof, although a few inactive issues trade in units of 10 shares.

routine expenses   Expenses that occur on a regular basis, such as food costs, dental checkups, church contributions, etc. These expenses may vary in amount, but they occur on a regular basis.

sector fund   Securities or other assets that share a common interest. Sector funds permit an investor to concentrate on a specific investment segment and yet diversify investments among various issuers. Sector funds entail more risk, but offer greater potential returns than funds that diversify their portfolios.

secured credit card   A credit card for a person without credit or with poor credit. The account limit on the card is guaranteed by funds held by the bank in an interest-bearing account. Usually, after 18 months, the funds in the bank account can be returned to the cardholder.

securities   Investments that represent evidence of debt, ownership of a business, or the legal right to acquire or sell an ownership interest in a business.

security deposit   Amount required by a landlord to cover expenses at lease termination if property is damaged by the tenant. The deposit, if held for more than two years, should be returned to the tenant with interest added if there is no damage.

SEP-IRA   A retirement plan for the self-employed that permits contributions up to $25,000 per year. Similar to an IRA except that the contribution limits are higher.

settlement   The settling of property and title on an individual or individuals; the transaction when you finally purchase the property.

shareholder   A person who owns shares in a corporation.

sheriff's sale   When a foreclosed property is sold at public auction in order for the lender to recoup his losses.

simple interest   Interest paid on an initial investment only. Simple interest is calculated by multiplying the principal times the annual rate of interest times the number of years involved.

simplified employee pension plan (SEP)   A special type of joint Keogh–individual retirement account, permitting contributions from employees and employers. The SEP was developed to give small businesses a retirement plan that is easier to establish and administer than an ordinary pension plan.

small-cap stock   Companies which have less than $1 billion capitalization.

speculation   Taking above-average risks to achieve above-average returns, generally during a relatively short period of time. Speculation involves buying something on the basis of its potential selling price rather than on the basis of its actual value.

standard deduction   The minimum deduction from income allowed a taxpayer for calculating taxable income. Individuals with few itemized deductions use the standard deduction instead of itemizing deductions.

stock   Shares of ownership in a company. These shares include common stock of various classes and any preferred stock outstanding.

stock fund   A mutual fund that limits its investments to shares of common stock. Common stock funds vary in risk, from relatively low to quite high, depending on the types of stocks in which the funds are invested.

stock market   The organized securities exchanges for stock and bond transactions. Major exchanges are the New York Stock Exchange, the American Stock Exchange, and the National Association of Securities Dealers Automated Quotation System (NASDAQ).

sublet   Leasing an apartment from the current tenant rather than from the landlord.

target benefit plan   An age-weighted retirement plan that is normally used by a company that wishes to have a specified sum available for an older employee (usually an owner) at the time of retirement.

tax attorney   A lawyer who has earned a Master's degree in taxation (LLM).

tax preparer   An individual who prepares a tax return according to the law.

tax-deductible   An expense that can be used to offset gross income when calculating your taxable gross income.

tax-deferred   Income that is earned, but neither received nor taxed until a later date, when the funds are withdrawn or mature. Tax-deferred assets include those within an IRA, 401(k) plan, 403(b) plan, tax-deferred annuity, tax-deferred life insurance, EE savings bonds, and others.

taxable income   Income that is subject to taxation; adjusted income minus standard or itemized deductions and exemptions.

term insurance   Life insurance in which the insurance company pays a specified sum if the insured dies during the coverage period. Term insurance includes no savings, cash values, borrowing power, or benefits at retirement. On the basis of cost, it is the least expensive insurance available, although policy prices can vary significantly among firms.

thrift   A financial institution that derives its funds primarily from consumer savings accounts set up to provide personal mortgages. The term originally referred to those institutions offering mainly passbook savings accounts. The word thrift often refers to savings and loan associations, but it can also mean credit unions and mutual savings banks.

total return   Dividend or interest income plus any capital gain, generally considered a better measure of an investment's return than dividends or interest alone.

Treasury bond   Longer-term (over 10 years), interest-bearing debt of the U.S. Treasury, available through a bank or brokerage firm or directly from the Federal Reserve. Treasury bonds are quoted and traded in thirty-seconds of a point.

Treasury note   Intermediate-term (1 to 10 years), interest-bearing debt of the U.S. Treasury. Treasury notes are quoted and traded in thirty-seconds of a point.

Treasury stock   Shares of a firm's stock that have been issued and then repurchased. Treasury stock is not considered in paying dividends, voting, or calculating earnings per share. It may eventually be retired or reissued.

trust   A form of property ownership in which legal title to the property is held by someone (trustee) for the benefit of someone else (the beneficiary).

trustee   A person or corporation appointed to administer or execute a trust for the beneficiaries.

value stock   A stock in which the price is considered below normal using valuation measures common to the market.

variable expenses   Expenses that are changeable, alterable.

variable interest rate   Interest, either paid or received (depending on whether you are borrowing or investing funds), that changes periodically, depending on the initial contract.

vested   To pass into possession. Usually this means working long enough in a company for an employee to have the right to the employer's contributions into the retirement plan.

vesting schedule   A schedule predetermined by an employer (within governmental guidelines) in which employees vest in the company's retirement plan.

warranty   A statement of promise or assurance in connection with a contract or purchase.

yield   The percentage return on an investment; also known as "return." The dividends or interest paid by a company as a percentage of the current price.

Index

Y–Z